APPLETON-CENTURY-CROFTS SOCIOLOGY SERIES

Edited by *John F. Cuber*, The Ohio State University

SOCIAL STRATIFICATION
IN THE UNITED STATES

Social Stratification
IN THE UNITED STATES

by

JOHN F. CUBER
The Ohio State University

and

WILLIAM F. KENKEL
Iowa State College

New York

APPLETON-CENTURY-CROFTS, INC.

Preface

THE FIELD of social stratification is at this writing without a published textbook, although a few months ago a voluminous and well selected book of readings appeared. Yet our research output in this field has been immense. For several years the American Sociological Society's Census of Research has recorded major research activity on stratification. The special issue of the *American Journal of Sociology* pertaining to stratification, in 1953, contained a bibliography of 333 items to which we could add at least another hundred titles without exhausting the available materials.

It seems that the time is now ripe for someone to attempt a reasonably brief integration of many of these scattered theoretical and empirical works, to present to advanced students a reasonably inclusive and consistent concept of the field of stratification, a basic vocabulary, some of the main ideas and issues and a representative cross section of the empirical materials and critical analyses of them. This we have tried to do. The book is in no sense encyclopedic; it is concerned with stratification in the United States only, and even for this society does not treat all of the possible theoretical problems. We have tried, in Chapters 2 and 3, to make our orientation explicit. We do not presume to have written a "standard" advanced textbook in the field, for the field is yet too fluid for anyone to know what is standard and what is tangential.

The plan of the book deserves a brief comment. Part I is a semantic, theoretical, and methodological orientation to stratification literature. A number of theoretical positions are taken and are, somewhat a priori, rationalized. Part II is a series of chapters, each devoted to a discussion and evaluation of one important study in this field. Emphasis is placed upon critical analysis rather than upon mere description, because it is our contention that unless empirical data can stand the test of close methodological scrutiny, they must be regarded as more factious than factual. In Part III we return to theoretical matters, re-examining the positions originally taken in Part I in the light of the data and criticisms presented in the main body of the book. In addition, a number of new theoretical and practical problems are discussed.

Acknowledgments for a book of this type are practically impossible. Hundreds of our predecessors and contemporaries have left us a rich legacy of theory and data upon which we have freely drawn. To some of these our indebtedness is conscious and apparent—Max Weber, Talcott Parsons, Kingsley Davis, C. H. Cooley, Robert Merton, and W. Lloyd Warner. Dr. Alfred C. Clarke, Dr. Russell R. Dynes, and Dr. Meno Lovenstein have read substantial portions of the manuscript and made helpful suggestions. But there are others whose influence has come more indirectly and whose contributions have been commingled with others' in the complex thoughtways of contemporary sociology. To the last acknowledgment is difficult, a fact of which we became acutely aware when we attempted to document our material at a number of places. Suffice it to say, that we are aware of profound indebtedness to many people—sociologists and others —and are under no illusions that our own contributions go much beyond integration and reappraisal of ideas which run through the sociological tradition.

While the authors have exchanged ideas freely, no attempt has been made to inhibit the individuality of either. The theoretical sections, Part I and III, were written by Cuber and Part II by Kenkel.

Doubtless this book has shortcomings. What is more, all will not agree as to what the shortcomings are, partly because social scientists possess a robust individuality and partly because we have attempted to present a structure in a large area with very few guideposts. We are reminded of a probably apocryphal instance in which an older man had finished imparting his wisdom to a younger one, closing with the observation that probably only half of what he had said was true, the main difficulty being that he did not know which half.

J.F.C.
W.F.K.

Contents

x

CONTENTS

Part III

CONCLUSIONS

SOCIAL STRATIFICATION
IN THE UNITED STATES

Part I
ORIENTATION

1

Working Concepts

LANGUAGE is both the hallmark and the bugaboo of the man of learning. Despite the emergence and more recent popularization of semantics,[1] confusion, inexactitude, and verbal impasse are manifest. Practically anyone who has listened to professional conversations among social scientists will have noted that two persons who are sharply at odds at the beginning of a discussion often discover by the end that they really meant the same thing. Language was the barrier. Similarly, two persons using identical terms frequently refer to radically dissimilar ideas. For these and other related reasons, it seems necessary to devote this preliminary chapter to setting forth a minimum basic nomenclature pertaining to social stratification in America, and a rationale for the concepts used.

There seems to us to be urgent need here and elsewhere in the social sciences for an *economical* technical vocabulary. The student in most of the social sciences encounters a plethora of verbiage with hair-splitting distinctions, inconsistencies in usage, and seemingly endless adumbration of impressive language.[2] We have endeavored ruthlessly to cut through this accumulation, using

[1] For a good semitechnical introduction to this field see Stuart Chase, *The Tyranny of Words* (New York, Harcourt, Brace and Co., 1938), especially pp. 96-140.

[2] H. W. Pfautz, e.g., writes: "Probably no area of current sociological interest suffers so much from the disease of overconceptualization." "The Current Literature on Social Stratification," *American Journal of Sociology*, 58 (January, 1953), p. 392.

rather rigid criteria of simplicity and utility, to fashion a nomenclature by which students of stratification can communicate efficiently.

1. Differential Status

Differential status refers to the obvious and omnipresent fact
that persons and groups in a society—even a democratic one—are
assigned or allowed to achieve statuses which differentiate them.
Much of the nomenclature used in the study of history consists
of words that represent categories of differentiated statuses, such
as serfs, freemen, noblemen, the third estate, slaves, indentured
servants, royalty, commoners, and so on and on. Merely mention-
ing each of these terms reminds us that the persons to whom they
applied were not only prestigially ranked differently from persons
in other categories in the abstract sense, but also that each rank
carried with it more or less specific rights and duties, privileges
and disprivileges, codified in statute and re-enforced by common
law and informal customs. It should not be overlooked, however,
that the persons within any one of these categories, such as serf
or indentured servant, were not all equal. Within each status
category were usually subcategories and sub-subcategories, so
that no person had exactly the same positional ranking that anyone
else did, even though in certain respects, for example, as in serfs
being "bound to the soil," all were alike.

A useful but by no means uncomplicated distinction is that
between status differences that are *assigned* to a person, like age,
sex, and color statuses, and statuses that are *achieved* by the person,[3] presumably as a result of some attributes or choices or accomplishments which pertain to him, such as the statuses suggested by the categories "doctor," "felon," or "playboy."

Many differentiated statuses are formalized and manifested in
a variety of obvious symbols. Titles, as used in military organiza-

[3] This useful distinction was apparently first introduced into social-science
literature by the late Ralph Linton, *The Study of Man* (New York, Appleton-Century-Crofts, Inc., 1936).

tions or in academic hierarchies, are familiar cases in point. Practically every formal institution in a society contains a number of differentiated roles (or "positions" or "offices") which hierarchically arrange the role-incumbents in a system of subordination-superordination. Even in informal relationships, differential status is manifest; and the various statuses are often sharply set off from one another. Language betrays the entire system, at least in its bolder outlines. Such expressions as "a leading family," "other side of the tracks," *nouveau riche*, "white-collar worker," or "social climber" rather forcefully reveal at least some distinctions which practically everyone recognizes. Other manifestations of invidious status distinctions are found in the customary display of deference toward higher-status persons and the granting of superior privileges to certain higher ranking individuals. The web of inferior-superior statuses in the modern community is indeed an intricate one.

These hierarchical systems of differential personal evaluation may be viewed in a number of *dimensions*. By "dimensions" we refer merely to the various ways in which differential status can be apprehended and measured. We turn now to some of these dimensions as they apply in contemporary United States.

a. Prestige. Very commonly Americans talk in terms of an abstract dimension which they call *prestige* or some synonym thereof.[4] Although this dimension is often difficult to measure or even describe in a strictly empirical sense, it does seem to constitute a reasonable inference from direct observations; there is a quality which a person is accorded by others when he *does*, or *is* or *owns* or *"stands for"* or is *associated with* something which is valued. Probably the emotions of pride and shame give tacit

---

[4] Kingsley Davis, e.g., draws a distinction between *prestige* and *esteem* which may be useful for some purposes. *Prestige* refers to the "invidious value" attached to a "status or office," and *esteem* refers to the valuation of the particular person occupying a given office. The two may be quite dissimilar, as in the difference between how we value the status "doctor" and some specific doctor who may be a drunkard or an abortionist. See Kingsley Davis, *Human Society* (New York, The Macmillan Co., 1949), p. 93.

testimony to the importance of the prestigial dimension in the minds of most people.

b. Privilege and *disprivilege.* Less abstract than prestige is the dimension of differential privilege and disprivilege found in any social group, from the aggregate society to the smallest group within it. Even in the most equalitarian social groups there are some perquisites bestowed on one person and disallowed to another. Moreover, it is a matter of common observation that one of the reasons people struggle to achieve valued things, like money or an education or a commission in the military service, is that these acquisitions entitle their acquisitors to certain privileges which some other people do not have. Some differential privileges are *established in the law,* for example, the voting franchise being limited to men in the United States prior to 1920. Others are the *logical extensions of some other privilege* or possession, such as the ability of a person of sufficient wealth to hire other people to do onerous things for him, which he would have to do for himself if he could not afford the servant. Finally, some "privileges" are simply the *differential probability* of certain categories of persons being able to achieve a desired goal. For example, the probability of a Negro becoming a United States senator is lower than that of a white man, even though legally there is no categorical rejection of the Negro.

In describing differentials in a social system, there is a tendency for observers to pay more attention to differential privilege than to differential *dis*privilege and/or *duty*. In American society, for example, the higher income of the so-called middle class is frequently cited as one of their "privileges" over members of the unskilled working class, which often seems to result in middle-class persons having better homes, automobiles, and more expensive vacations. It is easy to overlook the fact that these middle-class persons, as a rule, also have some attendant duties which the "working man," as a rule, need not perform. For example, the middle-class person is usually held to a higher standard of personal conduct and appearance, is likely to have a job calling for greater responsibility, and is much more likely to be called upon by the community to give time and money to activities and enterprises which the working man largely escapes. As a case in point, it is reported that numerous enlisted servicemen have in recent years declined commissions when they were available, because, all things considered, the privileges of the second lieutenant were judged by the master sergeant to be worth less than the disprivileges that went with the higher rank. It seems not unlikely that in civilian life this same judgment occurs with some frequency when a person assesses the changed duties and responsibilities which are intertwined with the beneficial aspects of a proffered "promotion."

In pointing out the duty and/or disprivilege aspects of differential status, it is not intended to imply that the disprivileges are in any sense commensurate with the privileges. *Both* privilege and disprivilege attend any given rank and the disprivileges are unevenly distributed also.

c. Power. A much-discussed dimension of differential status is that of *power*. Many times "power" is not defined,[5] or the reader is left with a vague inferential notion of what the term is supposed to refer to. We shall attempt a loose and proximate definition of what *we* mean by power, acknowledging that our concept is nothing more than an approximate consensus in a semantically confused maelstrom of usage. By *power* we mean *the ability of an individual to control some part or parts of other persons' behavior in conformity to the former's will.* There is *no implication of absoluteness* of power in this usage, for some of

[5] A brilliant exception to the tendency for sociologists to abstain from discussions of power is Robert Bierstedt, "An Analysis of Social Power," *American Sociological Review*, 15 (December, 1950), pp. 730-738. In Reinhard Bendix and Seymour Lipset, *Class, Status and Power: A Reader in Stratification* (Glencoe, Ill., The Free Press, 1953), despite the use of the term *power* in the title and substantial section of the book devoted to "Status and Power Relations in American Society," the term is not formally defined by the editors. There may, of course, be greater utility to a commonsense usage of language than to overformalization which so often renders sociological literature forbidding, even to the sociologist himself.

the greatest and most obvious concentrations of power are at the same time sharply limited by legal tradition, religion, or the competing power of someone else. For example, the rise of modern trade unions has reduced the employer's power over the working man, but he still has power of many sorts, and there always were some limitations on his exercise of power. We thus conceive of power as a *relative ability to control in accordance with the power wielder's wishes.* This implies, of course, the existence of contrary wishes on the part of the person over whom power is wielded; otherwise, if there were a mutuality of intent or goal or will, we could not speak of power.

It is recognized that there is one apparent difficulty in this concept of power that should be made explicit. Taken literally, the concept may appear to be psychologically naive in that it fails to account for the obvious fact that by indirect methods the person or group desiring to control often may influence the controlled one so subtly that the controlled party has the illusion of following his own wishes. Actually, his "own" wishes were fashioned for him without his knowing it. This is perhaps the reason for the existence of propaganda, with its galaxy of devious technique and subtlety. If, for example, through propaganda, employers can convince workers that unions are detrimental to the workers' best interests, then the workers will themselves destroy unions and employers will have achieved their objective without any apparent display of more naked power. To take a more current case, certain groups would like to restrict the "liberal" teaching characteristic of some departments of some universities. They usually lack legal power to do so; also many time-honored traditions like academic freedom stand in the way. But if parents, students, boards of trustees, and especially donors can be convinced that "liberalism" is a threat to other cherished values, then academic freedom will be destroyed without any overt exertion of power by the persons who originally effected the control. This is an old technique, but with the exception seemingly of only a few sophisticates, it is effective again and again, often to the enragement of those who think they see through the "conspiracy."

With the above qualifications, then, we feel that the rather uncomplicated concept of power which we have here set forth will be useful for our purpose, always bearing in mind that the term is used *relatively*. It is not necessary to demonstrate absolute and complete control of one person by another in order to demonstrate power. Power exists to the extent that any fraction of an individual's or group's action is controlled by someone else, by whatever means and however indirectly that control may be exerted.

It is fashionable in some quarters to decry the mere *fact* of power, as if in a utopian society no one would be controlled by anyone else. This naïveté has a primitive appeal, particularly to some who may still be chafing under the recalled restrictions of their childhood, even though now decades removed from the fact. It probably also has a sentimental appeal to practically everyone, at least at times. A little reflection, however, will readily demonstrate that this anarchistic notion is only a pleasant fantasy. Social order implies restriction upon individual action, however little and however genteel.

Obviously, in the kind of large-scale society which we have in America today, everyone cannot be his own censor. Some persons must be delegated to make decisions with which other persons must comply. But who should have what power and how much, and how much is too much, and what is fair and what unfair, and what should be changed and how should we change it? These are among the abiding enigmas of man in society and more especially in the kind of mass society which now characterizes Western civilization.

Whatever one's judgments concerning these troublesome issues, certain objective facts cannot be gainsaid—power over persons is a societal reality, power is very unevenly distributed in our and in practically all other societies, some inequities are probably inescapable in a mass society, and controversy over structure of power is one of the most explosive categories of social issues. Power thus has a twofold relation to the differential-status system: the distribution of power at any given time works as a perpetuator of the system and, because of negative reactions to it, differential power may also be a dynamic factor making for change in the system.[6]

2. Stratification

The term *stratification* is used in a wide variety of ways by American sociologists and other students of social science.[7] It is, like many social-science ideas, an analogical concept. When the geologist talks about rock "strata," he can demonstrate that physically one layer is above or below another, and precisely how one differs from the other. Somewhere, some early social scientists became impressed with the aptness of this "layer upon layer" pattern to characterize differences in status and other characteristics among members of a society. But analogies and analogical terms are almost always fraught with error. In this case, social "strata" are not as distinct or as permanent or physically juxtaposed as are the strata in a rock formation. The use of the analogical term may actually serve the disutility of giving the impression, particularly to the beginner, that "somehow there *must* be some kind of strata or we wouldn't use the word *stratification*." Such a fact needs to be *demonstrated, not assumed* at the outset.

To be sure, there is a kind of authority based on common observation, and certainly buttressed by popular language patterns, for conceiving of the population as nicely stratified. Everywhere one hears about persons who are "moving up" or "marrying down" and references to "lower class" or "the submerged tenth"

---

[6] This point is also made in Bendix and Lipset, *ibid.*, p. 13, although in a somewhat different context.

[7] See, e.g., Harold F. Kaufman, Otis Dudley Duncan, Neal Gross, and William H. Sewell, "Problems of Theory and Method in the Study of Social Stratification in Rural Society," *Rural Sociology*, 18 (March, 1953), pp. 12 ff.

are heard on every side. The image of vertically piled strata is further buttressed by the convention of constructing statistical tables along vertical rather than horizontal axes. That leads to the quick impression that, since the highest incomes and education are at the top of the table, and since categories are expressed in units of $1000, or of three years of education, then the persons to whom they refer must somehow also be lumped together in units. Stereotypes also give vitality to the stratum notion; thus, everyone knows what a "rich financier" looks like and what kinds of attitudes "a reliefer" has, and what the "middle-class housewife" does with her time. Actually, of course, these neat stereotypes bear little resemblance to the wide variety of actual persons falling into the respective categories. Nevertheless, the stereotypes, formalized often in hackneyed stage and fiction types, and embalmed in perennial joking patterns, persist. It is unfortunate that some of these stereotypes become uncritically incorporated into the professional thinking of some scholars and writers on stratification who ought to know better.

In spite of all that can and should be said about the semantic difficulties with the analogical term *stratification*, it would seem unwise to try to delete it from the professional vocabulary. Rather, it seems to us to be so firmly entrenched in our usage that it must be retained, but used with the full knowledge that it is a physical analogue and is fraught with serious danger of reification.

Mention should perhaps be made of a *dual usage* to be found among writers who use the word *stratification*. Most often it refers to a condition, *as if* one stopped the maelstrom of societal activity as he does a movie projector and observed the pattern of subordination and superordination in the status systems. Stratification would thus be defined as a *pattern of superimposed categories of differential privilege* or some similar formulation. The other usage makes stratification a *process*. This is logical language usage, too, because society is dynamic and, surely, there must be some activity that takes place, as a result of which the patterns of differential status are worked out. Some writers state or imply that stratification is this *process* of assigning and achieving differential status. In practice this distinction should give the student little difficulty, however, because it is usually apparent from the context whether the writer is using the static or the dynamic meaning of the term.

3. Social Class

Social class has been defined in so many different ways that a systematic treatment would be both time consuming and of doubtful utility. One central core of meaning, however, runs throughout the varied usages, namely, the notion that the hierarchies of differential statuses and of privilege and disprivilege fall into certain clearly distinguishable categories set off from one another.[8] Historically this conception seems to have much better factual justification than it does in contemporary America. Under feudalism, for example, the status categories of serf, freeman, and nobleman were clearly set apart from one another by law, occupational differences, marriage proscriptions, and style of life. With the possible exception of the Negro-white distinction—and very doubtfully even there—there is no such counterpart in contemporary America, or for that matter, in much of Western civilization. Radical differences, to be sure, do exist in wealth, privilege, and possessions; but the *differences seem to range along a continuum with imperceptible gradation from one person to another*, so that no one can objectively draw "the line" between the "haves" and the "have nots," the "privileged" and "underprivileged," or for that matter, say who is in "the working class," who is "the common man," or who is a "capitalist." The differences are not categorical, but continuous.

Despite these difficulties, the term *social class* may be useful

[8] See, e.g., Robert MacIver and Charles Page, *Society: An Introductory Analysis* (New York, Rinehart and Co., 1949), pp. 348-349. They define social class as "any portion of a community marked off from the rest by social status."

in an approximate sense, such as that implied in the phrases *middle class, professional class,* and so on. The possibilities for deception, however, especially by reification, are omnipresent, as is also the tendency to assume greater similarities among the persons falling into the stated class than the facts warrant. For example, persons in the "working class" currently may receive annual incomes from, roughly, $2000 to as much as $10,000. Moreover, many "professionals" are employed at incomes in the lower half of the above range. "Stockholders" may own one or two $10 shares or a million, and, what is even more important, may hold any number between these extremes.

4. Statistical Class

Considerable clarity would be introduced into the analysis of stratification if it became conventional to use the adjective *statistical* as a modifier of *class* in many discussions. For statistical purposes, any continuous series of data may be divided into *any desired class intervals* to facilitate the process of analysis. Thus, the population can be divided into college graduates and non-college graduates—two classes. Or, on the basis of completion of grammar school, high school, college, and professional school—four classes. Or the number of years of schooling divided into intervals of four years, thus making five classes. Or one-year intervals, making about twenty classes. Any one of these is an entirely legitimate classification, but confusion and deception may easily lurk in the unwitting assumption that "class three" *is set off from* "class four" by anything more inherent than the statistician's arbitrary decision.

A great deal of insight into the nature of social stratification can be secured by statistical analysis of overt behavior, attitude, possessions, personal attributes, and so on. These analyses would be rendered more useful, in most instances, if several class intervals were employed in the customary "breakdown" of the same data, such as was suggested in the illustration concerning education in the above paragraph. Because this is rarely done, students, and sometimes also their teachers, frequently get the idea that the "over $10,000" a year man is somehow "set apart" from the "under $10,000" a year man, whereas such is true only in a highly technical sense.

5. Caste

There is relative clarity in the use of the term *caste* among both professional and lay writers. It refers simply to a society which is characterized by clear-cut status, power, and privilege differences which are relatively permanent. That is to say, a person is virtually born into a class and is ascribed a pattern of privilege and responsibility, and style of life, and probably a particular occupational range which he follows, with very few exceptions, for the rest of his life. It should be stressed that caste is a term, that there is probably no actual society in the world today which exactly fits the theoretical model of the word just defined. When we use the term *caste* we have reference, usually in a comparative context, to the society which is relatively caste-like in its characteristics.

It is conventional to refer to the position of the Negro and other "persons of color" in the United States as representing a caste or caste-like group. The reasons for this designation are probably obvious—restrictions prohibiting the Negro from entering certain occupations and strictly limiting him on others, prohibition of marriages with whites, civil disabilities, and so on. It should be apparent, however, that the Negro's position is not entirely caste-like and is becoming less and less so. Educational opportunities and employment opportunities for Negroes are ever becoming wider. Civil rights, though by no means equal, are slowly becoming equalized and limitations on social intercourse are becoming less strict. Although we see no serious objection to referring to the American Negro group as a caste, it should be done with the full awareness that some of the caste-like attributes are being removed and some of them have already disappeared.

6. *Social (Vertical) Mobility* [9]

Social (vertical) mobility refers to the changing status of a person in the stratification system of a society. The term is a loose and approximate one only. Obviously the "log cabin to riches" hero has been socially mobile. But how much social mobility is normal in a society, and how are we to measure it? Customarily we do so by money and occupational title, so that, for example, if a man whose father did not go to college graduates from college and enters a profession, we say that the son was socially mobile because his father followed an occupation not requiring a college education and the son is in one which does. It is possible, however, that the son's income and standard of living and position in the community might be appreciably below that of his father, and thus the matter becomes more complicated. There is also difficulty in distinguishing between social mobility of an individual and the social mobility of an entire category, such as an occupation. For example, during the past thirty years the *relative* income of semiskilled industrial workers in the United States has materially increased, so that it is not uncommon for regularly employed industrial workers to support a level of living appreciably above that of many teachers and clergymen. During both periods, however, industrial workers were industrial workers. Have they been upwardly mobile as a group or not? How about the teachers and clergy? Were they downwardly mobile—or not?

There are further complications in our conventional ways of measuring social mobility. Many studies compare the occupation of father and son.[10] If an industrially employed father, for

[9] For a classic treatment of this concept see Pitirim Sorokin, *Social Mobility* (New York, Harper and Bros., 1927).

[10] See, e.g., Natalie Rogoff, "Recent Trends in Urban Occupational Mobility," in Paul K. Hatt and Albert Reiss (eds.), *Reader in Urban Sociology* (Glencoe, Ill., The Free Press, 1951) or Stuart Adams, "Trends in Occupational Origins of Physicians," *American Sociological Review*, 18 (August, 1953), pp. 404-410.

example, sends his son to college and his son enters a profession and remains in it for the rest of his working life, has the son been upwardly mobile or immobile? Conventionally this would often be called "upward mobility," because the son is in a higher ranking occupation than his father. But if his father's income provided the college education, is it not as logical to credit the upward mobility to the father as to the son? Also, if the son spent his entire life in the same occupation, was he upwardly mobile or stationary?

Considerable attention among sociologists and other social scientists has centered around such questions as whether the American status system is making upward mobility more difficult [11] and whether the handicaps to upward mobility are fair and just. On the whole, most sociologists seem to have concluded that the barriers are not "fair and just" and that considerable need for reform exists.

Barriers to social mobility may be loosely designated as of two varieties—*functional* and *arbitrary*. By functional we mean those barriers to higher occupational position which relate to the ability of the person to discharge the obligations of the position. For example, if a boy does not have the physical and mental ability to become a physician or an engineer, then it seems rational and moral to deny him the right to enter that profession. But all of the limitations to upward mobility are not functional. Some are *arbitrarily imposed and thoroughly undemocratic* in character. Such factors as color, religion, or father's social position have frequently been introduced to prevent persons of ability from entering certain occupations of high status. Leaving aside the dubious morality of such a procedure, there is the practical consequence that the society is thus deprived of the services of a competent trainee.

[11] See Gideon Sjoberg, "Are Social Classes in America Becoming More Rigid?" *American Sociological Review*, 16 (December, 1951), pp. 775-783.

7. "Open" and "Closed" Class [12]

The student of social stratification literature will frequently encounter such phrases as *open class* and *closed class* in the discussions of social mobility. These terms simply have reference to the (real or assumed) ease of changing one's status. The "closed" class system approaches caste, in that mobility is difficult and rare. The "open" class system, on the other hand, is presumably a system in which mobility is frequent and easy. It is, in short, a "democratic" system, where the barriers to mobility are of the functional variety discussed above and not arbitrarily imposed for the purpose of limiting competition.

8. Differential Aspiration [13]

In recent years attention has been drawn to *differential aspiration* for social mobility as a factor affecting the rate of upward social mobility in the United States. The concept briefly is this: Numerous potentially able people who could easily meet the requirements of training and entrance into positions of higher status do not aspire to such positions. Although the evidence is by no means clear as to what factors go into differential aspiration, it is apparent that differential aspiration exists, and that it is a significant factor affecting mobility. We do not know how much is due to an unwillingness or inability to postpone immediate gratifications in order to fulfill the requirements of training or education essential for the higher-status occupation. Furthermore, we do not know how much importance should be assigned to the conventional rationalizations, somewhat current among lower-class families, that it is "no use" to aspire to higher occupations because the "cards are stacked against poor kids," the "snobs will keep you out anyhow," and "it isn't what you know but who you know" that determines your success.

[12] The classic treatment of these terms is found in C. H. Cooley, *Social Organization* (New York, Charles Scribner's Sons, 1909), Chapter XXI.

[13] See especially Leonard Reissman, "Levels of Aspiration and Social Class," *American Sociological Review*, 18 (June, 1953), pp. 233-242.

It should be apparent by now that the analysis of social mobility is highly complicated as well as important. The purpose of this preliminary discussion is to call attention to the fact that some of the suppositions underlying criticisms and justifications of the status quo have not always been objectively arrived at, and that, even if theoretically clear, have not always been supported by the kind of factual evidence necessary to justify the criticisms or justifications which are offered.

9. Life-Chances [14]

Life-chances is a quasi-actuarial concept. It refers to the varying probability that a person in a given status will achieve some stated objective or suffer some stated disadvantage. For example, early in the interest in social class a study was made of the differential probability that newborn infants among the various income levels of the population of a city would live through the first year. As would be surmised, the lowest likelihood of survival was found in the lowest-income groups with the chances rising materially along with the income of the parents, although the very highest incomes seem not to have improved the chances over the moderately high. So we see rather literally that the "chances of life" for a newborn infant are related to the family's ability to buy and otherwise get for him those things which are necessary for survival during the first year—food, sanitation, medical care, and the like.[15] It soon became apparent that many of the other good things of life, as a rule, were conditional upon the status position of the person seeking them. There is now widespread recognition that the ideal of "equality before the law" [16] does not obtain in practice, that persons of higher income and social status receive better treatment and can afford to pay for better legal

[14] See, e.g., Pfautz, *op. cit.*, p. 401.
[15] A. J. Mayer and P. M. Hauser, "Class Differentials in Expectation of Life at Birth," *Revue de l'Institut Internationale de Statistique*, 18 (1950), pp. 197-200.
[16] Walter Reckless, *The Crime Problem* (New York, Appleton-Century-Crofts, Inc., 1950), pp. 57-60.

assistance than can their less opulent neighbors. As early as the
1920's the Lynds [17] showed, for instance, that in Muncie, Indiana,
the likelihood that a child of high intelligence would go to college was more dependent on the financial and social position of
his parents than upon the child's ability to do college work.
Criminologists have demonstrated that the probability of children
becoming delinquent is in significant part dependent upon the
neighborhoods they grow up in, the neighborhood, of course,
being strongly influenced by parents' occupation, education, and
income.

Further evidence could be marshaled at great length, but probably need not be. The point is that the conditions of social stratification tend to be self-perpetuating and tend to reinforce one
another. This statement of the matter has been sharply chal-
lenged by persons who adhere to what has been called "the American dream"—the notion that if a person is ambitious and virtuous
and able and "somehow has it in him," he will be upwardly
mobile, with no real limits. Presidents of the United States who
were born in log cabins, bank presidents who started as messenger
boys, and corporation executives who delivered newspapers when
they were boys are cited as evidence that "it *can* be done." And,
of course, it *is* done, but the crux of the issue is: How often?
What are the probabilities? We do not know exactly what the
probabilities are for given people, but we do know with reasonable
surety that the probabilities for achieving health, wealth, and
fame are *better* for a child of higher status than of a lower status.
The point is not that there is certainty of success for the high-
status child and certainty of failure for the low-status child, but
rather that the chances are appreciably better for the higher-status
child.

Despite the tendency to argue the opposite for patriotic and
moralistic reasons, most people give tacit evidence that they are
aware of the life-chances hypothesis. A considerable amount of

---

[17] Robert and Helen Lynd, *Middletown* (New York, Harcourt, Brace
and Co., 1929), pp. 185-186 and especially footnotes on p. 185.

the striving and "keeping up with the Joneses," which is such a conspicuous part of American goal-seeking, consists of the efforts which many people are making to improve their own and their children's life-chances wherever they can. An acquaintance with teenage children sells his comfortable home in order to move into an exclusive suburban section, so that his children can grow up "making the right contacts in order to get ahead in the world." A widow with a marriageable daughter moves to a college town, enrolls the girl in college because "that is the best place for her to find a husband; my grandchildren must have a better chance than my daughter did."

It appears likely that some reformists' zeal has overplayed the importance of differential life-chances. There has been much loose talk and writing about the "impossibility" of a lower-status boy achieving this or that status which a dozen other lower-status boys are achieving every day. Moreover, differential life-chances have been used as an alibi to mask personal failure in character or ability and to account for low aspirational levels when they may need explaining to oneself or to someone else. These vulgarizations to the contrary notwithstanding, however, the fact remains that life-chances are unequal and that they are roughly correlated with position on one or more vertical scales which measure the parents' social statuses and therefore the child's differential opportunity to achieve the "good things" in the society.

Other somewhat technical concepts than the aforementioned will, of course, be used throughout the book. It would seem to be unnecessary as well as cumbersome to define them all. Much of this nomenclature is, or ought to be, already familiar, because it is more or less standard in the social sciences, if not even in the language of the better-informed layman. In this category would fall such terms and concepts as *culture*, *role*, *value*, and *personality*.

SUMMARY

In this chapter we have attempted to set forth in very broad outline the minimal nomenclature which we regard as essential for undertaking our task of summarizing, criticizing, and integrating much of the extant literature on social stratification. Rather than simply defining these terms as one might in a glossary, we have attempted to add substance to them by discussing a few pertinent problems relating to each concept and commenting on the utility and disutility involved in a number of them. Equipped with these understandings, the student will be more adequately prepared to assume the task which lies ahead.

SELECTED READINGS

The selected readings for the first three chapters will be found on page 42.

2

Three Theoretical Themes

SOME OF THE basic aspects of our frame of reference were introduced in the preceding chapter. There a number of pivotal concepts were defined and something of their interrelationships suggested. The task of orientation is not yet completed, however, until we examine some larger theoretical issues and consider a number of methodological problems pertinent to the larger undertaking.

UNIDIMENSIONAL VERSUS
MULTIDIMENSIONAL STRATIFICATION

One of the persistent, but *often implicit*, theoretical difficulties which obfuscate efforts to analyze social stratification concerns whether stratification (or "class") is unidimensional or multidimensional. Writers with a strong statistical bent sometimes approach their task with either a tacit or expressed assumption that stratification "is" a hierarchical arrangement of persons measured or manifested by *a* difference—attitudes, style of life, differential power, prestige, economic role, or what not. In contrast stand a few sociologists, but growing in number, who apparently have been influenced, whether they know it or not, by the late Max Weber.[1] Weber distinguished among at least three stratifications

[1] See H. H. Gerth and C. W. Mills, *From Max Weber: Essays in Sociology* (New York, Oxford University Press, 1946), pp. 180-195, and A. M. Henderson and T. Parsons, *Max Weber: The Theory of Social and Economic Organization* (New York, Oxford University Press, 1947), pp. 424-429.

in a society: (1) the *economic order* ("classes"), that is, the relation of persons to the production and distribution of goods and services; (2) *the prestigial or honorific order* ("social order"); and (3) the *power structure* ("legal order"). A given person (or family) at any given time has at least these three, not one, relative positions in a society. The three positions may not correlate with one another—and often striking contrasts are manifest. Moreover, the interrelations among these three stratifications are not fixed, but rather are constantly changing.

Our own position on this issue is very well stated by Kurt Mayer.[2] (His use of the word *class* instead of *stratification* represents no inconsistency with our usage.)

Only a class theory which recognizes these three [or more] vertical dimensions as analytically distinct and which intends to trace their interrelationship can provide a realistic understanding of the class structure of complex, industrial societies. [It must also take cognizance of the fact that the interrelationships of the three dimensions are] in constant flux.

This is a larger order than might at first appear. To apprehend and measure the three (and there may be more) dimensions is a baffling and complex problem; to analyze their interrelationship is an even more subtle and exacting task. But the objective seems to us rightly stated by Mayer, and while we must be satisfied with less than full accomplishment for the present, we should also recognize that the goal is not truly reached when we fashion a quick "solution" by unidimensional analyses.

CONTINUUM THEORY VERSUS CATEGORICAL THEORIES

Categorical (or discrete classes) theories claim, in effect, that in American society the patterns of prestige, power, and other privileges and disprivileges result in the creation of more or less distinct groupings of persons. Such expressions as "the working

[2] Kurt Mayer, "The Theory of Social Classes," *Harvard Educational Review* (Summer, 1953), p. 165.

class is marked off from" some other class, imply that there is a line of demarcation which sets off the designated group of ranked people from some other group. One of these writers says, "A social class, then, is any portion of a community *marked off from the rest by social status.*" [3] In other words, it is postulated by some writers that there is in a community (or society) a collectivity of people of sufficiently similar privilege and disprivilege that they are "marked off from" other persons with different privilege-disprivilege configurations. This concept of stratification is further implied in such phrases as "class lines" and "class conflicts."

Some writers, conscious of the difficulty of defining precisely these alleged lines, point out that it is sometimes impossible to determine "just where" the line should be drawn, but that there is, "somehow," "more or less," some "sort of line" that everyone knows is there! Many persons are familiar, for example, with the upper-, middle-, and lower-class trichotomy, with the Lynds' "business class"-"working class" dichotomy,[4] and with the Warner group's sixfold class system.[5] When one attempts to place a *random* selection of individuals in their "proper" class categories, difficulties arise,[6] because the individuals in question have some attributes, say, of "lower-upper" and some attributes of "lower-middle." Where, then do they "belong"? Proponents of these categorical systems often allege that these unclassifiable cases are really only "few," are "exceptions to the rule," or are "individuals in transition" from one status category to another. Although there is undoubtedly some truth to each of these rationalizations, we shall subsequently demonstrate that such cases are *not* few, much less "exceptional," or "persons in transition."

---

[3] Robert MacIver and Charles Page, *Society: An Introductory Analysis* (New York, Rinehart and Co., 1949), pp. 348-349. Italics not in original.

[4] Robert and Helen Lynd, *Middletown* (New York, Harcourt, Brace and Co., 1929), and also their *Middletown in Transition* (1937).

[5] W. L. Warner, Marchia Meeker, and Kenneth Eells, *Social Class in America* (Chicago, Science Research Associates, Inc., 1949).

[6] See, e.g., Gerhard E. Lenski, "American Social Classes: Statistical Strata or Social Groups?" *American Journal of Sociology*, 58 (September, 1952), pp. 139-145.

It should be pointed out that not all persons who use the *nomenclature* of the categorical-class analyst necessarily subscribe to the above rigidity. Sometimes expressions like "middle class" or "upper-upper" are used in a loose way to designate an approximate range in a hierarchical system for comparative purposes. They do not imply lines of demarcation any more than a person who speaks of "middle age" or "old people" necessarily implies that the categories are clear cut. Considerable caution, therefore, should be observed in analyzing a writer's theoretical position, lest we confuse nomenclature with *conceptualization*.

By implication we have already defined the *continuum theory of stratification*, namely, the idea that there are several privilege, power, and status ranges, more or less continuous from top to bottom, with no clear lines of demarcation. For statistical purposes, of course, it is entirely legitimate to set up *statistical* classes in a continuous series of data, breaking the series at any point or points which suit the purposes of the investigation. Thus, for example, if we are dealing with age, we could, logically, define "old age" as beginning at 65, because then the person is eligible for social security payments; or at 70, because then he has outlived the average life expectancy at birth; or at 55 or thereabouts, because that seems a reasonable point at which to terminate the range called "middle age." Any of these lines of demarcation can be considered logical, so long as one does not assume that this statistical device gives him any particular grasp on reality and so long as he also realizes that any individual at a given age may fall into a number of different categories, depending on the purpose of the classifier.

Protagonists of the continuum theory of stratification in American society make a strong case for their theory.

1. First, they point out one criticism of the categorical theories, which is now more or less widely known: that there are almost as many systems as there are observers—three classes, six classes, two classes, and four classes!

2. No matter what the criteria may be, significant numbers of

persons cannot be readily categorized; this being the case, what shall we do with these numerous "fringe" people?

3. Moreover, the bases of ranking change from time to time, the privileges and disprivileges of persons change with the passing and repealing of laws and the obsolescence of occupations, and in many other ways the system is in perennial flux.[7]

4. A very important line of justification for the continuum theory devolves from the nature of the data. As everyone knows, students of differential rank have "discovered" that the possession of wealth and income, family background, education, ownership of status-giving goods, and prestige give a person or family a relative ranking in the local community or even in the nation. However, when we *measure* each of these attributes, a *continuous series of data emerges*. Income and wealth form a continuous series from the multimillionare to the person on relief. Occupational prestige has been measured and the findings form a series of scores from 96 (out of a possible 100 points) down to 33. (See pp. 138 to 139 for further comment on this study.) Wealth follows a pattern similar to that of income; and prestige goods and services, since they are largely dependent upon income, also follow the same pattern. Education, to be sure, does show some "natural" breaks in the series, due only, however, to the convention of terminating education at the completion of the eighth grade or of high school or of college or of a professional or other post-graduate school.

5. What is an even more important justification of the continuum theory derives from the fact that the alleged bases or criteria for ranking (whether prestige or power or privilege is focused upon) mostly do not show significant *correlations* with one another. A hypothetical case may be constructed to *illustrate* (not offered as "proof" of) this point.

[7] An excellent treatment of this point is to be found in Gideon Sjoberg, "Are Social Classes in America Becoming More Rigid?" *American Sociological Review*, 16 (December, 1951), pp. 775-783. See also M. E. Deeg and D. G. Peterson, "Changes in Social Status of Occupations," *Occupations*, 25 (January, 1947), pp. 205-208.

John Doe is a Jewish owner-proprietor of the largest mercantile establishment in a New England city of 100,000. Being the son of an immigrant, in a family which did not highly value education, he left high school at the end of his second year. Upon his father's death, he inherited a half-million dollar estate, including his father's old, but well-built, home in the "zone of transition" of the city. A Jew, he cannot belong to either of the two high-prestige country clubs or to any of the high-status Protestant churches of the city, and there is not a large enough Jewish population to support a Jewish Synagogue. One of his sons married the daughter of a highly respected professor in the local university. The other son remained in the military service after the end of the war.

Now what "class" does this man belong to? In terms of lineage, it is obvious that he belongs to a group long disvalued in the Western European culture. In terms of prestige goods—home, automobile, clothes, and jewels—his rating would be approximately average. His institutional affiliations (country club, church, lodge, etc.) would do little, if anything, to attach special prestige or power to him. His educational achievements are certainly below average; those of his children only slightly better. The details in this case are admittedly somewhat extreme, but cases of this *type* are not unusual. It is well known that some of our most highly educated persons (teachers, clergymen, scientists) are on the average relatively lowly paid, and some of our most highly paid persons and groups have little formal education. Many of the "old families" are no longer well off financially and the *nouveaux riches* are found in every community. The correlations among the various criteria of rank are mostly tautological ones: wealth and/or income and the possession of goods that require wealth or income in order to possess them. This is hardly a startling discovery.

It seems for these and other reasons that we are on more sound theoretical ground as social scientists if we proceed on the assumption that the American ranking system is more accurately conceived of as a continuum than as a set of discrete categories. A more detailed, documented defense of this position will be made at the conclusion of this book, after an examination of many kinds of "evidence" has been completed. It seems desirable here at the outset, however, to make clear that we do have this theoretical preference, and some of the reasons why we hold to it. The reader is further reminded that we do not rest our case at this point; to do so would be, at best, premature. There are numerous empirical studies which need first to be examined and also some additional theoretical problems with which we will need to struggle. There is, then, a great deal more to the continuum theory than has been presented up to this point.

THE ISSUE OF "FUNCTIONALISM"

A third theoretical issue concerns the *raison d'être* of a stratification system. What is its rationale? Two main views on this question can be found in present sociological literature.

The *functional* point of view, stated in simple terms, holds that the existing differential distribution of privilege and disprivilege derives from the efforts of a society to fulfill its necessary goals.[8] For example, a society needs leaders in government, religion, and education. These leaders require substantial periods of training and they must defer gratification of many of their personal wants and must submit to considerable discipline in order to secure their training. After the period of training is completed, they are required to assume positions of considerable responsibility, resulting often in more self-denial. As a reward for these disprivileges, and for the value of the service performed, these persons, it is claimed, receive the privilege of higher income, higher prestige, deference, and various kinds of other perquisites.[9]

Furthermore, talent is relatively scarce. Not everyone has the necessary intelligence, physical stamina, and emotional attributes, for example, to complete the conventional training for an M.D.

---

[8] For a clear and forceful statement of a functionalist position, see especially Kingsley Davis and W. E. Moore, "Some Principles of Stratification," *American Sociological Review*, 10 (April, 1945), pp. 242-249.
[9] *Ibid.*

degree and to practice medicine thereafter. Similarly for other professions and undertakings that require special skill. Therefore, it is further argued by functionalists, unequal privilege is also the result of unequal possession of talent.[10]

A conflicting view [11] stresses that, for American society at least, there are contradictions to the functional theory. The positions of highest societal responsibility—government, religion, the judiciary, and education—are financially not highly rewarded in the American system. Are we to conclude that liquor dispensers, entertainers (including athletes), and speculators have a higher "function" in American society? They, along with racketeers, certainly receive higher incomes and are further supported in the eyes of many by high prestige. Furthermore, what is particularly functional about the accent on lineage? Moreover, cases are legion in which persons of considerable talent are summarily denied the right to exercise their talents in socially responsible positions simply because they are Negroes, or because they are Jewish, or because otherwise they have not chosen their parents wisely.

An acceptable functionalist position would seem to need, then, to take account of several conditions: (1) "Rewards" to persons, which presumably motivate the able to defer gratification and otherwise translate their aspirations into actions in the public interest, should be understood to include psychic and prestigial income as well as financial returns. The low incomes of teachers and clergymen may be counterbalanced by such factors as high prestige, pleasant working conditions, long vacations, and other non-pecuniary advantages. (2) Alternative ways of handling recruitment and reward should be recognized as being compara-

---

[10] *Ibid.*

[11] For a vigorous critique of Davis and Moore's position on functionalism and stratification see Melvin Tumin, "Some Principles of Stratification: A Critical Analysis," *American Sociological Review*, 18 (August, 1953), pp. 387-394. A defense of their position by Davis and Moore follows Tumin's critique. The issue is reopened by Tumin again in a "Letter to the Editor," *American Sociological Review*, 18 (December, 1953), p. 672.

bly, if not equally, functional in meeting the needs of the society. In other words, the functionalist should so state his position that it could not be used by the supporters of the status quo in such a way that all new ways of recruitment and reward come to be labeled "disfunctional." Change can improve as well as impede the chances for a better society. (3) Goals (values) of those who judge functionality should be recognized as affecting judgments of what is and is not functional. For example, mass education is probably not "functional" to one with pro-fascist views. (4) What is "functional" will vary from time to time because societal arrangements are not functional per se, but rather are so in part *because of* the conditions imposed on the society from the outside. For example, a large military force is functional only so long as there is a real and present danger from the outside; otherwise it is a parasite on the economy. Examined in the light of these and probably other qualifications, a stratification system can probably be objectively evaluated, either in toto or in its various parts, as to its functionality.

SUMMARY

In this chapter we have examined three basic theoretical issues pertaining to social stratification—multidimensional versus uni-dimensional stratification, continuum theory versus discrete classes theory, and the issue of functionalism. We have taken a stand with respect to each prior to our examination of research findings because we believe that a position has to be taken in order to orient oneself. It may be necessary, in the light of the data which we shall examine, to change these positions. Therefore, these issues shall be reopened in the latter part of the book when we may be better equipped to consider them in a less *a priori* manner.

SELECTED READINGS

The selected readings for the first three chapters will be found on page 42.

3

Some Methodological Aspects
of Stratification Research

AN EMPIRICAL ORIENTATION

SOME critics have approached the study of stratification on an essentially intuitive basis. They have said, or implied, that people generally, or they themselves, "just know" about stratification and accordingly have felt free to state summary generalizations, assert cause-and-effect relationships, and present an altogether definitive treatment of the subject. Although upon occasion we and others have become impatient with the other extreme of too-narrow empiricism, often almost devoid of any theoretical orientation, we feel that the most reliable procedure for us is to *adhere rather closely to fact, and to subject our theoretical propositions and generalizations recurrently to the empirical test.* Thus, we do not intend to comment upon "the essence of class" or "the spirit of the age" or "the ethos of the proletariat." We leave this quasi-mysticism to the poet, the journalist, and possibly also to the social philosopher. (The politician will probably exploit the privilege anyway!) If we assert something to be "true" we shall accept the obligation to *demonstrate* it: (*a*) as a direct conclusion from facts gathered by some presumably reliable researcher, (*b*) as a reasonable inference from such data, or (*c*) as an observation which the reader could presumably make for himself or which others have made informally—an empirical observation, not fancy or guess.

We do not accept the rigid convention, however, that only elaborately statistical research is "empirical." Empiricism refers to any and all efforts to test generalizations by recourse to objectively verifiable information. A vast amount of available objective (verifiable) information has often been ignored by sociologists, possibly because some researchers have apparently overlearned their statistical lessons. Historical data, personal observation, and illustrative cases are all empirical and highly useful in this and in many other fields, even though they yield no coefficients of correlation or chi squares.

When we emphasize that our approach will be empirical, we do not mean that we shall not be concerned also with logical analysis. Actually, we consider that an important, though often neglected, part of empirical endeavor is logical analysis of the assumptions underlying statistical inquiry and of the assumptions implicit in drawing conclusions from statistical data. In fact, much of our evaluation of the various studies which constitute the core of this book will be logical criticism. We feel that the distinction between empiricism and theoretical endeavor has been too long overplayed—a liaison, in the field of stratification at least, is long overdue.

Nor do we mean to imply, either, that logic is any satisfactory substitute for empirical endeavor, any more than that the reverse would be true. Our position is that the logical analysis of a problem and of data which purport to be relevant to the problem are indispensable parts of mature empiricism. The stereotyped straw men, conventionally called "the arm-chair theorist" and "the raw empiricist," both seem to us to be of patent disutility. Rather, we shall seek a more inclusive form of inquiry, rigorous and relentless in its scrutiny of the so-called "facts." But facts we must have, else we know not whether we are dealing with reality or with the figments of some individual imagination or societal myth.

A TENTATIVE ATTITUDE TOWARD "DATA"

There is no dearth of allegedly factual material in the field of social stratification. But there *is* a dearth of data which can be considered truly reliable—reliable at least as a basis for drawing the inclusive and often dogmatic conclusions which are so frequently stated with confidence. Arnold Rose has aptly called our attention to this problem in a related connection. ". . . There is a growing science by analogy. The conclusion of many an excellent study based on a limited sample is couched in the form of a universal generalization." [1]

Not only are studies often overgeneralized, but frequently a given set of data lend themselves equally well to more than the one conclusion which the author has, for whatever reason, chosen to make. The point is not that his conclusion is wrong, but that another one, basically different from his, is equally right. Moreover, the techniques by which data are gathered and the techniques by which they are processed have a great deal to do with the kinds of evidence one gets. We are not implying that any appreciable number of American sociologists have deliberately set out to get inaccurate data, but rather that somehow they have often been misled regarding what they have found.

The following four considerations, more specifically, seem to justify the contention that the student of existing stratification data should be highly cautious in the conclusions he draws, even though the authors of the studies are persons of high repute and the statistics often sound impressive.

1. *The Local Nature of Most Research Data*

With a few exceptions, which we shall cite later, research materials on stratification have been of a local nature. Almost always the researcher has selected a city or village or hamlet or section of the open countryside and proceeded to analyze it somewhat

[1] Arnold M. Rose, "Generalizations in the Social Sciences," *American Journal of Sociology*, 59 (July, 1953), p. 49.

intensively. It is usually fairly easy to rationalize the alleged "typicality" of the community chosen; nevertheless, generalization beyond the local area actually studied involves more faith than scientific wisdom. Indisputably there are many uniformities in social relationships, probably even more than most persons realize, but it does not follow that one has a right to *assume uniformities of a specific sort that have not been demonstrated.* We do not, moreover, intend to imply that a locality study is not an entirely legitimate study. The point is, rather, that the locality study is *known* to be true only for the locality chosen—even if otherwise entirely satisfactory; we simply do not know how well, or even whether, it applies somewhere else. We are not asserting that it does *not* apply; we are simply insisting that we do not know *whether* it applies.

There are, to be sure, some exceptions to this general pattern of localized studies. Centers, for example (see Chapter 10), studied a sample of the national population, and North and Hatt used a national sample of white males in their study of the prestige ranking of a series of occupations.[2] But even the latter is limited—to whites and to males and to adults. We do not consider this a serious limitation, but it *is* a limitation.

2. The Factor of Obsolescence

No sociologist seriously denies that American society is "dynamic," and it seems an altogether reasonable assumption that the systems of stratification, whatever their attributes, are not exceptions to the general proposition. However, most researches take place at a particular point in time. This is necessary and entirely legitimate, but the conclusions from such undertakings are frequently cited as generalizations projected more or less indefinitely into the future. Centers' study showed, for example, that industrial workers were overwhelmingly "liberal" in their political philosophy and were supporters of the Democratic party.

[2] National Opinion Research Center, "Jobs and Occupations: A Popular Evaluation," *Opinion News*, 9 (September 1, 1947), pp. 3-13.

This was presumably accurate in the 1940's when the study was made. Obviously, it would at least be doubtful that this condition is still true, since in the last presidential election in sections of the country where the preponderant vote was a working-class vote, sizable pluralities for the Republican party (surely the less "liberal" party) were amassed. On the basis of Centers' data this would have been highly unlikely, if not impossible. Certainly Centers is not to be held responsible for people having changed their minds! Our criticism, of course, is not of Centers at all, but of people who use Centers' data as if they were as true today as a decade ago when they were gathered. Illustrations of this sort could be multiplied; we may not even have used the most glaring one in our reference to the Centers' study. It should be stressed again and again, however, that conditions change and that unless studies are repeated in comparable form at fairly frequent intervals, which they almost never are, then the obsolescence factor intervenes as a potential invalidating influence. We have said a *potential* invalidating influence, because it is quite possible that some aspects of stratification do persist over long periods and are highly resistant to change. But in the absence of *data documenting* that fact, one has no right to *assume* it.

3. *Research Methods Strongly Influence the Results Secured*

Anyone who has had practical experience in conducting or guiding or advising research enterprises will readily recognize that the research designs used and the techniques employed in gathering and interpreting data are almost inevitably compromises and sometimes rather devious compromises. Almost never can we find out exactly what we want to know, from exactly the persons from whom we want to get it, and exactly in the place and in the quantity and in the form we ideally prefer. To get what we would ideally desire is usually too costly, or too time-consuming, or the persons having the information will not give it or cannot give it. Another persistent difficulty is communication. One cannot be sure when he asks an informant "What social class do you belong to?" that the informant will understand the question the way the interrogator means it. This is true even when the question is accompanied by careful explanations. Although considerable progress has been made in the art of question-asking and of scale construction in recent years, numerous problems still persist.

Moreover, verbal data do not always correspond to "reality" in other dimensions. A man may say he "belongs to the working class," but what does he *do* because of it, and *what difference does it make* in his life whether he says "working class" or "middle class" or what not? We usually assume, when a person makes a choice of class affiliation, that the response indicated something more than a verbal claim. But how do we *know* that it does? Too often this is left to simple faith. In some studies, to be sure, overt behavior data have been collected and to these, of course, this caution does not apply.

Other cautions pertain, however, to the gathering even of overt behavior data. For example, suppose that a study shows conclusively that persons of a certain occupational and income category —often termed *a class*—usually marry other persons from the same group. Superficially, the conclusion may be drawn by some that either these persons had preferences for their own class or were left with no alternative because they were rejected by other classes. Quite possibly neither is the correct explanation. Residential propinquity studies, for instance, show that substantial numbers of persons, even in large cities, marry persons who live close by.[3] Perhaps residential propinquity and other kinds of propinquity, like job and recreational participation, simply multiply the chances for exposure to potential mates of similar socioeconomic level. The supposition of *preference* for a class per se or a *rejection* by other classes may be quite as much a delusion of the interpreter as a necessary derivative from the data.

The problem of choosing *indices* is especially perplexing.

[3] See, e.g., Alfred C. Clarke, "Residential Propinquity as a Factor in Mate Selection," *American Sociological Review*, 17 (February, 1952), pp. 17-23.

Rarely can one secure the actual information he wants. Suppose, for example, it is an investigator's objective to test the hypothesis that persons on different socio-economic levels in the same community have different styles of life, that is, have different recreational patterns, food habits, and household routines. How do we measure these? Do we ask people? If so, whom do we ask: the husband or the wife, the neighbors, or the children, or all of them? But maybe they are unable or unwilling to tell the truth. Are we to assume, if family *A* owns a $500 TV set, and family *B* a $250 one, that TV viewing is more important to one than to the other? Are we going to use amount of time spent as a satisfactory index for comparing the relative importance of movie attendance among different people? If we are interested in vacation patterns, which is the best index: how many miles people travel, how much the vacation costs them, how long it takes, or what? One fairly well-known scale utilizes a set of facts recording the content of living rooms as an index of a family's socio-economic status.[4] Another study finds that a composite index of occupation, source of income, community of residence, and type of house are sufficient indices to place a person reasonably accurately in the status system of his community.[5] But what results would one get if he used *another* set of indices on the same persons? Would the community "stratify" in the same way, and who is to say which index is the better, even for the purpose stated?

Sometimes the choice of different indices results in diametrically opposite conclusions. In an unpublished study of a group of university fraternity and sorority members, one student, using the index of part-time employment, concluded that sororities and fraternities were becoming more democratic, that is, reaching a

[4] F. S. Chapin, *Scale for Rating Living Room Equipment*, Institute of Child Welfare, Circular Number 3, Minneapolis, University of Minnesota Press, 1930, and also "Socio-Economic Status: Some Preliminary Results of Measurement," *American Journal of Sociology*, 37 (January, 1932), pp. 581-587.

[5] W. L. Warner, Marchia Meeker, and Kenneth Eells, *Social Class in America* (Chicago, Science Research Associates, Inc., 1949).

wider economic range because, as time went on, a larger and larger proportion of the members of these fraternities and sororities were employed part-time. Employment was interpreted to mean financial need. Another student, studying the same fraternities and sororities—in fact, using the same informants—drew the opposite conclusion by using a different index, namely, whether the student's father or mother had been a fraternity or sorority member. This student found that as time went on, a larger percentage of members had mothers or fathers who were also sorority or fraternity members. Our point is obviously not to attempt to answer the question of democratization of sorority and fraternity membership, but rather to point out that, depending on the index used, a given hypothesis or its opposite can frequently be sustained. Ideally, of course, a research ought to be designed with multiple indices and the data examined in the light of alternative hypotheses, but this is not often done.

Summarily, then, the student is admonished to be cautious in accepting the alleged "results" of inquiries into stratification phenomena. This admonition stems from our observations that the results are strongly influenced by the kind of indices used, the sample chosen, and many other kinds of methodological compromises which necessarily have to be made. Again, it should be stressed that caution in the evaluation of conclusions does not mean a summary rejection of conclusions. The student may find, after scrutinizing some research carefully and critically, that its results stand up. This should be the *conclusion*, however, of the inquiry, and not taken for granted at the *outset*.

4. Bias

Finally, we come to the question of bias, conscious or unconscious, on the part of the investigator making the study. This problem is a subtle and highly important one. Despite conscientious struggle with the problem, almost since the beginning of social-science research, our methods for handling it are not altogether satisfactory. To begin with, we must understand that every study has one or more biases. We cannot eliminate bias. At best, perhaps, bias can be *rendered explicit*, so that the reviewer of an investigation can determine for himself whether the bias has seriously affected the conclusions or the initial formulation of the problem. To illustrate, let us assume that two persons, one an "intellectual Marxist" and one a conservative, "free-enterprise" oriented person, both set out to study "class influence" on education. The Marxist, committed as he is to the underlying notion of an inevitable conflict of interest between the proletariat and bourgeoisie, would quickly note much evidence of bourgeoisie domination of the school system. He would observe that school boards are almost always chosen from among the bourgeoisie and that most administrators also are, that they largely indoctrinate children rather than educate them, and that many lower-class children of ability do not go on into higher education. For each of these charges he could supply abundant statistical evidence. Our free-enterprise student, on the other hand, could point out, also with evidence, that comparatively few industrial workers have either the interest or the necessary skills to become members of school boards with their myriads of responsibilities and time-consuming activities. He would probably point out that, of course, public school teachers and administrators are largely re-cruited from the middle class, because it is in the middle class that children characteristically learn the kind of values and skills nec-essary to training and success in college. Finally, he could show that many of the children of working-class parents who may be *able* to do college work do not *want* to go to college. Instead of seeing in the system a sort of conspiracy by the bourgeoisie to restrict the educational plum to themselves, he could present statistical evidence to show that large numbers of the working class wish to have no part of it anyway. Here we have some of the main lines of an important controversy. Both analysts are able and presumably persons of integrity. Their conclusions are diametrically opposed, however, because of their prior commit-ments to philosophical *premises which are essentially independent*

of the specific data in the immediate inquiry. Yet both can present statistical data to support their hypotheses in such a way as
to sound convincing.

For all of these reasons, then—the local nature of most research,
the constant danger of obsolescence, the fallibility of our research
methods and indices employed, and the unavoidable problems of
bias and philosophical commitment—it seems to us that the careful
student cannot but be highly cautious in his interpretation of our
so-called "data."

AN OPEN MIND

Students who are familiar with the thoughtways of contemporary sociology are quite aware of the existence of schools of
thought based either on philosophical or methodological commit-
ments. We have our theoreticians and our empiricists, our func-
tional-anthropological schools, our Warner school, our pro-Marx-
ists, and our persistent American Dreamers. Like the apocryphal
blind men examining the elephant, each is very, very sure that he
has a firm grip on reality. And he can prove it with statistics—or
he refuses to "stoop" to prove it with statistics!

What, then, is the student to make of this seething cauldron
of data and more data, claim and counterclaim. Helpful advice is
not easy to give, but it would seem to us that an open mind is
the safest and soundest position. Probably no one has a monopoly
of the facts or of skill in their interpretation. Likewise, probably
no one's research is wholly without value. Unlike the bigoted
blind men arguing about the nature of the elephant, it seems to
us that men with eyes could apprehend that there are large measures of truth and also of falsity in the conflicting testimony, and
that it is incumbent upon *them* somehow to integrate, somehow to
put together into a meaningful and more or less consistent whole,
those data and conclusions which make sense and to rake up and
burn such other rubbish for which they can see no further use. The
professional worker in the field will probably store the rubbish

in the attic, because he may have need of it someday. And there may even be diamonds in the debris!

SUMMARY

We have divided the discussion of our working frame of reference into two categories, theory and method, although of necessity the two have been somewhat co-mingled. We have tentatively chosen the multidimensional over the unidimensional concept of stratification, and the continuum theory over the categorical theory of American social stratification, chiefly, but not completely, because the former does not preclude the other, and seems much easier to document with existing evidence. Similarly, we have cast our lot with those who hold that our stratification system is a qualifiedly functional one, thus rejecting at least the more sweeping implications of some of the functionalists. Finally, we have committed ourselves to an empirical orientation, but to a tentative attitude toward empiric data. Our rationale for each of these commitments has been tersely set forth in this and the preceding chapter.

SELECTED READINGS

Comprehensive bibliographies of stratification materials have been published elsewhere. We doubt the wisdom of reproducing them here in their totality. Articles and books not appearing in the bibliographies listed below will be included in our lists, as will also those of special significance. If the student has need of comprehensive bibliographies, he is referred to:

The American Journal of Sociology, 58 (1953), pp. 407-418 (333 items are cited).

Bibliography on Status and Stratification (New York, Social Science Research Council, 1952), mimeographed (approximately 800 items).

Class, Status and Power (Glencoe, Ill., The Free Press, 1953).

(While these three collections duplicate one another to some extent, they are sufficiently different to warrant careful attention, each in its own right.)

The following list of suggested readings is only a small fraction of the total harvest. It has been compiled with the needs of the advanced undergraduate and beginning graduate student in mind. It contains a less-than-complete orientation to the field of stratification, but the coverage is good enough to constitute an adequate start.

BIERSTEDT, Robert, "An Analysis of Social Power," *American Sociological Review*, 15 (December, 1950), pp. 730-738.

COOLEY, C. H., *Social Organization* (New York, Charles Scribner's Sons, 1909), Part IV, especially Chapters XXI to XXV.

DAVIS, Kingsley, and MOORE, W. E., "Some Principles of Stratification," *American Sociological Review*, 10 (April, 1945), pp. 242-249.

LENSKI, Gerhard, "American Social Classes: Statistical Strata or Social Groups," *American Journal of Sociology*, 58 (September, 1952), pp. 139-144.

MAYER, Kurt, "The Theory of Social Classes," *Harvard Educational Review* (Summer, 1953), pp. 149-167.

PFAUTZ, Harold W., "The Current Literature on Social Stratification; Critique and Bibliography," *American Journal of Sociology*, 58 (January, 1953), pp. 391-419.

ROSE, Arnold, "Generalizations in the Social Sciences," *American Journal of Sociology*, 59 (July, 1953), pp. 49-59.

SOROKIN, Pitirim, *Social Mobility* (New York, Harper and Bros., 1927).

TUMIN, Melvin, "Some Principles of Stratification: A Critical Analysis," *American Sociological Review*, 18 (August, 1953), pp. 387-394.

VEBLEN, Thorstein, *The Theory of the Leisure Class* (New York, The Macmillan Co., 1899).

WILLIAMS, Robin, *American Society* (New York, Alfred A. Knopf, 1951), especially pp. 78-135.

Part II

FIELD STUDIES OF SOCIAL STRATIFICATION IN AMERICA

As WE HAVE already noted, the concept of social stratification is well rooted in sociological thought and literature. It is only within the last several decades, however, that the more empirically oriented social scientists have turned their methods on American cities and towns in order to gather *objective data* on social stratification. Those acquainted with the large and growing body of empirical field studies of social stratification will realize that they are as varied in their approaches as they are numerous. Some are particularistic, others are of a generalizing nature. It is our purpose, in this section, to investigate some of these studies. The voluminous body of significant studies pressed for the inclusion of critiques of many, but the practical considerations of space can not be ignored. The final selection of eight studies rested both upon their typicality and their uniqueness. The techniques employed in the investigation and the scope of the research problem were also considered.

The first four studies in this section were primarily designed to investigate the social-status system of a particular community with implications, in some cases, for the United States as a whole. The first is a study of a small farming community in the central Southwest, the next describes the social stratification system in a New England "mill town." The third selection presents a method that has been used to analyze the social-stratification system in several relatively small communities, while the fourth is a study

43

of social stratification in a Midwestern city of about 400,000 people.

The final chapters in this section represent critiques of researches that have analyzed social status somewhat incidental to other purposes. One, for example, was designed to investigate the relationship between the social status of adolescents and their behavior. Two studies deal with the relationship between a person's social status and certain of his attitudes and beliefs. Finally, in the last chapter of this section we shall see how social status operates in the American school system.

4

"Plainville, U.S.A."[1]

IN 1950 THERE WERE in the United States over 100,000 towns and villages with fewer than a thousand persons. The fifty-eight and a half million people who live in these towns or in "unincorporated territories" can attest to the fact that life in rural America can be as "complex" as it is held by urbanites to be "simple."

In 1939 James West, an anthropologist, began to tap this large source of data. Originally, his interest was in learning "how one relatively isolated and still 'backward' American farming community reacts to the constant stream of traits and influences pouring into it from cities and from more 'modern' farming communities." [2] With this in mind, he began to search the southern Midwest for a town that met his requirements. To begin, he sought a town with not over a thousand inhabitants. In addition, the town he wanted should be as close to a traditional farming community as possible. Finally, he hoped to find a place with no recognized social classes and "where the people were all living as nearly as possible on the same social and financial plane." [3]

West felt that he had found the community for which he was looking when he arrived in Plainville.[4] Its size and economic base

---

[1] James West, *Plainville, U.S.A.* (New York, Columbia University Press, 1945). While our discussion is written in the present tense, it should be realized that we are writing as of about ten years ago when West made his study.

[2] *Ibid.*, p. vii.

[3] *Ibid.*, p. viii.

[4] The names of all places and persons have been altered. This was done by West (also a pseudonym) to assure complete anonymity for the people of "Plainville."

45

fitted his requirements and the townspeople were proud to tell him that "This is *one* place where ever'body is equal. You don't find no classes here." [5] He was not in the town long, however, before he realized that this commonly voiced expression of "equality" was, at best, a myth. West was early convinced that he was dealing with "a discrimination system of enormous complexity." [6] Therefore, he amended his original objective to include an investigation of the social-status system to discover "... whether or not this system of discrimination took a form which should be described under the label of rigid social classes." [7]

West's interests were to be channeled in still another direction. The uniqueness of Plainville and its inhabitants prompted him to ask the question, "How does a newborn Plainville boy or girl gradually come 'to pull the skin of the local culture' over him or her, and become the adult male or female Plainviller?"

Thus, the investigation of this community had three aims: (1) to study culture change—how Plainville has reacted to the traits and influences from the "outside world"; (2) to study the social-status system—how the system of differential rewards and privileges operates in a relatively isolated community; and (3) to study the everyday life in Plainville, with particular reference to how its young gradually learn the standards, mores, and traditions of the community. These three aims sometimes become merged into a description of Plainville and its inhabitants. But when we learn "what life is like to people who are born in Plainville and live out their life-span there," [8] we learn also some of the answers to these three major problems.

Methodology

West conducted his study of Plainville through use of the participant observer technique, combined with formal inquiry. On

[5] *Ibid.*, p. 115.
[6] *Ibid.*, p. xii.
[7] *Ibid.*
[8] *Ibid.*, p. xiv.

the one hand, he shared in the life of the community as much as he could. At first this consisted merely of "idling" about the town and talking with whomever would talk, until gradually he was "adopted" by some of the people. "I went to church bazaars, basket dinners, and funerals; to basketball games, pie suppers, and other school entertainments; to picnics, public sales, Saturday afternoon 'drawings,' and to many other public events." [9]

On a more formal level West conducted many "notebook interviews." He held formal interviews with more than fifty people, "totaling from two hours to several hundred hours each," [10] and was able to have at least a few words with about half of the adults who "traded" in Plainville. In addition, eight adults wrote "life histories" ranging from 30,000 to 75,000 words each. Ten cents an hour was paid to two high school boys and two high school girls for writing their autobiographies (15,000 to 50,000 words each). Through the use of these documents obtained from both adults and adolescents it was hoped not only that "facts" would be uncovered but also that the meaning of these facts to the persons involved would be revealed.

Finally, West made use of various records: back issues of the county weekly, collections of letters, and a *History of Woodland County*, published in 1907. Fourteen months after his arrival he was able to convey to others what it is like to live in Plainville, U.S.A.

Plainville and Its Hinterlands

Over a century ago settlers from the hills of Kentucky and Tennessee traveled westward in search of better land. Some went no farther than what is now Woodland County of a state in central United States. By 1870 these and later migrants had occupied most of the bottom and timbered land which make up about two thirds of this county. It was not until nearer the end of the nineteenth century that the prairie which cuts through the

[9] *Ibid.*, p. xiii.
[10] *Ibid.*

county was "homesteaded," for it was then that men first realized that a plow could "break the prairie."

Plainville is situated near the center of Woodland County where the prairie and the "hill country" meet. Surrounding the little town of 275 people are 200 farms, some of them "prairie farms" and some of them "hill farms." But Plainville is not only a geographical hybrid. Its way of life reflects the influences both of the "hillbillies" farther south and of the plains farmer in the Midwest.

The people of Plainville are white, Protestant, and largely Anglo-Saxon. The town boasts a Church of God Holiness, a Christian, a Methodist, and a Baptist church; most of the believers worship in one of these four churches. The rest are mostly Dunkards, who have no church in town. Perhaps as many as a third of the Plainvillers can be called "nonbelievers" in that "they no longer believe the received tenets of fundamentalistic Protestant theology, or they at least discredit any literal interpretation of the Bible." [11]

Plainville is strictly an agricultural community. Even the townspeople are "close to the land" and produce much of their own food. The best farms, however, are those few which are situated in the river bottom. The next most desirable farms are on the prairie, but heavy erosion and leaching have lessened their productivity. A prairie farmer can expect to get nineteen bushels of corn, seventeen bushels of wheat, or twelve bushels of oats to the acre. The poorest land is in the rocky "hill country," much of which is in scrub timber. However, a considerable amount of it is farmed or is used as pasture land. It is here that we find the smallest farms, the poorest farmers, and the largest families.

Plainville could scarcely be called a modern community. Although many of the farmers have automobiles, some farm wagons and buggies are still seen. The "big wagon," however, competes successfully with the mere hundred trucks in the entire county. Almost all the farmhouses have kerosene lamps, but two

[11] *Ibid.,* p. 142.

thirds of the houses in town "have lights." This means that the half of the farmers who have radios must operate them on batteries whereas more than half of the townspeople can use utility electricity. A few crystal sets are still in use. The undertaker, the doctor, and the produce dealer live in the only three houses in the community that have bathrooms, flush toilets, and hot running water.

The average house is heated by a wood-burning kitchen range and a living-room stove using the same fuel. Most of the farmers "get up" their own wood. Water for everything from cooking to the weekly bath in the "galvanized washing tub" usually comes from the well. In the "hills" the people have only the natural springs. The ideal standard of "a bath a week" is seldom met by the men. The women more nearly approach this ideal, if only with a sponge bath. "Children are often bathed in series in the same water, the larger ones or the girls before the smaller ones and the boys." [12]

With this quick overview of Plainville in mind, let us focus our attention on more specific aspects of the life in this small town. The section that follows will describe how Plainvillers earn their living. Next, attention will be given to the social-status system.

EARNING A LIVING IN PLAINVILLE

"Nearly every Plainviller is in two separate and simultaneous economic systems, a 'money economy' and a 'subsistence economy.'" [13] Apparently, the latter is the more important, not only for the hill and prairie farmers but for the townspeople as well.

To the farmers, "getting a living" means getting food on their tables. Some farmers raise almost everything they eat while the vast majority produce most of what they eat. Potatoes head the list of vegetables that are grown and consumed. Farmers may dig as many as fifty bushels each year. Other common vegetables are

[12] *Ibid.*, p. 37.
[13] *Ibid.*, p. 40.

grown on a far smaller scale and some of these are "put up" for winter use.

The most commonly eaten meat is "hogmeat." A family may consume three to six hogs a year which are butchered and cured on the farm, often with the help of friends and neighbors. Plainvillers have no objection to beef but the inadequacies of refrigeration and slaughtering facilities and his greater size make it unfeasible to slaughter a steer. Game, especially rabbit, squirrel, quail, and fish, is eaten when it can be caught or hunted. Some of the hill folk are known to "run hounds" in the hopes of being rewarded with 'possum. Muskrat and woodchuck are more rarely eaten. Wild blackberries are gathered and eaten rather freely but otherwise little fruit is consumed. A certain portion of the fruit takes the form of jams or "sweet preserves."

"The experts consider Plainville diet, as well as sanitation, to be poor, pointing out the high, but unmeasured, incidence of rickets and tuberculosis among the children." [14] The Plainvillers, on the other hand, consider that they eat well enough and boast that no one need ever go hungry in their town. The confusion, of course, is largely between quality and quantity of food consumed, a point most Plainvillers fail to comprehend.

Farming is not the only occupation in the Plainville area. There are some thirty-two "business houses" in the town, including five filling stations (four of which are on the county road), two general stores, a "cash grocery," and a hardware store. There are only six "really paying propositions": the undertaking establishment, the doctor's practice, the Produce House, the Ford agency, one of the general stores, and the liquor store. Some businesses employ a clerk or a helper but the liquor store and many of the smaller businesses are operated by the owner alone.

Some of the hill folk make their living from a combination of activities such as hunting, trapping, wood chopping, and odd jobbing. Apparently these are sufficient for their not-too-great needs.

[14] *Ibid.*, pp. 45-46.

"Gub'ment money" of various sorts finds its way into the community.[15] In 1937 some two hundred people drew "pensions" (Old Age Assistance). In 1940 over fifteen Plainville men and women earned WPA money. The men did road work while the women "milked their needles" at the WPA Sewing Room. NYA checks, veterans pensions, and ADC payments brought still more money into Plainville. The people of Plainville are critical of all this "gub'ment money," but even a strong dislike does not seem to deter them from collecting payments. A widow (her husband managed to commit suicide with an ax) was able to tap ADC, NYA, and WPA funds. "And every day she roams up and down the street cussin' Roosevelt and the New Deal...." [16]

All in all, money is scarce in Plainville. A farmer may realize from $50 to $100 a year from his salable crops and livestock. The women folk supplement the income with a small amount of "butter and egg money" (now actually from cream and eggs) which is spent "just running the home." It has been estimated that from $1 to $12 passes from farmer to merchant each week.

The average non-farming job pays between $30 and $50 a month. "To most Plainvillers, $50 a month means 'good money' and $100 a month means 'great big money.' To a merchant, profits, above interest on debts, of $80 to $150 a month provide a good living...." [17]

In view of the amount of money in circulation in Plainville about 1940, it is not surprising that prices seem considerably lower than present-day city prices. A young man can "start up good" in farming for $1000, while with $300 he can buy a poor team, furniture, tools, chickens, a cow, perhaps, and still have "a little money to run on until something starts coming in." [18] A youth from the "hunter-trapper class" can buy some timber land

[15] The various abbreviations for federal aid and income include: Aid to Dependent Children (ADC); National Youth Administration (NYA); and Works Progress Administration (WPA).
[16] *Ibid.*, p. 30.
[17] *Ibid.*, p. 52.
[18] *Ibid.*, p. 23. It is to be noted that these are pre-World War II prices.

for $25 to $100. For another $100 he can build a home comparable to his parents and he is then ready to "marry, settle down, and start raising a bunch of children and dogs." [19]

Housing is generally inexpensive. The newest small homes can be built for no more than $300. Larger homes, of course, are more expensive but the one-time show place of the community built at "no regard for expense," cost $3000.

In the town almost as little money is required, provided a garden is maintained. "A widow drawing Old Age Assistance of twelve dollars a month . . . if she owns her home, lives well according to Plainville standards as long as she is able to tend a few hens and work her garden." [20]

All in all, then, the answer to the question, "How do Plainvillers get their living?" is a simple one: "From the land."

SOCIAL STRATIFICATION IN PLAINVILLE

We will recall that when West first came to Plainville he was told that "this is *one* place where ever'body is equal. You don't find no classes here." [21] We have already seen the various ways in which Plainvillers earn their living as well as something of the different styles of living in Plainville. The doctor, for example, lives in one of the three "modern" houses in Plainville and is said to have one of the few "paying propositions" in town. Back in the hills we find families living in shacks costing $100 or less and subsisting by hunting, trapping, or odd jobbing. Evidence of this sort leads us to suspect at the outset that everybody is *not* equal.

While West was living in Plainville he observed that some people were more "respected" than others, that it was "better" to live on the prairie than in the hills, and that it was not quite "right" for a man to make his living by hunting and trapping. "Good families" were contrasted with "bad stock" and the inde-

19 *Ibid.,* p. 24.
20 *Ibid.,* pp. 40-41.
21 *Ibid.,* p. 115.

pendent farmers were favorably compared to the poor ones. Since references such as these were made with a certain frequency, it became clear that Plainvillers do recognize differences among themselves. In addition, different kinds of behavior were expected of different people, according to their social status, indicating that a certain degree of repetitiveness was associated with the differential-status system.

In short, there appeared to be a well-recognized system of social stratification in Plainville, despite the fact that people did not always agree on just how "high" or "low" a person should be rated. From his interviews, however, *West discovered that the social stratification system "looks different" to the various Plainvillers, depending largely on their own place in the system.*

The Social-Stratification System as Seen by the "Better-Class" Adult

The average "better-class" adult who "bothers to think about it" recognizes two general types of persons in the Plainville area, the lower class and the upper class, although he seldom speaks of them in these terms.

"This upper class includes about half the people in the community. *Though its members vary in relative rank, the class does not break up into clear subdivisions.*" [22] Occasionally a quasi-subdivision, called the "upper crust," is used for categorizing the people at the very top of the upper class. No one of the upper class, however, identifies with the "upper crust" and it seems that the category, as well as the label, is not generally employed in a wholly complimentary context.

The remaining half of Plainvillers are known as the "lower class." Although the upper-class people do not recognize sharp subdivisions within their own ranks, they identify three subclasses of the lower class. In order of descending social status they are known colloquially as (1) "good lower-class people," (2) the "lower element," and (3) "people who live like the animals."

22 *Ibid.*, p. 119. Italics not in original.

Using this four-class description of the stratification system as a reference, let us turn to the criteria used to differentiate the statuses of Plainvillers. Then, we will indicate how the stratification system appears to each of the above-mentioned classes.

The Criteria of Social Status

Plainvillers do not fully agree on which things are important in deciding the social status of their friends and neighbors. In addition, not all of the criteria used are equally important at all levels within the stratification system. Basically, however, there are six criteria that are frequently employed, in some combination, to differentiate the various classes in Plainville.

Residence. As evident in Figure 1, a schematic representation of the way the class system appears to the upper-class adult Plainviller, the people can generally be placed in one of the two broad classes on the basis of where they live. Most hill folk are lower class and most prairie dwellers are upper class. The main exceptions occur when hill folk are found "living like prairie dwellers" and people physically located on the prairie are known to "live like hillbillies." In either case, the exceptional people probably possess most of the remaining criteria for the class that is not usually found in their geographical part of the community. Generally, then, knowing whether a person lives on the prairie or in the hills is sufficient basic information to place him in one of the two large classes identified by the "better-class" Plainviller.

Although this criterion is strictly applicable only to the farming population, it is occasionally employed, in a somewhat different sense, to discriminate between townspeople. An expression such as "his family lives in the hills" is indicative of the pervasive nature of this criterion. The prairie-hill split does not seem to be useful, however, for differentiating the several subclasses of the lower class.

Earning a living. The "way a man makes a living" partially determines his rank in the Plainville status hierarchy. For the farmers, this criterion can be called "technology," which indicates which aspects of making a living are important in differentiating between farmers. On the larger, less rocky, and more fertile prairie farms are found most of the modern farm machinery that exists in Plainville. In other respects, also, more modern farming practices are followed and a greater variety of crops are produced. It is the prairie farmer, and not his hill cousin, who

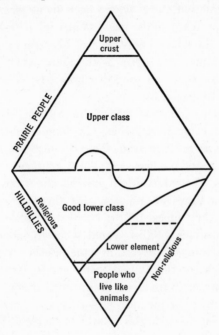

FIG. 1. The class structure as seen by upper-class Plainvillers. (Redrawn from James A. West, *Plainville, U.S.A.* [New York, Columbia University Press, 1945], by permission)

recognizes the differences between pure-bred and "scrub" livestock. "In the hills 'old-style patch farming' has survived better, as has the even older pattern of living from stream and woods—from fishing, hunting, trapping, gathering, and from woodchopping."[23]

23 *Ibid.*, p. 120.

The criterion of "technology" is closely related to the first criterion and can be thought of, perhaps, as a refinement of it. Take the case of a farmer who is living on a prairie farm but is merely "scratching out a living" without the aid of modern machinery and with a seeming lack of interest in the up-to-date agricultural practices of his fellow prairie dwellers. On the basis of the first criterion alone—where he is living—we would probably place him in the upper class. When we determine his class position with the added knowledge of his farming practices and equipment we may not arrive at the same conclusion. This, in part, is what is meant by saying that prairie farmers who live like hill people are lower class.

The criterion of "how a man makes a living" is also used to rate the townspeople of Plainville. The doctor and the undertaker receive the most prestige from their occupations, with business owners, clerks, odd jobbers, and WPA workers receiving progressively less. The information given us about the non-farming occupations in Plainville indicates that they are ranked in the same order as they appear on the North-Hatt scale for the Prestige of Occupations.[24] This would seem to indicate that the differential-status system agrees, in some respects, with that found in other sections of the United States and in larger towns and cities. However, a Plainviller's occupation, although important, is not considered to be the most important characteristic in determining his social status. In this respect Plainville is different from our larger towns and cities; Warner, for example, in his statistical analysis of various status factors, attaches the largest weight to "occupation"[25] and Centers sums up the opinion of many a status analyst when he states that "occupation seems generally agreed upon as the most satisfactory single index of stratification...."[26]

[24] Cecil C. North and Paul K. Hatt, "Jobs and Occupations: A Popular Evaluation," in Logan Wilson and William L. Kolb, *Sociological Analysis* (New York, Harcourt, Brace and Co., 1949), pp. 464-473.

[25] W. Lloyd Warner, Marchia Meeker, and Kenneth Eells, *Social Class in America* (Chicago, Science Research Associates, Inc., 1949), pp. 181 ff.

[26] Richard Centers, *The Psychology of Social Classes* (Princeton, Princeton University Press, 1949), p. 15.

The large percentage of Plainvillers who are farmers probably account for the fact that it is not *what* a man does (farm), but the closely related points of *how* he farms (technology) and *where* he farms (prairie or hill) that is important as far as social status is concerned. Thus, "how a man earns a living" is still quite important in Plainville, but most Plainvillers cannot be ranked accurately by unrefined occupational titles.

The criterion of lineage. "A third and very important criterion is lineage. 'Good families' (so labeled by any number of synonyms) are contrasted with 'poor families,' or 'low class,' or 'lower element,' or 'no-account,' or 'trashy' families." [27] In view of the difference, sometimes subtle, in the adjectives used to describe families, it may be that lineage would be useful not only for placing people in one of the two broad classes in Plainville but also for determining their relative position within the classes. Lineage apparently is equally applicable among the townspeople as it is among farmers. It will be noted that "lineage" does not appear on Warner's objective scale for determining social class. [28] It did, however, play an important part in his more informal method for placing individuals. This perhaps tells us something about the use and applicability of this criterion of status. In informal situations with people of a quite small community, where "everybody knows everybody else," the mention of a family name recalls various status characteristics of the family and serves as an adequate summation of these characteristics. As a method, however, it is hard to quantify and structure. Thus, whenever an objective scale for measuring social status is desired, or whenever a technique is needed that will be applicable in communities of various sizes, "family name" is usually ignored. The analyst of a small town, however, cannot ignore this criterion.

Wealth. "Many people, when asked outright, 'What gives a man a rank among his fellows?' will answer, 'The only thing that counts in other people's eyes is, how much money has he

[27] West, *op. cit.*, p. 121.
[28] See Chapter 6, pp. 116-121.

got?' " [29] Although most Plainvillers would probably say that this is not entirely true, they would also agree that wealth is one criterion of social status in this town. The average wealth of a prairie dweller is greater than the average wealth of the hill farmer. This is true not only when wealth is measured by the items already included in "technology," such as farming machinery, tools, equipment, and number and type of livestock, but it is also true when wealth is measured by other possessions. Usually the larger and more expensive homes are found on the prairie farms. Prairie farmers most likely have more expensive home furnishings, clothes, and cars, than do the hill farmers. The prairie dweller usually has, or has more of, many other items to which a money value can be attached.

Once again we see why it is that where a Plainviller lives is indicative of his placement in either the lower class or the upper class. It is also becoming more evident why we cannot make a sharp distinction between the people of this town on the basis of whether or not they live on the prairie. Wealth, as well as the other criteria already mentioned or yet to be discussed, has a tendency to "blur" the picture.

Morals. "As a fifth criterion, 'morals' is given much local lip service. The common moral traits which most people agree in stressing are 'honesty' . . ., willingness to do hard work, 'temperance' (regarding alcohol), and performance of all domestic duties." [30] West discovered several interesting facts with regard to morals as a criterion of social-class placement: (1) The people of Plainville differed in their opinions of what constitutes moral behavior; some had a "severer" moral code than others. (2) Morals are not a sufficient reason for placement in either the upper or lower class. Moral traits do affect a person's relative position *within* the two classes but "no one ever crosses the main class line . . . as a result of moral distinction or moral delinquency

---

[29] West, *op. cit.*, p. 121.
[30] *Ibid.*, p. 122.

alone." [31] (3) Morals seem to be more important in judging lower-class than upper-class people. In Plainville the highest two subclasses of the lower class are differentiated chiefly by the morality of their members; an upper-class person, however, who continually and seriously broke the moral code would probably lose the respect of his friends and neighbors but they would still consider him in their class. Specifically, then, morality seems to be the chief characteristic for distinguishing between the "good lower-class people" and the "lower element."

The "good lower-class people," numerically a large group, are allegedly moral. Part of the evidence of their morality lies in the fact that most of them who are past adolescence have been "saved" in the sense that this expression is used in Plainville's Holiness Church. More of the evidence of their morality lies in the fact that most of them possess the traits of morality previously given. Whether or not they have been "saved," the people of this subclass are generally hard-working, ambitious, law-abiding citizens. Apparently, their morals are as good as those of the people of the upper class. Still, a combination of hard work and ambition has not been enough to supply them with the other traits and possessions necessary for entrance into the "better half" of the society.

The people in the subclass directly beneath the "good lower class" are collectively referred to as "the lower element." They are generally not considered to be moral individuals, although the degree of their moral delinquency varies. The least respected members "get in trouble with the law," usually for stealing. Others cross the path of justice because of their fighting, drinking, and related behavior (disturbing the peace, drunken driving, and the like). The worst indictment against others is that they are "mighty rough" or "mighty ignorant" and "never darken a church door."

People in the lowest subclass of the lower class are not even "in

[31] *Ibid.*

the race" with respect to morals. They are referred to as the "people who live like animals" and are not held accountable, morally or legally, for what they do or fail to do. Ignored by the law and the churches ("... even the Holiness people treat this sharply set-off group as if it has no souls to be saved"),[32] the people of this subclass build shacks "way back in the timber" and manage to live by some combination of "scratching out a living" from their small gardens, hunting, occasional odd jobbing, stealing from fields or henhouses, and receiving gifts of food from neighbors.[33]

Manners. "The sixth criterion of class is of enormous complexity, because it involves all the other criteria, renders them meaningful, and in a sense supersedes them. At the same time it governs interclass relationships and is critical in matters of class mobility. This criterion is 'manners.' "[34]

Included in the criterion of manners is a seemingly infinite number of traits, habits, and tastes that combine to form two

[32] *Ibid.,* p. 129.

[33] It will be noted in a later section that a study specifically designed to discover the relationship between social behavior and social status largely substantiates the Plainville findings that moral behavior varies with class position. In the study referred to, the frequency with which the youth who are the subjects of *Elmtown's Youth* generally engaged in tabooed pleasures was inversely related to their status position in the community. (See page 178.) In addition, at least one other study summarized in this book seems to substantiate West's findings that "morals" serve as the chief factor for differentiating the two subclasses of the lower class. When Centers asked his sample, "What would you say puts a person in the lower social class?" a fairly large percentage of them mentioned such items as poor character and low morals, laziness, drink, and crime. (See Chapter 10, p. 246.) In his study, even people engaged in more menial types of occupations refused to classify themselves as "lower class" because they seemed to reserve this category for individuals who have low morals in addition to being poor. Morals, however, was not mentioned as a good criterion of placement in any of the other three classes, upper, middle, or working, utilized by Centers. This study is certainly not parallel to West's but it does serve to indicate that people seem to identify a group of morally low people at the bottom of the "social heap." Warner would call these the "lower-lower class" or, more colloquially, the "Lulu's." (See Chapter 6, p. 111.) Lenski, in turn, reports that some of his respondents talked of a "notorious" and "depraved" group at the very bottom of the social structure. (See Chapter 5, p. 91.)

[34] West, *op. cit.,* p. 124.

distinct ways of life—life in the hills and life on the prairie. It is not so much that the hill folk ride in wagons or old jalopies, live in unpainted shacks, and "eat the grub they eat," but that they are said to *like* their way of life. A preference for this style of living, in turn, is accredited to ignorance. They are said to reject modern farming technology not because they cannot afford it but because "they don't know nothing except hoes and axes, and doin' it the *hard way*." [35] They don't know how to act, cook, "talk proper," or dress. The expression, "They don't know nothin' excep' ignorance!" [36] seems to sum up the way upper-class Plainvillers look upon the manners or way of life of the lower class.

Prairie farmers, on the other hand, drive later model cars, have up-to-date farming practices, and use modern farming implements and equipment, because they somehow feel that people *should* do these things. In short, "manners" as a criterion of social class seems to include the value that people attach to a "way of life" as well as the way of life itself.

Differential Perception of the Class System

"What the Plainviller says he does in judging another is 'add everything I know about him up in my head and strike an average.'" [37] Since the six criteria of social status are not weighted the same by all the people, the average they "strike" is different. As a consequence, the stratification system "looks different" to each class of Plainviller. There is, however, a certain amount of agreement even among segments of the community as to how the system *really* is and how it operates. For example, West's experiences led him to believe that most upper-class Plainvillers would more or less agree with the four-class (or five, if the "upper crust" is included) description already presented. People within certain other segments of Plainville society can be said to agree essentially on how the system "looks to them."

[35] *Ibid.*, p. 125.
[36] *Ibid.*
[37] *Ibid.*, p. 118.

1. The class structure as seen by "good religious people." The greatest modification of the upper-class impression of the class system occurs when the "good religious people" rank themselves and their neighbors. The accent is on "salvation" and pious morality and only after that are the criteria of residence, lineage, technology, and wealth employed.

The Holiness people appear to have the most integrated viewpoint of those who rank according to morality. As Figure 2 indicates, their definition of the lower element and "the people who live like animals" is about the same as that of the upper-class people. No longer, however, is there a "good lower class," an upper class, or an upper crust; these people are placed in one large class. Within the class, however, individual differences in rank are recognized chiefly according to how the person "stands with God" but also according to the other criteria of status. As shown in the diagram, a good religious hillbilly is ranked lower than a good religious prairie farmer, indicating a certain amount of agreement with the upper-class Plainviller.

Set apart from the community, as seen by the religious people, are the otherwise "good citizens" who "don't live right." It is significant to note that a *vertical* line separates these people from the world of the "good religious" ones. Rank for rank, they seem to be granted the same status as their "real believing" neighbors. Thus it appears that the good religious people ". . . are aware that their main criterion does not agree with dominant standards of the community, though they live as if it did, and 'hope that a day will arrive when all will live godly lives.' " [38]

2. The class structure as seen by other lower-class people. Some lower-class people who are not able to see the class structure in "the Holiness way" view it about the same way that upper-class people do. Others in the lower class, mostly those that the "uppers" would call good lower class, but probably also some from the lower element, describe the stratification system in a way that is quite different from the upper-class picture. As

[38] *Ibid.*, p. 129.

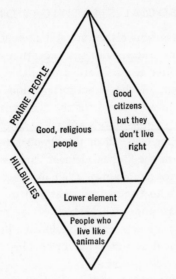

FIG. 2. The class structure as seen by "good religious people."

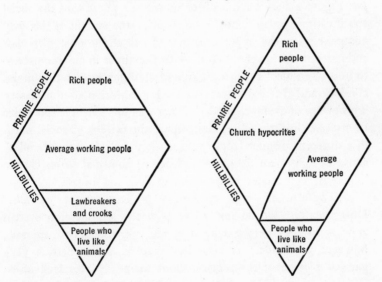

FIG. 3. The class structure as seen by some lower-class people.

FIG. 4. The class structure as seen by "nonreligious" lower-class people.

(Redrawn from James A. West, *Plainville, U.S.A.* [New York, Columbia University Press, 1945], by permission)

shown in Figure 3, four classes are still present but the lines are drawn at different places, with the exception of that separating "the people who live like animals" from the rest of the community. The segment of the structure previously defined as the lower element is now reserved for the "lawbreakers and crooks." ("Of course *every* community's got a few of *them*.") [39] Some of what was the upper class, all of the "good lower class," and the law-abiding part of the "lower element" are merged to form the "main bulk" of the community ("all us good honest everyday working people who try to live right and do right").[40] Above this large group are the "rich people" or the "people who *think* they're better." In this segment are included all of what the upper class loosely defined as the upper crust plus about half of the remaining upper-class people.

3. *The class structure as seen by nonreligious lower-class people.* Figure 4 shows a still different way of perceiving the social stratification system. Those who describe the system in this way comprise what the upper class would call the good lower class and parts of the lower element. What they have in common seems to be a resentment toward the role of churches in dictating moral conduct and this is reflected in their description of the classes. This group of average, good (but not religious) people recognize four classes in Plainville. They employ the criteria of social status in a different manner from the way they have been used and so arrive at a different definition and description of the four classes. The only segment retaining its boundary is the lowest.

4. *The class structure and the "people who live like animals."* Unfortunately, we do not know how the stratification system appears to the "people who live like animals." They are said, however, to "have no very clear picture, or, at best, a very garbled picture of the society about them." [41] This lack of an understanding of the society is attributed to two factors: their

39 *Ibid.*, p. 131.
40 *Ibid.*
41 *Ibid.*, p. 133.

real or apparent mental subnormality, and the efforts of some of
the rest of the community to confuse them, through their joking,
with respect to their own and others' social status. The story is
told, for example, of the attempts of a group of men to convince
one of the lower-status Plainvillers that his woodcutting and odd-
jobbing were great enterprises. It was strongly suggested that he
run for a political office and he was promised the unanimous support of the community. In addition, he was asked, in a quite
serious tone, why his wife (local folklore had it that the man had
purchased her from his brother for $6 and a shotgun) didn't join
one of the neighborhood clubs. Lower-status Plainvillers, of
course, would *like* to believe the implications of such suggestions,
and it seems they do put some credence in them. The extent to
which this sort of joking influences their picture of the stratification system is hard to ascertain.

Significance of Differential Perception

The phenomenon of differential perception of the social-stratification system has, in general, received little attention from status
analysts.[42] In the studies summarized in this book it seems to have
been avoided with two exceptions. Lenski made a point to mention that apparently the way individuals viewed the stratification
system in the New England community studied by him was not
related to their own social status.[43] In Centers' study, on the
other hand, the people in any one of his four classes tended to
agree among themselves concerning the criteria for membership
in that class more than they did with members of other classes.[44]
As we shall see later, due to the structuring of Centers' study, we

[42] A notable exception can be found in Allison Davis, Burleigh B. Gardner,
and Mary R. Gardner, *Deep South* (Chicago, University of Chicago Press,
1941), pp. 63-73. The authors conclude: "Not only does the perspective on
social stratification vary for different class levels, but the very bases of class
distinction in the society are variously interpreted by the different groups"
(p. 72).

[43] Gerhard E. Lenski, "American Social Classes: Statistical Strata or Social
Groups?" *American Journal of Sociology*, 58 (September, 1952), p. 142.

[44] Centers, *op. cit.*, pp. 89-106.

cannot tell whether respondents of different statuses thought in terms of different numbers of social classes.

In still other studies it was apparent that people had dissimilar definitions of the make-up of the stratification system and of the criteria on which it is based. Since this was not systematically related to their own social status by each author, it is difficult for us to do it at this point.

Thus, the problem of differential perception of a stratification system is far from being solved. Perhaps the presence or absence of this phenomenon is related to the rigidity of the system as well as the size of the community under study.

Cliques, Clubs, Churches, and the Class System

In Plainville, nearly every friendship clique, lodge, club, church, and other organization can be ranked according to its position within the social-stratification system. For example, there is a social clique of young married women, called the Leaders, who are very near the top of the upper class. The Leaders ("our 400—only they ain't but a dozen of them")[45] are an exclusive clique who exchange luncheons, engage in mutual visiting, and go on shopping trips to large towns together. As their name implies, no lower-class person would stand a chance of joining the group and most upper-class women are also excluded.

Many other friendship cliques exist, for both adults and adolescents, and usually, it seems, the members are more similar than dissimilar. Apparently this is also true of the formal organizations in Plainville. The Boosters Club (includes the Leaders and others) is said to be "very high." Home Economics clubs draw only upper-class women. The Masons is an upper-class organization and somewhat beneath it are the Odd Fellows and the Woodmen who might have a few lower-class names on their rolls.

The four churches in Plainville can also be fitted into the social-stratification system. Members of the Christian Church as well as most nonreligious people would rank the churches in the follow-

[45] West, *op. cit.*, p. 106.

ing manner: Christian, Methodist, Baptist, and Church of God Holiness.

Lower-class people do not join the Christian Church because "they wouldn't feel comfortable there." [46] Apparently for the same reason, upper-class people do not usually join the Holiness Church. One upper-class woman did, however, join the Church of God Holiness and was said to have lost the respect of her friends, although her more objective status remained the same. Her friends from the upper class, when visiting her on her death-bed, made an effort to call when they would be least likely to find "them ignorant Holinists" present.

There are differences in the type of worship and the manner in which services are conducted between these religious bodies at opposite ends of the status scale. In Plainville the Christian church alone is without a "mourners' bench" where hardened souls, sometimes aided by their friends, can vociferously petition heaven for salvation. In the Holiness church it is not unusual for sinners to feel the "burden of their sins" roll away after such supplication, and services are conducted with this intention.

The next contender for the place of the Christian Church is the Methodist. At one time, in fact, their social positions were reversed, but a combination of factors allowed the Christians to attain the higher status. Not the least reason seems to be the size of their respective church buildings. Spurred on by a gift from a former Plainviller, men from the Christian Church started a building fund with the slogan, "Let's build something that'll make the Methodist Church look like a woodshed" [47] (some said "back-house"). Apparently this appeal to the competitive, if not strictly religious, nature of man was successful, for since the completion of their large church (it is the only place in town large enough to hold the high school commencement exercises) and the failure of the "Methodist Bank," the Christians have been Plainville's "ee-light."

[46] *Ibid.*, p. 160.
[47] *Ibid.*, p. 146.

Interestingly enough, when the Holiness congregation does the ranking, the positions of the churches in Plainville are reversed. A clear difference of "values" is evident, since for the same reasons for which Christians rank them the lowest, "Holinists" rank Christians the lowest. The Holiness people consider the services of the Christian Church as the most "cold and worldly" and thus the least appealing to God. Christian, as well as Methodist, Baptist, and nonreligious people criticize the more emotional type of services characteristic of "Holinists." Apparently, their "clappin' and hollerin' " is not considered devout.

Thus, the Holiness congregation, by virtue of the fact that they are judging largely by "non-worldly" standards, come up with a different picture of the social-stratification system in Plainville. The churches, as well as individuals, receive different ranks when judged by different Plainvillers.

Various other studies have indicated that churches can be ranked according to the general status composition of their members.[48] Sometimes the rank of a given church denomination is not the same in different communities. The Methodist Church which was near the top in Plainville chiefly attracts people from the middle-status range in Elmtown, whereas Warner found it to be the lowest-status Protestant church in one New England community. There is, however, a certain amount of agreement regarding the social evaluation of the religious denominations in the United States, despite the fact that regional differences and the ethnic make-up of the community must be considered. Warner concludes that "Episcopalians and Unitarians generally rank higher than Methodists and Baptists. Congregationalists, Presbyterians, and Christian Scientists are centered in the middle class." [49] To this we might add that the Pentecostal, the Pilgrim Holiness, and the Church of God Holiness usually have about the lowest status of Protestant denominations. Roman Catholic churches usually

[48] See especially Liston Pope, "Religion and the Class Structure," *The Annals of the American Academy of Political and Social Science*, 256 (March, 1948), pp. 84-91.
[49] Warner, *op. cit.*, p. 96.

draw most of their members from a low social level up to about
the middle of the status range.

Vertical Mobility in Plainville

In Plainville it is not unusual to hear that "any feller can git
just about where he wants to be, if he's got the grit and determination." [50] Others express this sentiment as a fact of yesterday,
but only a dream of today. "They used to say any boy could be
President. A boy's got about the same chance of bein' President
nowadays as he's got of bein' Charley McCarthy ... Still, you
find some of 'em thinks they can make it." [51]

Despite the motivation presumably supplied by nurturing the
dream of mobility, we are told that in Plainville, "Movement
across the line separating the upper class from the lower class is
virtually impossible, without leaving the community." [52] Even
when they leave Plainville, as do about half the children of each
generation, most men become day laborers either on farms or in
the cities. Some men, of course, "make good" when they leave;
the man who struck it rich in "Oklahomy oil," a couple of college
teachers, and a few others are used to illustrate the point that it
can happen.

Actually, among the people still living in Plainville, *three* cases
of vertical mobility between the upper and lower class have
occurred. Two involved social climbing whereas the other, said
to be the more difficult one, was a case of descent from the upper
class. Movement within the lower class is not difficult. Particularly is this true with regard to movement from the lower element
to the good religious people or vice versa. By salvation a man can
rise above the lower element, while evidence of backsliding will
return him to his former status. This process, or part of it, can
be repeated; as long as a man indicates by his behavior that "his
conversion meant business" he will be numbered among the good

[50] West, *op. cit.*, p. 134.
[51] *Ibid.*, p. 135.
[52] *Ibid.*

religious people, especially by those Plainvillers who emphasize the criterion of religion.

Mobility within the upper class probably occurs, too, as evidenced by the mention of families who successfully competed for "top position" in Plainville. However, West presents fewer cases of movement among the prairie farmers. Perhaps this is due to the lack of clean-cut subdivisions in the upper class which may make "rises" or "falls" harder to spot.

Social Stratification and the Life Cycle

The impact of differential social status is felt by most Plainvillers "from the cradle to the grave." Most babies are born in their mother's home. If the family can afford it, the doctor is in attendance. He may, however, refuse, if money is still due him for the last baby. In such cases an older woman, who is a neighbor or a relative, will officiate at the birth. In rare cases, the lower-class baby's mother is the only one to hear his birth cry. In equally few instances the child is born amid all the conveniences and cleanliness that the "Largetown" hospital can offer. If the new baby is born to a lower-class Plainville family, it is not likely that his birth was "planned." He is likely to be greeted by, or in later years to greet, a number of siblings.

It would take an entire study, specifically oriented to the purpose, to describe the effects of differential social status on a child's early years. Soon in his young life, however, he is taught "how to act" when in the presence of family members, other children, and adults. In all classes boys and girls are taught separate sets of behavior patterns. The patterns themselves, particularly those that concern modesty, vary among the classes. Most Plainville children soon learn to be "careful" with regard to exposing their own sexual organs to the sight of another, including members of their family. Some "modern" (upper-class) families, however, instill less prudishness in their children by consciously rejecting the "nakedness taboo" among all family members. In some families near the opposite end of the status scale a similar pattern is followed but seemingly not because of the parental structuring of the situation. It is said that in these families "They think nothing of nakedness. . . . A girl will show her brother her body and she can see his." [53]

The Holiness and other lower-class religious families stress modesty more than any other group. The usual taboos regarding bodily exposure are intensified with the result that short skirts, low necklines, and bobbed hair seem immodest to them. Apparently, it should be added, religious beliefs or motives are not the determining factor in enforcing modesty and other aspects of the moral code. "Many nonreligious people train their children to rigid sex morality, 'guard their daughters' reputations,' and are otherwise 'just as moral as anybody.' " [54]

In ways not always very subtle, the Plainville child is taught how to treat children from socially inferior or superior families. A boy or girl from the upper-class families is told, "You don't want to play with Johnny *Jones! He* (his family, people like *that*) don't know how to *act* . . . Why don't you walk home from school with the *Smith* children? You'd like to be *seen* with people like that . . . The *Joneses* keep hounds. . . ." [55] And so in this way all of the child's friends and acquaintances, as well as other people, are fitted into the social-status system through comparison with his own family's status. It does not take long before the upper-class child realizes approximately where he stands with respect to the rest of Plainville.

When we listen in on a similar lesson being taught to a lower-class child, his parents sound somewhat on the defensive or the "excuse-giving" side. The child may be told that he is "as good as anybody" or that he should act like he's "just as good as anybody." Upper-class families, particularly those whose children are believed to have slighted the lower-class child, are spoken of as "cold," "selfish," or "stuck-up." The lower-class child is told

[53] *Ibid.*, p. 178.
[54] *Ibid.*
[55] *Ibid.*, p. 197.

that such people merely *think* they're good and in reality they're just hypocrites. Perhaps repeating to a lower-class child that he's "just as good as anybody" is the most painless way of impressing upon him the falsity of the assertion!

And so the children of Plainville become its adolescents. By this time each boy and girl has a good idea concerning his family's (and thus his) social status in the community. The upper-class male adolescent realizes he must never date a girl from the "good lower class" because of parental fear that such habits will result in his marrying such a girl. He knows too, that it is even worse to date a girl from the "lower element" because "everybody knows what he's after." We are told it would be "inconceivable" for an upper-class girl to have a date with a lower-class boy.

Among the Plainville males, men as well as boys, status distinctions are not so rigid. Boys may play or hunt together almost regardless of status, and may even "stay all night" at the home of a pal whose family is not "his kind." Men may borrow, "neighbor," or trade with one another whereas their wives merely "treat each other with respect" and their daughters are not allowed to play with each other.

By the time a Plainville boy is ready to marry it is almost as if the "die has been cast." He talks, acts, works, and maybe "thinks" like a hillbilly or a prairie farmer; like a "good religious person," or like a man from the lower element. The strongest of social pressures are brought to bear to assure that he marry his own "kind" of girl. If the boy has lived his life on the prairie farm, the chances are great that he will somehow be able to get a similar farm. A parental gift or loan of $1000 will be sufficient to enable him to "start up good." One third of this amount and perhaps some system for farming the "family place" would see the newlyweds off to a decent start.

A boy from "way back in the hills" requires much less in order to emulate his parents' life and achieve their social status. A hundred dollars, earned or borrowed, will buy him a piece of timber land. The house he builds on this land seldom costs more than this. With this investment he can settle down and raise "a bunch of children and dogs" and support them by some combination of hunting, fishing, woodcutting, or trapping. The life cycle is nearing completion.

As a man, from any class, grows older and his function as the head of a family decreases, he gradually loses the respect of his younger neighbors and friends. He may attempt, and almost succeed, to delay this process by becoming (or remaining) active in various organizations within the community. If, at age of seventy, or thereabouts, he joins the "old man's loafing group" that gathers daily at the Plainville square, he enters into what West calls a "classless limbo." Only a trace of each man's former status is still present, but from the group's conversation of the "old days" a listener could probably rank them as once they were ranked. In addition, a line of distinction is drawn between those old people who have saved enough on which to live and those who are forced to accept a "pension" (Old Age Assistance check). However, at this age few seem concerned with status.

To say that "When death comes to a Plainviller it marks the last time in his life that status distinctions can be made between him and his neighbors," may be quite obvious. His family is expected to utilize as many of the artifacts and practices from the "funeral and graveyard" segment of Plainville culture as possible. Some Plainvillers are laid to rest without the benefit of expensive metal caskets and bought flowers and their graves are left unmarked; others are "put away properly" by their relatives. The former economic positions of the deceased can be judged, with some accuracy, by a rank order of the size of their tombstones.[56]

Summary of Major Findings

The following eight points represent what are thought to be some of the major findings of this study which relate particularly to social stratification.

[56] W. M. Kephart, "Status After Death," *American Sociological Review,* 15 (October, 1950), pp. 635-643.

1. Despite vocalizations to the contrary, a system of differential social status was evident in Plainville.

2. When comparing Plainviller to Plainviller, the range of status differences may seem great; but when the community is compared to an urban society, the Plainville status range would probably coincide with about the lower half of the range usually found in a large city.

3. Six criteria were used by the people of Plainville to evaluate the social position of their friends and neighbors. These included, residence (prairie or hill), technology (modern farming practices and equipment or their lack), wealth (all possessions to which a money value can be attached), manners (way of life plus value attached to it), and morals.

4. These six criteria are weighted differently by different Plainvillers. In addition, not all the criteria are equally important over the entire status range.

5. The stratification system in Plainville is perceived differently by various inhabitants. Three factors contribute to this phenomenon: (a) the differential importance attached to the status criteria, (b) the varying degree of their applicability for the complete status range, and (c) the tendency for Plainvillers to deny, vocally, the existence of status differences.

6. Some agreement was found, however, in the way that certain segments of the community described the stratification system. The upper-class Plainviller described two major social classes; the lower of these had three subdivisions; the higher had one quasi-subdivision. Three different types of lower-class people described the stratification system in terms of four classes, but neither among themselves nor between any one of them and the upper class was there any agreement concerning the definition and delineation of the classes. The only exception to this occurred with respect to people with the very lowest social status; a small group of people who "live like animals" was identified by all of the different groups of raters.

7. From the foregoing remarks, it seems safe to conclude that

the recognized system of social stratification in Plainville apparently does not consist of one given number of social classes which are recognized by all, or even most, of the community and which are defined similarly by them.

8. Vertical mobility is given much lip service in Plainville (but not as much as formerly) and selected cases illustrate it *can* happen. It is least likely to occur between what upper-class Plainvillers call the upper class and the lower class; it is most likely to occur between the subdivisions of the lower class.

EVALUATION

In practically every study there are valuable contributions, sometimes many of them, for which the work will be remembered. The experienced student also becomes aware of the inadequacies that exist in most studies. From both the positive contributions and the recognized inadequacies the student can profit.

In our evaluation of West's *Plainville*, it was thought best to isolate certain problem areas and present both a positive and a negative critique of each.

Methodology

As was noted earlier, the manner in which West gathered his data on Plainville and its inhabitants consisted of two basic methods, the participant-observer and the interview method. These were supplemented by a few case histories and autobiographies.

When skillfully employed, the value of the participant-observer method, in terms of the results and insights obtained through its use, is not to be disputed. Basically, it consists of becoming, as nearly as possible, a member of the group which is under study. It is not merely being *with* the group, nor does it consist of being an onlooker to the group activities. Rather, it is a matter of having a part, active or passive, small or large, to play in the group's activities. From his own description of his stay in

Plainville, it is clear that West was able to take part in many of their social activities. Perhaps it was by attending funerals that he learned that Plainvillers strive to "bury their dead right" but that not all succeed in doing so. His knowledge of the kind of food that Plainvillers eat and, perhaps more important, his knowledge of their attitudes towards this food—what is "right" to eat and what is not, which food is particularly good, what comprises a "company meal," and the like—this knowledge was at least partially obtained at Plainville supper tables. The list could be extended almost indefinitely.

The important question is: Did West (or for that matter, could *anyone*) really participate in *all*, or even *enough* of the phases of the life in this community? The answer to this is almost certainly negative, and our concern is directed to discovering what aspects of the life in this small town may have been missed. There is some evidence that West was accepted more by the higher-status people of Plainville than by the lower-status individuals. Perhaps this started when he acquired temporary lodging with the County Agent and was intensified when he substituted as a high school teacher and took an active part in a community reform project. Even if West could enjoy a good 'possum dinner with the "people who live like animals," it is doubtful, in view of his other activities, whether his host and hostess and their "brood" could accept him as an equal and participating member of the group. Perhaps he was never invited to such a feast; we were not told at whose homes he took part in family meals.

We were told, however, that it was harder to discover some of the child-rearing practices of lower-status families. Again, we learned very little about how the social-status system appears to the "people who live like animals." This may be further evidence that West was more readily accepted by the upper-status members of Plainville than the lower-status people. It is difficult to ascertain how great was the effect of this tendency toward "upper-class bias." It is certain that we do not receive any entirely one-sided picture of life in Plainville, but what we *do not* know about the "people who live like animals" and somewhat higher status individuals may be as important as what we have learned about them. In any case, the student should be aware of this limitation in the methodology and make possible allowances for it.

A bias in the same direction may have been present in West's selection of interviewees. No doubt he tried to conduct formal interviews with "all kinds of people"; more than likely, he succeeded to a certain extent. We were not told exactly how many people were formally interviewed nor were we given any indication of the position in the social-status system occupied by the interviewees. It is suggested, then, that any bias that may have been present probably tended toward an upper-status bias. It would be in this direction, it is thought, because of the evidence that West was participating somewhat more in the higher-status segments of Plainville society and because of the admittedly easier task involved in talking with people of more nearly one's own social status.

All of what has been said regarding selection of individuals for formal interviews applies to an even greater extent to the selection of people for informal "chats." Living in the town itself meant that the possibility of chance meetings with "hill folk" was not as great as that for a similar meeting with townspeople or those who could readily get to town (prairie farmers and hill farmers with good transportation).

Again, we have no way of knowing anything about the social status of the adults and high school students who wrote histories and autobiographies. Other studies have indicated that the lower-status segments of society contribute a higher percentage of the children who do not go to high school.[57] Thus, the odds are again in favor of the students coming from higher-status families.

Some of the above quarrels with West's methodology may appear to be overemphasis of "fine points." They are made be-

[57] See especially W. Lloyd Warner, Robert J. Havighurst, and Martin B. Loeb, *Who Shall Be Educated?* (New York, Harper and Bros., 1944). Chapter 11 of this book is devoted to a discussion of *Who Shall Be Educated?*

cause it is felt that an awareness of their existence is necessary for interpreting the findings. In a sense, they are made, too, because it is felt that basically the methods used by West were sound and apparently had good results. It seems worth while to suggest improvements on an already good technique.

Not everyone, to be sure, could have participated in as many and as varied activities as did West, and not everyone could have learned so much about Plainville and Plainvillers. As we shall learn later, West has made some valuable contributions to the field of social stratification in addition to his vivid description of life in this mid-Southwestern town.

Differential Perception of the Status System

One of West's more significant contributions lies in his analysis of the social-stratification system in Plainville and the different perception of it by various segments of Plainville society. Rather than analyzing the stratification system through use of an instrument designed to distinguish a fixed number of social classes, West approached the study armed only with his blank notebook. The people of Plainville told him how the system appeared to them. Through use of this method, West discovered what probably could not have been discovered by a highly structured instrument, namely, that the system "looks different" to different Plainvillers, depending, apparently, on their place within it. West's description of how the system appears to "good religious people," to the "lower element," and the "upper class," are quite vivid and clear.

There are only two negative criticisms important enough to be made concerning this section of the Plainville study. The first regards our lack of information about how the status system appears to the very *lowest* status people—"the people who live like animals." The second has to do with the *unstated implications* of the differential perception of the social-stratification system.

The people who live like animals. All in all, we probably learn less about this segment of Plainville society than we do about any other one. This is particularly true with regard to the lowest-status people's view of the social-stratification system. We are simply told, "The small group of people who 'live like animals' have no very clear picture, or, at best, a very garbled picture of the society about them." [58]

Personal experience with people of extremely low status has led us to conclude that many of their actions may be interpreted as "proof" of their "garbled" picture of the society about them. Nevertheless, they have *some* picture and can usually relate it. What does the Plainville society look like to "the people who live like animals"? What criteria do *they* use to rank their fellow citizens? To which description of the Plainville status system is their viewpoint the closest? These are some of the questions that are left unanswered in West's study. A more pervasive and all-inclusive question can be phrased, *"Was West ever close enough, physically, socially, and psychologically, to the lowest-status Plainvillers to discover what they thought about the social-stratification system?"*

Interpretation of the differential perception. It is not altogether clear how West interprets the fact that people from different parts of the status hierarchy view the stratification system in different ways. Sometimes his comments seem to indicate that there is one most correct way (the upper-class way) of describing the Plainville stratification scene. The expressions themselves would not be meaningful out of context, but unmodified references to the upper class, the lower element, and even the upper crust sometimes leave the impression that West accepts the upper-class description of the stratification system as the most accurate one.

At other times it seems that West feels there are as many "correct" descriptions of the stratification system as there are people describing it. If this is the right interpretation—and there seems to be somewhat more evidence that it is—then it would seem that the Plainville status hierarchy does not take the form of a "class

[58] West, *op. cit.*, p. 132.

system" in the traditional usage of the term. According to the first interpretation, there is one certain number of social classes which have definite boundaries but a fairly large proportion of Plainvillers fail to recognize them completely. According to the second interpretation, there is no given number of social classes that is recognized by all, or most, of the community and which are defined similarly by them. Let us repeat that the evidence seems to favor the latter interpretation; it is unfortunate, however, that the confusion exists at all.

The Criteria of Social Status

West has made a positive contribution to the field of social stratification by isolating the most important criteria by which Plainvillers judge the social status of one another. He has indicated that no one criterion is sufficient to ascertain accurately the status position of a given family. We are told that the knowledge of a family's name or knowing where the family lives could probably be used with a high degree of accuracy for distinguishing the upper class from the lower class. We learn also of the extreme emphasis placed on religiousness and morality by some Plainvillers. In a sense, then, we are given an idea about the relative importance of the six major criteria of social status.

A stranger going into Plainville may experience some difficulty in ranking the people, because of insufficient information on hand regarding the weight to be attached to each criterion. A student of social stratification would probably want to know more about the relative importance of the criteria in order better to understand how the status system operates in this small town.

Social Status and the Everyday Life of Plainvillers

It would be most difficult to list the many aspects of a Plainviller's life that are affected by his social status. A man's informal relations with his neighbor, his dating, courtship, and marriage patterns, his political behavior, his membership in formal clubs and associations, and even the way he worships God are somehow related to his position within the status hierarchy of the community. This is made clear in the original text, and it is hoped that enough of it is retained here to let the reader feel that it is an important contribution of the study.

The effect of social status on some aspects of the lives of the people receives more attention than its effect on others. It is clearer, too, how social status enters into the lives of some segments of Plainville society than it enters into others. This is probably largely inevitable, but it would have been useful to learn more about how social status operates in the lives of the lowest-status people. It is not stated with a certainty whether this small group has withdrawn, as it were, from the "race" for social position or whether, in spite of their efforts, they are the habitual losers in the race.

With this one exception, then, it can be said that throughout West's *Plainville* we are afforded meaningful glimpses of how status operates in the Plainviller's everyday life "from the cradle to the grave," bearing in mind that it was not the intent of the study to go into detail on this point.

The Dynamic Aspects of Social Status

In general, West's description of how the Plainville stratification system looks and operates today is better than his description of how it "got that way." In a similar vein, his description of how families at a given social level are living is better than his explanation of how they achieved their social statuses. These and other dynamic aspects of social status (admittedly more difficult to analyze) could stand fuller treatment.

As far as the first point is concerned, we do not learn explicitly how the "people who live like animals" became almost set apart from the rest of Plainville. Nor do we discover how the loosely defined group at the top of the status hierarchy—the "upper crust"—came into being. Perhaps, it is a vestige of a once clearly defined "upper-upper class" that is losing its identity; perhaps, it is the "upper-upper class" of tomorrow.

We learn that little social mobility takes place in Plainville, and especially that "Movement across the line separating the upper class from the lower class is virtually impossible, without leaving the community." [59] Why is this so? Specifically, what barriers are set up across this line, and why are they so rigid? Apparently, there seems to be an economic thread running through many of the criteria of status and, therefore, many of the attributes that have to be attained to gain recognition as an upper-class Plainviller. The more productive prairie farms cost money and, in turn, make their owners larger profits. Technology, as a criteria of status, includes the presence of shiny tractors and other items that can be purchased. But how, we should ask, are economic achievements translated into "power" so that these same achievements are denied the lower-class people? In a general sense we have some of the answers to this question, but not those specific answers that are unique, perhaps, to Plainville.

Let us ask, too, why mobility was analyzed only in terms of the upper-class description of the stratification system. It is possible that more or less mobility would be evident if, for example, one of the lower-class pictures of the system was used. In some descriptions, it will be recalled, the line separating hill from prairie folk was apparently not very rigid and appeared only *within* one of the classes. The use of such a description may have indicated more mobility within the middle section of the status hierarchy.

And, finally, we might ask about the future of the stratification system in Plainville. Are the social forces that operate in this small town conducive to a more rigidly defined stratification system, or to one that is even less well defined than today's? Is the trend toward greater or lesser differences between the extremes of the status hierarchy? That is, is Plainville society becoming more equalitarian, or will it be even less true fifty years hence than it is today that "everybody here is equal"? These are the kinds of questions that the social scientist should be prepared to answer, not in terms of generalizing forecasts but by way of careful hy-

[59] *Ibid.*, p. 135.

potheses based upon the best and most accurate data he can obtain in his delimited field.

SELECTED READINGS

DAVIS, Allison, GARDNER, Burleigh B., and GARDNER, Mary R., *Deep South* (Chicago, University of Chicago Press, 1941), pp. 63-73.

HIMMELWEIT, H. T., HALSEY, A. H., and OPPENHEIM, A. N., "The Views of Adolescents on Some Aspects of the Social Class Structure," *British Journal of Sociology*, 3 (June, 1952), pp. 148-172.

USEEM, John, TANGENT, Pierre, and USEEM, Ruth, "Stratification in a Prairie Town," in Logan Wilson and William Kolb, *Sociological Analysis* (New York, Harcourt, Brace and Co., 1949), pp. 454-464.

WARNER, W. Lloyd, and LUNT, Paul S., *The Social Life of a Modern Community* (New Haven, Yale University Press, 1941), Chapters XX, XXI, and XXII.

5

Status and Wealth in a New England Mill Town[1]

IN THE SUMMER of 1949 Gerhard E. Lenski began a study of social stratification in Danielson, Connecticut. This small textile mill community became his "laboratory" for a study designed to examine the relationship between social status and wealth. His subjects were a sample of the nearly two thousand families in this New England town.

Specifically, Lenski's study was designed to answer two questions: "First, to what degree are the prestige status and the wealth of families in modern industrial societies correlated? Second, what are the causative factors producing this relationship?"[2] Since the answers to these questions would necessitate an analysis of the community's social-status system, Lenski formulated a hypothesis concerning the nature of this system. The hypothesis had to do with the existence of "true" social classes and read as follows: "Social classes exist as discrete, perceived groups in the community of Danielson, and therefore all 'well informed' members of the community are aware of the existence of such groups, and are also aware of the membership limits of such groups."[3]

[1] Data in this chapter have been used with permission of the author from two sources: Gerhard E. Lenski, *Prestige Status and Wealth* (unpublished Ph.D. dissertation, Department of Sociology, Yale University, 1950); and Gerhard E. Lenski, "American Social Classes: Statistical Strata or Social Groups?" *American Journal of Sociology*, 58 (September, 1952), pp. 139-144.

[2] Lenski, *Prestige Status and Wealth*, pp. 1-2.

[3] Lenski, "American Social Classes: Statistical Strata or Social Groups?" p. 141.

When the above hypothesis and the two major questions are combined, three phases of the research problem emerge: (1) the investigation of the social-status system, (2) the investigation of the economic-status system, and (3) an analysis of the relationship between the two. In this summary, somewhat greater emphasis will be placed on the first phase—the methods and findings relevant to the social-status system of Danielson.

Danielson, the Town and the People

Danielson is located in the east-central section of Connecticut, just 27 miles due west of Providence, Rhode Island. It is situated near the site where Captain James Danielson, the first settler in the area, purchased his large tract of land in 1707. Nearby also is the river where the grandson of Captain Danielson erected a cotton spinning mill about a century later.

As late as the first quarter of the nineteenth century, almost everyone in Danielson was a Yankee and a Congregationalist. Today, less than one third of the people can call themselves Yankees. Two thirds of them are Catholic and the remaining churchgoers are divided among many Protestant denominations. The heavy and continuous influx of French-Canadians partially accounts for the change in both the religious and the ethnic make-up of the town. Today fully 48 per cent of the 6000 people of Danielson are of French-Canadian extraction. The 300 Irish are the most numerous of the remaining eight national groups that have come to the town throughout the years.

Danielson has long been a "mill town." Recently, however, a producer of nationally advertised food products has established a branch plant that employs a hundred local workers. During World War II a large manufacturing concern built an assembly plant in Danielson where an additional 300 workers now earn their living. Despite these recent attempts at diversification, the textile mills form the basic industry. One mill, in fact, usually employs about half of the town's industrial workers. A large payroll cut by this company in the late 1940's proved once again to

Danielson that "it is basically a one-industry, and even a one-company town." [4]

How typical is Danielson? The town is probably not too unlike many of its size in the New England region. The fact that in 1948 about three fourths of its population earned less than $3000 a year indicates that it is not a prosperous town. It lacks some of the conveniences and services offered by large cities; about one fourth of the families, for example, cook on wood or kerosene stoves. Still, the town cannot be called poor. It is not atypical in the sense that a "college town" or a "resort town" would be. In the general region in which Danielson is located it is not unusual to find a town in which two thirds of the people are Catholic. Finally, Danielson seems to be growing despite the fact that "each generation a larger proportion of the children of the older stock leave . . . since its opportunities for the college-trained are limited." [5]

This, then, is a brief glimpse of the town in which Lenski spent four months interviewing families, examining their tax records and credit ratings, and nine additional months "just talking" with the townspeople.

Selecting a Study Group

There is often little that can be gained from studying the entire population of a town that cannot also be derived by examining an *adequate sample*. Since the method that Lenski had planned to use included long personal interviews, he limited himself to a sample of 150 of the nearly 2000 families in Danielson.

Fortunately, Lenski had at his disposal a recent list of the names, addresses, and occupations of all the Danielson families. From this list he drew 150 names at random (a 7.5 per cent sample of the total). Certain ethnic, occupational, and residential groups were not represented in this sample in the same degree that they appeared on the master list. Anticipating that he might have to

---

[4] Lenski, *Prestige Status and Wealth*, p. 72.
[5] *Ibid.*, p. 66.

correct for this, Lenski first determined the actual composition of the town. Occupations were derived from the town census data; the ethnic factor was roughly determined from the surnames contained on the same list; and the addresses plotted on an ecological map indicated the number of people who lived in each of the areas of the town. By withdrawing some names and adding others, the sample was "adjusted" so that it conformed very closely to the known categories in the total population.

SOCIAL STRATIFICATION IN DANIELSON

Methodology

Lenski determined the social status of his study group by what is called the "rater" or "judge's" technique. Basically, this consists of selecting a certain number of individuals from the community and asking them to rate the community members, or a sample of them, in terms of the members' social status. The specific techniques, including the instructions furnished the raters, vary; but an individual's final rank usually reflects the rank assigned to him by several of the judges. It is thought to be better if the raters represent a cross section of the community as far as is possible.

The raters. Lenski has this to say about the raters selected by him to rank the 150 Danielson families: [6]

Since the information to be obtained from the raters was considered to be of a delicate nature, it was necessary that they be individuals with whom the investigator could establish rapport.... The ratings finally used were obtained from twenty-four local residents and the writer. Seventeen of the raters were lifelong residents of Danielson. Five others had lived in the community for at least ten years. Only three of the raters, including the writer, had lived in the community for less than ten years. The raters came from many walks of life. Included among them were mill-hands, a mill foreman, a mill owner, a school teacher, a doctor, a paperhanger, a town official, an engineer, a laundry routeman, an artist, and a saleslady. Other raters included

[6] *Ibid.*, pp. 74-76. Italics not in original.

were the *wives* of millhands, businessmen, an electrician, a butcher, a doctor, and a mill official. The Protestant, Catholic, and Greek Orthodox faiths were represented among the raters. Individuals of British, French, Irish, Italian, and Greek extraction were included. Six of the raters were under thirty years of age, eight were in their thirties, three in their forties, four in their fifties, and four were over sixty years of age.

The rating technique. Having received the consent of these twenty-four people to act as raters, Lenski then went to their homes, one by one, and obtained their impression of the relative social status of the families in the study group. The first step in this procedure was to give each rater a stack of cards which contained the names and addresses of the families. Each was then asked to separate the families he knew from those he did not.[7]

Next the rater was asked to rate those families that he knew *according to their standing in the community*. Since he had already been doing this informally during the discussion that preceded the rating process, the raters seldom had difficulty with the actual process. The investigator usually sat beside the rater at a table while the ratings were being made. As the rater separated the cards, he usually gave his reasons for rating each family as he did. Such statements afforded a wealth of information about the factors the raters considered relevant to the prestige status of a family.

When the interview had been completed, the investigator gathered together the cards in such a manner as to preserve the order given them by the rater.

It is significant to note that Lenski apparently furnished his raters with a *minimum of directions*. In this way, it was thought, the viewpoints of the raters were more likely to be preserved than if they were given detailed instructions including, perhaps, what factors to keep in mind when they were rating a family, or into how many groups the cards should be sorted.

Status factors considered by the raters. "Almost without exception the raters felt obliged to justify their rating of each family, whether its rating was high or low."[8] These "justifications,"

---

[7] *Ibid.*, p. 77.
[8] *Ibid.*, p. 46.

coupled with the informal discussions of social status that preceded the actual ratings, give us insight into the kind of things
the raters considered relevant to social status.

Basically, it seems, the raters tried to relate the family's activities to the values of the community, with particular reference to
how their activities "contributed to the continued existence and
well-being of the community." [9] To evaluate a family's every
action in terms of its worth to the community would be a long
process indeed. Often the raters were forced to take short-cuts in
the rating process. Lenski has summarized the various factors that
the raters considered when they rated the Danielson families: [10]

A. What a family is
　　1. Ethnic background
　　2. Kinship ties

B. What a family does
　　1. Economic activities
　　2. Religious activities
　　3. Political activities
　　4. Educational activities
　　5. Leisure time activities
　　6. Domestic activities
　　7. Sexual activities

C. What a family has
　　1. Friends
　　2. Possessions

It would be virtually impossible to describe how the twenty-
five raters weighed and considered each of these status factors.
At best we could provide a few illustrations. Perhaps the matter
can best be summed up by Lenski's remark, "In short, it can be
said that the raters considered *the total way of life* of a family
relevant to that family's prestige status." [11]

Compiling the ratings. When all the judges had ranked the
families they knew, Lenski discovered that there was no clear

[9] *Ibid.*, p. 170.
[10] *Ibid.*, p. 83.
[11] *Ibid.*, pp. 83-84.

agreement among the raters concerning the number of groups into which the families were divided. "One rater used a three-level breakdown, four used a four-level breakdown, seven used a five-level breakdown, nine used a six-level breakdown, and four used a seven-level breakdown.[12] *No one type of breakdown was used by more than 36 per cent of the raters.*" [13]

West, in his study of Plainville,[14] discovered that although either four or five was consistently suggested as the number of social classes, the levels were defined differently by people from different portions of the status hierarchy. West handles the matter by presenting several different descriptions of the status system without concluding that any one number of classes, defined in any way, represented the true picture.[15]

In a later section we will see that in still another study the problem of raters describing the system differently was not encountered. Hollingshead, in his study of Elmtown, discovered that nineteen of his twenty-five judges placed thirty families in five groups.[16] The entire rating procedure will be described in more detail in a later chapter and possible explanations for this phenomenon will be introduced; at this point suffice it to say that here is a case where the judges seem in essential agreement regarding the "right" number of categories to employ.

Since Lenski's judges did not agree on the groups to be employed when rating the families, and since there was apparently

---

[12] Lenski notes that, "The number of levels used by a rater in describing the prestige status system of the community had no significant relationship to his own prestige status. Neither was the prestige status of the rater related to the limits or bounds of the strata he identified" (Lenski, "American Social Classes," p. 142). This is apparently contradictory to the findings of West in Plainville (see pp. 61-65). A time difference, differences in the location, size, and economic life of the communities, and the separate techniques used to investigate the social-stratification system in Danielson and Plainville, render a comparison between the two studies, on this particular point, somewhat difficult.

[13] Lenski, *Prestige Status and Wealth*, p. 77.

[14] See preceding chapter.

[15] See pp. 61-65.

[16] See pp. 161-162.

no indication that any one system was more "correct" than any other, he set out to devise a means for obtaining *a simple rating for each family based upon the various ratings assigned by the judges who knew it.* To obtain a composite rating, Lenski placed the scores of the families on a 100-point scale. If a rater, for example, had divided the families into four categories, these categories were weighted 100, 67, 33, and 0. The highest value was assigned to the group the rater considered highest, a score of 67 was given to his next higher group, and so on. If another rater had used five groups, they were weighted 100, 75, 50, 25, and 0. Each person this judge had placed in the lowest group received a score of 0; everyone in his second group received 25 points. For each of the 150 families there then existed as many scores as there were judges who knew the family.

Before averaging these scores, Lenski found it necessary to make some technical revisions in his technique: [17]

> During the analysis of the ratings it was observed that although all of the raters used the same criteria to define the top of the prestige structure, not all used the same criteria to define the bottom of it. Eighteen of the twenty-five raters created a bottom level of families which they described as "vicious," "notorious," or "utterly worthless." Invariably, when a family was placed in this level, the rater would recite one or more tales that illustrated the "viciousness," the "depravity," or the "worthlessness" of the family. The other seven raters, however, did not form such a level. The families that belonged to their bottom level were described in general terms as "hard-working people who never seemed to get anywhere." One rater summed up this type by saying, "They come to town, work here awhile, die or move on, and no one knows that they were here or cares that they are gone." No fascinating tales were told about these families. The seven raters' description of these families corresponded exactly with the other eighteen raters' of the families in their *second from bottom level*.
>
> Under these circumstances it would have been incorrect to weight the bottom level of the eighteen raters and the bottom level of the seven raters both zero.

[17] *Ibid.*, p. 79.

Lenski compensated for the discrepancy by extending the bottom level of the scale 25 points. "Thus *the adjusted scale* ran from plus one hundred to minus twenty-five. The bottom level of the eighteen raters was weighted minus twenty-five. The bottom level of the seven raters and the second from bottom level of the eighteen raters were both rated zero." [18] For each rater it was necessary to determine whether his lowest category chiefly contained families of the "notorious type" or the "plain hard-working type."

Following this adjustment a new set of scores was computed for the 150 families. Then, all of the scores for each family were averaged. [19]

The Social-Stratification System

The averaged scores, ranging from 86 to 6, were plotted on a scale. The resulting figure was inspected in order to investigate the nature of the stratification system in Danielson. If, for example, all of the scores "clustered" about three values, 10, 40, and 70, it would be necessary to investigate further the possibility of Danielson's having a three-class system. If some other number of clusters or no clusters were discovered, this too would be significant. Following an examination of the plotted scores, Lenski had this to say: [20]

It was impossible to discover a system of clearly defined, discrete social classes. The groupings that could be identified were, for the most part, vague and ill-defined and were in that part of the prestige structure in which there were the fewest cases, so that large gaps between ratings were bound to exist. The Danielson prestige structure appeared to resemble a *continuum* more nearly than it did a system of

[18] *Ibid.*, p. 80.

[19] The computation of final scores was actually preceded by another technical adjustment to the rating procedure. This one was felt necessary to compensate for the fact that some of the judges tended consistently to overrate people (as compared with the other judges) while some tended to underrate. In those cases where the effects of the deviant judges would not cancel out one another an inaccuracy was thought to be introduced. See Lenski, *Prestige Status and Wealth*, pp. 81-82.

[20] *Ibid.*, p. 84.

discrete social classes. This raised a fundamental question. *Was this failure to depict a system of discrete social classes due to inadequate research or inappropriate mathematical techniques, and was this chart, therefore, a misrepresentation of reality? Or was this chart a reasonably accurate picture of the structure of the family prestige system in Danielson?*

The additional evidence that was brought to bear on the subject can be classified as follows:

1. Disagreement concerning number of strata. Not more than one third of the twenty-four raters could agree on the number of social strata existing in Danielson. "This seemed to point to the conclusion that no system of discrete, perceived social classes existed in the community." [21]

2. Disagreement in definition of strata. Even those raters who divided the families into the same number of groups disagreed concerning the nature and boundaries of each strata. Some of the eight raters, for example, who had divided the sample into six strata, "defined their top stratum in extremely narrow terms, including only two or three sample families in it. Others, by contrast, defined their top stratum so as to include a dozen or more families." [22]

3. The arbitrary nature of the groupings. "... Most of the raters, in the course of the rating interview, constantly changed the number of strata they were using to classify the sample families. For example, one rater began by classifying the families into three strata. Later he subdivided two of these original three strata, and for a period of time he worked with five categories. Still later, two strata were combined so that in the end he had a total of four strata." [23]

4. Some raters suggested use of a continuum. "... Several raters *volunteered* the information that they could subdivide the families in the study group almost indefinitely. As one woman put it, "I could do a much better job of this if I had more time to

[21] Lenski, "American Social Classes," p. 142.
[22] *Ibid.*
[23] *Ibid.*, p. 143.

spare. I could probably separate these families into twenty or thirty levels or more; but that would take all day to do." [24]

5. Many raters sought directions. ". . . Many raters in the initial stages of rating asked the writer the number of categories into which the families should be divided. This would seem to indicate that the raters lacked any specific frame of reference when they began the task. It would seem from this that the raters were not accustomed to thinking of the community as divided into a series of discrete social strata." [25]

Thus, to the original evidence in the form of the continuous or "non-clustering" nature of the status scores, we add five additional types of evidence. Lenski cautiously recognizes that the findings are still subject to two interpretations: [26]

First, the findings could be interpreted as proof of the absence of any system of discrete social classes which are recognized by even the "well-informed" members of the community. Second, the findings could also be interpreted as indicating that the research techniques employed were inadequate and failed to uncover the true nature of the prestige status system which existed in Danielson.

The second interpretation, he holds, is unwarranted largely because the research techniques were such that a well-defined system of social stratification was discovered. The raters seemed well aware of this system and essentially agreed regarding its nature, as evidenced by their consistency in rating the families. Despite the fact that they used a different number of categories as an aid to ranking the families, more than 87 per cent of the 1792 ratings fell within 15 points (lower or higher) of the final rating score of each of the families.

In view of all the evidence, Lenski concluded: *"In short, prestige differentiation existed in Danielson, but it was not structured in the form of clearly defined, discrete social classes."* [27]

[24] *Ibid.*
[25] *Ibid.*
[26] *Ibid.*
[27] Lenski, *Prestige Status and Wealth*, pp. 86-87.

It should be noted that this conclusion is restricted to a definition of social classes as groupings of people of similar status, clearly set apart from the rest of the community and recognized as such by community members. If by a "social class" is meant some kind of a psychological group—a number of similar-status people who have attitudes or beliefs in common or who claim membership in a "class"—then there *may* be social classes in Danielson.[28]

Social-Status Levels

In order to continue his investigation of the relationship between social status and wealth, Lenski divided the social-status continuum into six segments. The difference between these constructed segments of a continuum and discrete social classes is made clear by Lenski's definition of the prestige levels: [29]

The term "prestige level"...may be defined as a group of families of somewhat similar prestige status. But it should be noted that a *prestige level* is not a real group any more than are men who earn from $2,000-$2,999 per year. Nevertheless the concept of prestige level is highly useful as a tool in social analysis. The boundaries or limits used...were determined by the investigator who created them and were chosen in such a manner as to provide the greatest aid to analysis.

Table 1 represents Lenski's definition of the six prestige levels.[30]

TABLE 1. The Six Prestige Levels (after Lenski), Their Score Ranges, and Number of Families in Each Level

Level	Final Score Range	Number of Families
I	82 to 86	3
II	54 to 69	6
III	32 to 46	20
IV	8 to 28	35
V	—1 to 7	73
VI	—6 to —2	13

[28] For a study of social class that employs this concept see Chapter 10.
[29] Lenski, *Prestige Status and Wealth*, p. 88. Italics not in original.
[30] *Ibid.*, p. 89.

THE WEALTH OF THE DANIELSON FAMILIES

Lenski considers the wealth of a family as consisting of all its money and all its possessions that have a money value. Defined in this manner, the total wealth of a family is difficult to measure. The family itself would be hard pressed to state its wealth; its possessions may be numerous or concealed; and the value of its possessions may fluctuate.

Since wealth can take so many forms, the measure of only one form, for example, savings, cannot accurately describe the total picture. In this study, therefore, a series of indices of wealth were used. Questions appeared on the schedule regarding the amount of money a man and his wife earned in a year. The spending habits of the family were investigated by asking such questions as whether or not they had had domestic help during the past year. In addition, a long list of questions related to the families' tangible possessions. Ownership of a vacuum cleaner, an electric mixer, a gas or electric stove, an automatic washer, a piano, and sterling silverware were some items thought to be indicative of the total wealth of a family. Questions also were asked on subjects ranging from the kind and amount of insurance owned to the price the women usually spent for dresses. All in all, forty independent indices of wealth were used.

Taken separately, many of these indices showed that the average family [31] in a given social-status category was wealthier than that in the lower categories. Some of the indices failed to show any significant difference in wealth between the average families in adjacent status categories, and a few indicated that apparently the average family in a lower category was wealthier than the average family in the next higher one.

"To summarize the findings," concludes Lenski, "it may be said

[31] The expression, "the wealth of the *average family* in a status category," is used to describe the wealth-level *occurring most frequently* among families within the status category. The expression should not be confused with, "the *average wealth* of families . . ." which would refer to the simple mean of the wealth of *all* families within the category.

that the wealth of the average family in each of the top four prestige levels was greater than the wealth of the average family in each of the next lower prestige levels. It also appeared probable that the average family in Level V was wealthier than the average family in Level VI, but the evidence pointed to the conclusion that the degree of difference in wealth was less than between other levels." [32]

The Final Wealth Scale

In order to compare statistically the total wealth of families with their social status, the collective effect of the various financial indices should be considered. Since it cannot be assumed that all of the items are equally as important in the total picture of wealth, a seemingly endless problem of weighting would be necessary in order to incorporate the forty indices used in this study into a single scale.

"After careful consideration, four of the most important of the forty indices were selected as the basis for the scale. The four were (a) current annual income of the head of family, (b) value of real estate . . . , (c) value of automobiles owned, and (d) face value of life insurance policies and annuities carried on head of family.[33] Each $1000 of current annual income was weighted 1.0, as was each $1000 worth of life insurance, real estate, or automobile owned." [34] Thus the problems connected with the relative weight of each item have been avoided; a thousand dollars is a thousand dollars, whether it represents the *value* of a life insurance policy or *money spent* for an automobile.

A total wealth score was computed for each of the families in the study group and this was compared with their final social-status rating. After computing the coefficient of correlation (plus 0.77) between these two scores, and testing the significance of

[32] *Ibid.*, p. 131.
[33] For comments on the advisability of using face value of life insurance as an index of wealth see p. 105.
[34] *Ibid.*, p. 138.

this coefficient, Lenski concludes that "A high degree of correlation . . . existed between the prestige status and the wealth of the families. . . ." [35]

THE RELATIONSHIP BETWEEN SOCIAL STATUS AND WEALTH

This study, we will recall, was designed to answer two questions. "First, to what degree are the prestige status and the wealth of families in modern industrial societies correlated? Second, what are the causative factors producing this relationship?" [36] The evidence was presented in the foregoing section to answer the first question. The same evidence, however, that indicated that the wealth of families and their social status is related also indicates that this relationship is not a *simple* causative one. That is, in view of the correlation discovered, wealth cannot be the sole cause of social status nor can social status be the only cause of wealth. Other factors are involved.

Lenski explains the relationship between these two variables by analyzing, first, why the relationship is so high. Next, he investigates some of the reasons that prevent the correlation from being perfect or near perfect.

The Common Factors in Status and Wealth

Part of the reason why there is a significant relationship between social status and wealth lies in the fact that there are factors common to both of the variables. In other words, if a person has certain attributes or performs certain activities he will "score high" in both social status and wealth.

1. Occupation. Perhaps the chief of these common factors is occupation. It is the usual source for achieving wealth. In addition, it was said by the raters to be the most important single factor affecting social status. "More than this," Lenski states, "it

[35] *Ibid.*, p. 143.
[36] *Ibid.*, pp. 1-2.

was found that the *relative degree* of financial reward received from these occupational activities corresponded closely to the *relative degree* of prestige status reward received. For example, mill owners and executives were rewarded for their activities both with greater wealth and higher prestige status than were their subordinates." [37]

2. *Material possessions.* Possessions were the second factor common to both social status and wealth. By definition, possessions *are* wealth. They also entered into the social-status picture. The following illustrates how possessions influenced the social-status scores of the Danielson families: [38]

> During the preliminary discussions that preceded the actual process of rating, most of the raters stated that the only thing that determined a family's prestige status was what that family had, or had not, done. When, however, these same raters were faced with the problem of actually rating a specific group of families, it was observed that they allowed other factors than activities alone to influence their decisions....
>
> Lacking complete knowledge of the past and present activities of all the families they were rating, the raters frequently turned to the families' possessions as a clue to the unknown activities. If a family owned a large, new automobile and an expensive, well-equipped house, the raters made the assumption (barring knowledge to the contrary) that the family had been, and was at present, engaged in activities of importance to the community. If, on the other hand, a family lived in a poorly furnished tenement in an undesirable section of town and drove an antiquated automobile, the raters assumed that the poverty of possessions indicated that the family "had never done anything to amount to much." In this manner possessions were frequently used as a clue to unknown activities. *The less known about the past and present activities of a family, the greater was the reliance placed upon possessions as a clue to activities.*

It is difficult to estimate the influence of possessions on the social-status ratings. To do so we would need to know not only how frequently the raters relied upon possessions as a key to a

[37] *Ibid.,* pp. 176-177.
[38] *Ibid.,* p. 170.

family's social status, but also how heavily they weighted them as compared to other factors.

In summary, then, the fact that occupation and material possessions contributed to both the prestige rate and the wealth score partially explains the high correlation between the two scores.

Why Not a Perfect Correlation?

Lenski cites several factors to account for the fact that wealth and social status were not found to be perfectly correlated.

1. Differential occupational rewards. Some occupations pay more in "psychic income" and prestige than they do in dollars. Take the classic case, the school teacher. Usually the salary received from this occupation is not as much, relative to the other members of the community, as is the social status. In other words, it will often be noticed that people of a status similar to the teacher are wealthier than he is.

On the other hand, a person's occupation may bring him more money than it does prestige. The occupation of bartender or garbage collector could perhaps illustrate this type. Presumably many Americans attach little prestige to such occupations but often the salaries these jobs carry is higher than, or as much as, those of more prestige-bearing positions.

Thus the discrepancies that existed between the financial and prestige rewards of occupations formed one explanation of the lack of perfect correlation between social status and wealth.

2. Rewards in status only. "According to the raters, certain types of activities that *were not* rewarded in terms of wealth *were* rewarded in terms of prestige status." [39] In this category would fall various kinds of civic and social activities. Members of the Board of Education, church and civic leaders, and officers of some social clubs seemed to be rewarded only by the prestige attached to these positions. This situation would help "upset" the relationship between wealth and status.

[39] *Ibid.,* p. 180.

3. *Punishment with respect to status only.* The slogan, "Crime does not pay!" may sometimes be more true of status rewards than financial ones. In Danielson, for example, members of several families were known to have engaged in such presumably remunerative activities as prostitution and theft. Such activities lowered their social status.

Other individuals engaged in activities that brought them no financial reward but did contribute to their loss of status. Personal habits such as drunkenness, slovenly housekeeping, and known deviant sexual behavior may fall into this category.

4. *The use of ethnic background as a guide to status.* The final factor cited by Lenski to explain the lack of complete agreement between a family's social status and its wealth has to do with the manner in which the raters used ethnic background, kinship ties, and friendship ties to help decide the family's social status. This is illustrated in the following excerpt: [40]

If a family was related to certain Old Yankee "clans" that "had never amounted to much," or if it was of French-Canadian or eastern or southern European immigrant stock, the raters assumed that that family would probably make little contribution to the welfare of the community. A family in this category would have to prove its worth to the community before it could expect any higher status in the prestige structure. In marked contrast, certain old Yankee families received their status almost wholly "on credit."

Thus, four factors—(1) differential occupational rewards, (2) activities that received status rewards alone, (3) activities that received punishment with respect to status only, and (4) the raters' use of ethnic and family background as a guide to status—were found to be important reasons why the correlation between social status and wealth does not more nearly approximate a perfect one.

[40] *Ibid.*, pp. 181-182.

SUMMARY OF THE MAJOR FINDINGS

Throughout this review emphasis has been placed on those aspects of the study that have a general reference to social-stratification theory. Some findings, not necessarily less important, have been omitted only because they have a more specific reference to Danielson in 1949. Other factors that were relevant to Lenski's purpose have not been discussed because it was felt they were somewhat extraneous to our purposes. With these limitations, it is thought that the following summarizes the major findings of the research:

1. A high degree of agreement seemed to exist among the raters regarding the social status of the Danielson families. This would indicate that there exists in this town a well-defined social-stratification system.

2. The social-stratification system did *not* take the form of clearly defined, discrete social classes. Lenski concluded that the system resembled a continuum.

3. An analysis of the wealth of the Danielson families pointed to the conclusion that the average family in a given segment of the status continuum was wealthier than the average family in the lower segments.

4. The coefficient of correlation between the wealth and the social status of the 150 families was found to be plus 0.77.

5. The most important factor in the determination of both wealth and social status was found to be the occupation of the family heads. This helped account for the relatively high degree of relationship between social status and wealth. The fact that possessions, a form of wealth, were used in judging social status also helped explain the correlation.

6. Other factors were discovered that prevented the correlation between wealth and status from being perfect. Included are various types of activities that were rewarded differentially in terms of status and wealth.

EVALUATION

The evidence uncovered in one small New England "mill town" led the author to conclude that the town's stratification system was not characterized by clearly delineated social classes. Since this represents a departure from the findings of the "typical" stratification study, it is well to investigate carefully the steps that led to the conclusion. Following this investigation we will address some remarks toward the other findings of the study, that is, those relevant to the determination of the wealth of Danielson families and those concerning the relationship between their prestige status and wealth.

Measurement of Social Status in Danielson

Basically, the social status of Danielson families was determined by the way in which they were rated by twenty-four residents selected by Lenski. Several sources of difficulty inhere in this system of determining the status placement of individuals.[41] In the first place, one often entertains a few doubts about the raters. How were they selected? What was *their* position in the status hierarchy?

The raters or judges that are used for purposes such as these must be individuals with whom the researcher can establish rapport. They must be able, too, to understand the task that is before them and, of course, they must be willing to perform it. Perhaps a "sophistication bias," but at least a "co-operativeness bias" is

[41] Various researchers, particularly those who have employed the technique, have commented on some of the problems associated with the "judges' rating" technique for determining the social status of community members. See especially Otis D. Duncan and Jay W. Artis, "Social Stratification in a Pennsylvania Rural Community," *The Pennsylvania State College of Agriculture, Bulletin 543* (October, 1951), pp. 22-26; Harold F. Kaufman, "Members of Rural Community as Judges of Prestige Rank," *Sociometry,* 9 (February, 1946), pp. 71-85; Harold F. Kaufman, "Prestige Classes in a New York Rural Community," *Cornell University Agricultural Experiment Station, Memoir 260* (March, 1944); Merton D. Oyler, "Neighborhood Standing and Population Changes in Johnson and Robertson Counties, Kentucky," *Kentucky Agricultural Experiment Station, Bulletin 523* (August, 1948).

present. The characteristics that can be associated with co-opera-tiveness or, for that matter, unco-operativeness, are difficult to ascertain; they may be associated with the issues under inquiry.

The raters utilized by Lenski appear to come from various "walks of life." There appears to be no readily discernible selec-tive bias with respect to the occupation or social status of the raters. No group of twenty-four persons, however, can be truly representative of a town of 6000 persons.

A more important question can be raised concerning the methods by which the actual ratings were conducted. It will be recalled that a minimum of directions were furnished the status-judges. The judges, therefore, were not likely to be influenced by Lenski's own theories about the stratification system.

There seems to be some confusion and ambiguity, however, concerning the criteria by which raters judged the Danielson citizens. We were told that they considered "the *total way of life* of a family relevant to that family's prestige status" and we were furnished a rather extensive list of the characteristics the raters considered. It is probably not realistic to assume that all the raters utilized the *same* characteristics and *weighted* them con-sistently when ranking specific families. There may even have been a consistent bias present. Perhaps the less well known a family was to the rater, for example, the more importance was attached to its material possessions; the families better known to the raters may have been rated more on their activities in the community, their friendship patterns, and the like. In short, we would find it hard to isolate the objective characteristics, the possession of which result in a certain status in the community. Perhaps, then, an objective scale may have given a better indica-tion of the status placement of Danielson residents; some signifi-cant status factors would probably have been missed, but we would then have the assurance that all residents were judged ac-cording to the same criteria.

Basically, however, Lenski's conclusions regarding the non-classlike nature of Danielson's stratification seem to be warranted by his data. His conclusions in this respect resulted from an analysis of the rank scores of the community members, buttressed by additional evidence obtained throughout the rating process.

Determination of Wealth of Danielson Residents

It is recognized that a direct measurement of the total wealth of a family would be difficult to obtain. What Lenski attempted to do, therefore, was to isolate the *more important* indices of the total wealth of Danielson families. The four indices appearing on the final scale were: (1) current annual income of the head of the family, (2) value of real estate, (3) value of automobile, and (4) value of life insurance policies and annuities carried on head of family. Each of these factors was weighted equally, that is, $5000 received per year in income was given the same score as $5000 invested in real estate, or the possession of an insurance policy with a face value of $5000. Put differently, an individual could "achieve" the same increase in wealth (as measured by this scale) by (1) augmenting his yearly income by $10,000, (2) purchasing a house $10,000 more expensive than his present one, or (3) buying a $10,000 insurance policy (at a cost of approximately $200 a year). This should indicate why it is suggested that the weighting system for the various indices of wealth could stand further refinement. In isolated cases, it would appear, the system of equal weighting could produce unrealistic results; it is not certain, moreover, that in most cases the weights used result in the most accurate estimates of wealth.

The Relationship Between Status and Wealth

Lenski states the primary aims of his research in these terms: "This project was designed to answer two important questions: First, to what degree are the prestige status and the wealth of families in modern industrial societies correlated? Second, what are the causative factors producing this particular relationship?"

The answer to the first question was given in statistical form: the coefficient of correlation between status and wealth scores of

Danielson residents was found to be plus 0.77.[42] The analysis of the *causative* factors producing this relationship, to use Lenski's term, seems to have been dismissed by an analysis of (1) why the correlation was so high, and (2) why it was not perfect.

Lenski did not emphasize the implications inherent in the fact that one reason the relationship between status and wealth proved to be considerable was that *both characteristics were, to some extent, measured by the same means.* Although he pointed out, for example, that the prestige status of families was partially determined by their material possessions, that is, their wealth, he did not seem to stress the fact that the ranking system and the wealth scale were, to a limited extent, measuring the same characteristic—wealth. As long as the judges were, even partially, ranking the families on the basis of their wealth, it is not surprising that there is such a high degree of relationship between wealth as determined in this manner, and wealth as determined by evaluating material possessions!

In short, it seems that the second question posited by the author, "... what are the causative factors producing this particular relationship" [43] [between prestige status and wealth] has not been fully answered. The dynamics of the relationship, that is, the way in which Danielson families translate their wealth into prestige, was investigated only briefly. In other respects, too, it is felt that the presentation of a statistical measure of the relationship between the variables, and the interpretations of the magnitude of this measure, have not fully qualified as an explanation of the "causative" factors responsible for the relationship.

[42] Kaufman discovered a similar relationship inasmuch as the coefficient of correlation between the score on twenty-four items of economic possession (from the Sewell socio-economic scale) and the class ratings of the population of a New York rural community was +0.61. When twelve additional items from the Sewell scale, pertaining to social participation, were included, the coefficient of correlation was discovered to be +0.71. See Kaufman, *op. cit.*, pp. 10-11.

[43] Lenski, *Prestige Status and Wealth*, pp. 1-2.

SELECTED READINGS

DUNCAN, Otis D., and ARTIS, Jay W., "Social Stratification in a Pennsylvania Rural Community," *The Pennsylvania State College of Agriculture, Bulletin 543* (October, 1951), pp. 22-26.

HETZLER, Stanley A., "An Investigation of the Distinctiveness of Social Classes," *American Sociological Review*, 18 (October, 1953), pp. 493-497.

KAUFMAN, Harold F., "Members of a Rural Community as Judges of Prestige Rank," *Sociometry*, 9 (February, 1946), pp. 71-85.

——, "Prestige Classes in a New York Rural Community," *Cornell University Agricultural Experiment Station, Memoir 260* (March, 1944).

OYLER, Merton D., "Neighborhood Standing and Population Changes in Johnson and Robertson Counties, Kentucky," *Kentucky Agricultural Experiment Station, Bulletin 523* (August, 1948).

SCHULER, Edgar A., "Social and Economic Status in a Louisiana Hills Community," *Rural Sociology*, 5 (March, 1940), pp. 69-83. Especially pp. 71-76.

6

"Social Class in America"[1]

Anthropologist W. Lloyd Warner is one of the recent social scientists who have employed empirical field methods in studies of social stratification. In the early 1930's he was already gathering data for what is now a series of studies designed to investigate and analyze the social-class system of America. In addition, others have granted Warner's hypotheses and used his methods in studying the social stratification of various communities and in analyzing the relationships between social status and characteristics ranging from the incidence of psychosomatic disorders to high school grades. There can be no doubt that Warner and his followers have made an impression on sociological thought, theory, and research.

It is not necessary, however, to review or comment separately upon the various studies by Warner and his associates, since he has recently published a "manual of procedure for the measurement of social status"[2] which embraces the major hypotheses set forth in his earlier volumes. This volume, *Social Class in America*, supplies the methods used by Warner to study social class in several communities but especially in "Jonesville," a small Midwestern community. It is to this volume, then, that we will direct our attention in an effort to examine Warner's theories about social class and the methods he used in formulating these theories.

---

[1] W. Lloyd Warner, Marchia Meeker, and Kenneth Eells, *Social Class in America* (Chicago, Science Research Associates, Inc., 1949).
[2] *Ibid.* (Subtitle of book)

THE AIMS OF THE BOOK

Social Class in America has, according to its author, three distinct aims. (1) It was written to present "basic material about social class in America," [3] that is, the generalities and uniformities about American social classes, what social class is, and how it functions in our everyday lives. (2) It was written to provide its readers with a method which will enable them both to identify the social classes in *any* community and to find the class level of any individual within that community. (3) The third aim perhaps should be regarded as a byproduct of the two major ones. Warner strives "to provide a corrective instrument which will permit men and women better to evaluate their social situations and thereby better adapt themselves to social reality and fit their dreams and aspirations to what is possible." [4] This last aim should not be taken lightly, although ameliorative motives are not usually a part of sociological research.

We feel, however, that Warner's methodology warrants primary attention since it is basic to his entire theory. In the first place, it is the same methodology that he supplies for those of his readers who wish to engage in formal research or informal study of social class. If there are any serious inadequacies or obscurities in his methods, then he has not fully fulfilled one of the major aims of his treatise. In the second place, the "facts" about social class in America uncovered by Warner must be viewed in the light of *his* particular methods for obtaining these facts. And, in the third place, the extent to which he enables his readers to adjust to social reality depends upon the extent to which his methods allow him to gain an accurate picture of this "reality."

[3] *Ibid.*, p. vi.
[4] *Ibid.*, p. 5.

WARNER'S BASIC METHOD—EVALUATED PARTICIPATION

Warner's basic method of determining the number of social classes in a community and the placement of individuals within the classes is called Evaluated Participation (E.P.). This method consists of six separate techniques to be used for categorizing the information obtained from comprehensive personal interviews. Let us see how the method works.

Matched Agreements

Our first instructions are to establish ourselves in the community and "acquire a number of good informants with diversified social backgrounds." [5] Through interviews with these informants we then obtain a number of *Social Class Configurations*. That is, we should abstract from this general-interview data everything the informants had to say concerning the way the stratification system of the community "looks to them," particularly any remarks they may have made concerning the number of "classes" in the town and the people who belong to them. Warner apparently has discovered that informants will name a certain number of classes and will volunteer the names of individuals belonging to each class.

After this type of data has been abstracted, it becomes the task of the researcher to determine the extent of agreement between the respondents. If, for example, all informants referred only to *the* upper class and *the* lower class and the correspondence among their lists of class members was high, the researcher might have reason to believe that the community was characterized by a two-class system.

Apparently, however, it is usually not so simple a matter to compare the configuration of various informants and determine the extent of agreement on the number of classes in the community. Warner presented the detailed description of the social-class

[5] *Ibid.*, p. iii.

structure of "Jonesville," a Midwestern community of 6000 people. The descriptions came from interviews with six informants, a "substantial citizen," two "church members" (both professional men), a "city official," an "adolescent girl," and a "mill laborer." [6] The informants were not further identified.

The social-class configuration of the "substantial citizen" differed markedly from the configuration of the "adolescent girl," while both of these were different from the "social-class configuration of two church members" who themselves disagreed as to the number of social classes found in this community. In all of the interviews cited by Warner, individuals named three, four, five, and six as the number of social classes found in Jonesville.

The Matched Agreement technique also makes use of the list of individuals that informants may have mentioned during the course of the interview. Each name that appeared on more than one list can be paired, and the researcher can determine whether all informants have defined that individual's social status similarly. In Jonesville, for example, Warner abstracted lists of names from the interview data obtained from ten informants. These ten included three professional men, two merchants, and one politician, accountant, "farm expert," laborer, and school girl. The names on their combined lists totaled 340, but the number of names that appeared on more than one list was not definitely stated. It appeared, however, that as many as 125 different people may have been named.[7] In any case, the ten informants agreed on the class placement of the individuals rated by more than one informant more frequently than they disagreed.

After comparing the social-class configurations of the informants and "matching" the names on their respective lists, Warner concluded that there were five social classes in Jonesville. He has labeled these the "lower-lower," the "upper-lower," the "lower-middle," the "upper-middle," and the "upper" class. In other commmunities the upper class is subdivided into a lower-upper

---

[6] *Ibid.*, pp. 47-62.
[7] *Ibid.*, p. 64. Computed from data in Table 2.

and an upper-upper. It is this "six-class system" that typifies Warner's studies.

After the number of classes in a community has been discovered, the next step would be to determine the class placement of the community members. Warner presents several techniques for doing this, but cautions that they are based on the foregoing one, the technique of Matched Agreements.

Status Reputation

One of these techniques is called Status Reputation and, in the words of Warner, it "covers the whole range of American behavior." "Anything," says Warner, "which is evaluated as superior or inferior is utilized. Moral, aesthetic, intellectual, educational, religious, ethnic, and personal behavior, as well as many other categories of social activity, are constantly being used.... Such characteristics are definitely part of a person's Status Reputation. They help place the man." [8]

One man, for example, may have the reputation of being dirty, illiterate, and a "ne'er-do-well." Another may be called a "real joiner" and "an average citizen." Even without knowing the community in which these men live, we would hazard the guess that the "ne'er-do-well" is of lower status than the "average citizen." Perhaps after we were acquainted with Jonesville we would be able to place the "ne'er-do-well" in the lower-lower class and the second man either in the lower-middle or upper-middle class.

A person's status reputation can frequently be judged from the everyday remarks that others make about him. Unfortunately, however, Warner is not very explicit concerning how the reputational information about an individual is systematically categorized and, finally, translated into terms of membership in a definite social class.

[8] *Ibid.,* pp. 73-74.

Institutional Membership

Another technique for establishing the social-class placement of individuals is called Real Interconnectedness or sometimes Institutional Membership. Basically, it consists of rating informal social cliques and various formal associations, such as civic and social clubs, churches, and fraternal societies on a seven-point social-standing scale. The frequency of an individual's participation in these groups is also determined (little, some, much) as well as the seriousness of his participation (core or peripheral member).

To determine the class placement of a particular person the researcher then tabulates the number and kind of associations to which he belongs, the seriousness of his participation in each of these, and the frequency of his participation. In Jonesville, for example, a man who was a member of and participated freely in the Country Club, the Federated Church, and the Rotary Club would be tentatively classified as upper class. This rating would be reinforced if, in addition, his circle of close friends was rated "very high" because of the statuses of its members. Another Jonesville resident may belong to no formal association other than the Gospel Tabernacle church. From the church records it may be determined that he attends services quite irregularly and does not take part in other church activities. A personal interview with the individual should yield a list of his friends. Perhaps they have a reputation that would tend to put them lower than the middle of Jonesville's status hierarchy. The researcher may then tentatively classify the man in question as either upper-lower or lower-lower.

The Technique Called Comparison

"More often than not, the informant will place someone by saying his status is above or below that of another person whose social status has already been established." [9] This is the technique

9 *Ibid.*, p. 79.

called Comparison; admittedly it is highly dependent upon other techniques.

This technique would be particularly useful *if the researcher was satisfied that a certain number of classes typified the community he was studying* and that some residents had been correctly placed in their respective classes. If, for example, Mr. Carleton had been previously placed in Jonesville's upper-middle class and it was reported by several informants that "Withington is about like Carleton," or "Withington ranks as high as Carleton," it would probably be safe to classify Mr. Withington as upper-middle. Interviews may also disclose that Mr. Smythe is generally considered a "good bit" higher than either Carleton or Withington. He would probably be placed in Jonesville's upper class, for that is the only class higher than the upper-middle. Other cases may not be so simple. Upper-class informants, for example, may not be able to make meaningful comparisons between lower-lower and upper-lower class respondents.

Symbolic Placement

"Informants often refer to the social place of another individual by Symbolic Placement, which can be divided conveniently into three common types: (1) symbolism by structure, (2) symbolism by region, and (3) symbolism by social traits." [10]

Symbolism by structure refers to various symbolic references to the groups (family, kinship groups, social or fraternal groups, etc.) to which a person belongs. Expressions, such as "One of the Cabots," "The Bakersmith Tribe," or "The Garden Club Crowd," would be examples of symbolism by structure.

Regional symbolism refers to the symbolic and often picturesque titles that are attached to the various sections of the community under study. A list of these names could be drawn up for any city or town; in Jonesville, expressions such as "Hill Streeter," "Riverbrooker," and "Back of the Tannery" are heard.

Trait symbolism apparently refers to the descriptive titles that

[10] *Ibid.,* p. 72.

are used in reference to a person's social behavior. Such expressions may refer more directly to a person's social status than do regional symbolism or symbolism by structure, but the meanings of the expressions are often obscure unless one is acquainted with the community. In one community, Warner discovered that the term *Yellow Hammer* was used to indicate low status. The symbolism is derived from the fact that the yellow hammer (a woodpecker) is native to the southern woods where the "poor whites" sometimes live. Other trait symbols such as "high hats" and "the 400" are not so difficult to interpret. Warner comments, "At the beginning of a study, Symbolic Placements are particularly useful for placing people and establishing the extremes of high and low status in the community." [11] Perhaps this remark should be interpreted as a caution regarding the limited use of this technique; many researchers would probably be hard pressed to use Symbolic Placement for assigning individuals to a specific social class. At any rate, specific directions for class-typing individuals on the basis of this technique were not furnished.

Simple Assignment

The final technique, Simple Assignment, amounts to the statement, by an informant, that a person is or is not in a given social class (previously determined by Matched Agreements). The procedure is assuredly simple. It would be reliable as well, if the researcher could be certain that the community under study was characterized by a clearly defined class system and that all of the informants recognized and understood this system. Thus, if two informants said that "Green is in the middle class" we would want to be sure that both were referring to the same portion of the status hierarchy when they used the term *middle class*.

The researcher, moreover, must be careful not to overlook "simple assignments" that are made in colloquial terms. "The Society Crowd," or "the 400" may be generally understood to mean "the upper class" in a given community. Unless, however,

[11] *Ibid.*, p. 73.

there is good reason to believe that the status terms are equated with the names of social classes it is probably better to treat them simply as status reputational terms.

THE INDEX OF STATUS CHARACTERISTICS

Warner readily acknowledges that the method of Evaluated Participation, with its six techniques, could require a generous expenditure of both time and money. To combat this he has developed another method for measuring social status which he calls the Index of Status Characteristics. This is a more objective measurement and is simpler and less costly to employ; the data used can be acquired with a minimum of or no interviewing.

The Index consists of a weighted total of scores obtained on four socio-economic status scales: occupation, house-type, dwelling area, and source of income. The total score is then translated into terms of social class—a score of a given magnitude indicates an individual is "in" a certain social class.

Occupation

Warner developed a seven-point or seven-level scale for rating occupations. The occupational scale was designed to measure the differences in prestige attached to various jobs and the amount of skill required to perform them.[12] In order to rate factory jobs, however, Warner found it necessary to base the distinctions on the hourly wage paid for the job.[13] Professional men received either a rating of one or two, depending on the amount of training required for their particular profession.[14]

Administration of this scale, in many instances, is a quite simple matter. It usually involves merely asking an individual what he does for a living. If he is unwilling to disclose this information it can often be obtained from a neighbor or even from the city

[12] *Ibid.*, p. 133.
[13] *Ibid.*, p. 138.
[14] *Ibid.*, p. 135.

directory. Once a person's occupation is discovered it can be compared with those listed on the scale; the complete scale contains from eight to twenty different occupations as examples of each level. Thus, if the occupation in question is one of those listed on the scale, the person is merely assigned the score value equivalent to the level at which his occupation falls.

Some difficulty might arise, however, in rating those occupations not contained on the scale. Warner refers us to the occupational scales of two other students for help in evaluating such jobs. The researcher may still experience difficulty, however, since the scales to which we are referred have a different number of categories than Warner's. In the final analysis, the researcher must be prepared to assign an occupation not contained on Warner's scale to one of the seven levels by comparing it to a job contained on the scale or to one found on some other scale. When the occupation is finally assigned to a level, the person simply receives the score equivalent to that level.

House-Type

The kind of a house in which a person lives is usually thought to be related to his social status. One's house, in any case, can be thought of as part of his wealth which, in turn, correlates with social status. If we can measure, therefore, the differences between the houses in a community, we should also have a rough and indirect measure of the social standing of their occupants.

Warner includes a house-type scale in his Index of Social Characteristics. After considering the various criteria by which houses could be judged, and thus differentiated, Warner concluded that "size and condition were the most objective and easiest to judge." [15] His original effort resulted in an *a priori* classification of houses with five categories for size (very large, large, medium, small, and very small) and five categories for condition (very good, good, medium, bad, and very bad). Condition, it should be added, included not only the external appearance of the

---

[15] *Ibid.*, p. 143.

structure itself but also the "size and condition of garden and lawn, extent to which the place was landscaped, placement of the house on the lot, and nearness to adjacent building." [16] With this classification, twenty-five different ratings are possible, ranging from "very large houses in very good condition" to "very small houses in very bad condition." [17]

The final house-type scale. The final house-type scale contained the following types of housing (the numbers refer to Warner's score for each type): excellent (1), very good (2), good (3), average (4), fair (5), poor (6), and very poor (7).

In order to rate a house, then, the researcher simply decides in which of the seven categories it best fits, on the basis of its over-all appearance and size, and assigns the score-value equivalent to that category. Warner's final scale also contains a brief description of the seven categories which should make the rating task easier. Average houses, for example, are described as follows: [18] "One-and-a-half to two-story wood-frame and brick single-family dwellings. Conventional style, with lawns well cared for but not landscaped."

If a researcher had the entire scale before him and was fairly well acquainted with the community under study he would probably be able to classify many of the houses with little difficulty. He may, however, find it necessary to develop some standardized procedure for classifying the "difficult cases," trailers, resident hotels, houses that seem to fall between categories, and the like. Although such cases apparently were not discovered in Jonesville, Warner did have to make a decision concerning apartments. "The best way to rank apartments," he concluded, "seemed to be on the basis of the size of living unit per individual family and the building's exterior condition." [19]

16 *Ibid.*
17 *Ibid.*
18 *Ibid.*, p. 150.
19 *Ibid.*, p. 150.

Dwelling Area

One of the things we like to know about a person if we are trying to determine his social status, is "the section of town" in which he lives. It makes a difference whether he comes from the "Northside" or the "Eastside," whether he lives "up on the hill" or "down by the river." A person's geographical position in the community reflects his social position.

Warner has attempted to quantify this characteristic by deriving a scale to measure the differences between the various dwelling areas in Jonesville or any other community. Recognizing that it is probably a whole cluster of traits that taken together make some residential areas more desirable than others, he has established several criteria which were used in differentiating the dwelling areas of Jonesville. These can be summarized as follows:

1. General appearance of the area—"A superior area has an air of orderliness and cleanliness with wide streets and many trees. An inferior area is littered with paper, dirt, and debris, and has an air of barrenness caused by the lack of trees, grass or flowers." [20]

2. General appearance of the houses—The over-all appearance of the houses in a neighborhood was taken into account since the "typical" housing of an area affects its status reputation.

3. Class membership of residents—"Further evidence is offered by noting where the members of the various classes live. . . . It was found that members of the same class tended to live in the same part of town; certain sections had a high concentration of lower-class families." [21]

On the basis of these criteria, Warner was able to distinguish sixteen separate dwelling areas in Jonesville. Although each could be distinguished from adjacent areas on the basis of the above criteria, it was soon discovered that some areas were socially equivalent. A town may perhaps have two "very low" areas at

[20] *Ibid.*, p. 152.
[21] *Ibid.*

opposite edges of the town. It may be discovered, furthermore, that lower-class people live in both areas. Such areas may well be socially equivalent.

When the equivalent areas were grouped together, *seven* types of dwelling areas emerged. These were labeled and assigned a score value in the following manner: very high (1), high (2), above average (3), average (4), below average (5), low (6), and very low (7).

In order to classify areas on the basis of this scale, the researcher should first acquaint himself with the various neighborhoods in the community. He should roughly determine the total range of areas, that is, he should attempt to establish what the highest area and lowest area are like. Since the dwelling-area scale has seven categories, there is a middle category with three categories below and three above. A specific area, then, can be rated by determining first whether it is approximately average, below average, or above average for the community. If the area does not seem to fit the middle category the process can be repeated. Does it fall at the highest extreme, the middle, or the lowest extreme of the three remaining categories?

The researcher can be guided, in classifying the areas, by Warner's description of the seven area types. Areas that receive a rating of 6, for example, are described as follows: "These areas are run-down and semi-slums. The houses are set close together. The streets and yards are often filled with debris, and in some smaller towns, like Jonesville, some of the streets are not paved." [22]

The Source of Income Scale

The final characteristic measured on the Index of Status Characteristics is the source of a person's income. This measure takes into account the fact that a person's prestige is affected not only by *how much* money he has but also by *how* he "gets it." Since Warner discovered a relatively high correlation between these

[22] *Ibid.*, pp. 153-154.

factors, and since it is sometimes easier to determine merely the source of an individual's income, he used only the "principal source of known income" [23] in his Index of Status Characteristics. He categorized the sources of income on a now familiar seven-point scale. Ranging from the highest status source of income to the lowest, the seven classifications were:

1. Inherited Wealth—a "fortune" large enough to live on that was inherited from an earlier generation.

2. Earned Wealth—"This category implies considerable wealth, for the individual lives on interest from capital and has amassed sufficient money so that he does not need to work." [24]

3. Profits and Fees—the fees of professional men and the profits of businessmen; also includes the royalties of musicians and writers.

4. Salary—This category includes fixed income that is paid on a monthly or yearly basis and salesmen's commissions.

5. Wages—the income of workers that is determined by an hourly rate. It is usually paid daily or weekly.

6. Private Relief—donations of money by friends, relatives, or those agencies that do not reveal the names of those receiving funds.

7. Public Relief and Non-Respectable Income—Public relief includes money that is received from a government agency or from a charity organization which will reveal the names of those receiving funds. Non-respectable income includes money obtained from engaging in illegal activities.[25]

The researcher may experience a little difficulty with this scale, particularly in scoring an income that is derived from two or more sources. Usually in such cases Warner assigned the rating of the "principal" source of income, but if he discovered that the income was about evenly received from two (or more) sources he averaged the scores assigned to the sources.

[23] *Ibid.*, p. 138.
[24] *Ibid.*, p. 22.
[25] The reader may or may not agree that these two sources of income are of equivalent status value.

Final Scores from the Index of Status Characteristics

The purpose of the four scales, Occupation, Dwelling Area, House Type, and Source of Income, is to furnish an estimate of the social-class placement of individuals for whom time or other factors prevent the detailed interviewing necessary for social-class placement by the method of Evaluated Participation. Each scale, it will be recalled, consisted of seven levels or categories, making it possible to achieve a score of from 1 to 7 on each sub-index. The final Index of Status Characteristics consists of a weighted total of the scores on the four scales. The weights were obtained by determining which weighting system provided the greatest correlation with social-class placement by the Evaluated Participation method. The results were: occupation, 4; source of income, 3; house type, 3; and dwelling area, 2.

An example of the computation of an individual's total score on the Index of Status Characteristics is as follows: Mr. Jones is a carpenter and derives all of his income from this source (wages). He lives in what might be called a "small house in medium condition" which is situated in an "average" section of the city. His score would be computed thus:

Status Characteristic	Score	Weight	Total
Occupation	5	4	20
Source of Income	5	3	15
House Type	5	3	15
Dwelling Area	4	2	8
		Total score	58

Knowing that Mr. Jones has a score of 58 on the Index of Status Characteristics is meaningful only if we also know the score of the residents of his community (or the United States) or have some other way of giving score a broader reference. Warner has attempted to do this by predicting the class placement for individuals with various scores on the Index of Status Characteristics. The score ranges for each social class were computed; they are based on the scores attained by those who were placed in a given class by the Evaluated Participation method. Table 2 indicates this score-class relationship.

We would predict, then, that the carpenter whose total score we computed to be 58 would be in the upper-lower class. In a similar manner, the class position for all members of a community could be predicted. A researcher may prefer, however, simply to rank the community members on the basis of their Index of Status Characteristics scores without converting them into terms of social class.

TABLE 2. Relationship Between ISC Scores and Social Class * (after Warner)

Score Range	Predicted Social Class
12—22	Upper Class
23—37	Upper-Middle Class
38—51	Lower-Middle Class
52—66	Upper-Lower Class
67—84	Lower-Lower Class

* Adapted from data in Table 19, "Predicted Social-Class Placement for Various Weighted Totals of Four Status Characteristics, for Old Americans" in W. Lloyd Warner, Marchia Meeker, and Kenneth Eells, *Social Class in America* (Chicago, Science Research Associates, Inc., 1949), p. 183.

EVALUATION

Warner's approach to social stratification has been evaluated on various bases. For our purposes, it is thought best to direct our appraisal of *Social Class in America* so that it will help the student answer two questions: (1) To what extent can the methods proposed by Warner be used in "any kind of a community" to determine both the social-stratification system of the community and the status of individuals?, and (2) To what extent is the six (or five) class scheme resulting from these methods an accurate and realistic portrayal of the American social-stratification scene?

Evaluated Participation

Of his two methods, Warner considers Evaluated Participation the more basic. It is largely through use of one aspect of this method, the technique called Matched Agreements, that the specific number of social classes in a community are determined. If a true class system exists in a community, all or most of the members of the community would have to view it in the same way.

As an example in the technique of Matched Agreements, Warner presented various "social-class configurations" or pictures of the class structure of Jonesville. These class configurations, as well as the individuals named by informants as belonging to each class, should then be "compared for agreement and disagreement." *At no point, however, are we told what constitutes agreement or disagreement.* Earlier in this chapter it was noted that there appeared to be no consensus among the informants who presented their version of the social-class structure of Jonesville. Of the six informants, one spoke of a three-class system, two of four classes, two of five, and one of six. How, then, were these descriptions compared for "agreement and disagreement" and how was the conclusion drawn that Jonesville is characterized by five clearly defined social classes? At what point, we might ask, are the disagreements so frequent that we should conclude that the community is not characterized by a *specific* number of social classes that are recognized by all or most of the community members?

The names of people who are assigned to particular classes by informants are also compared for the extent of agreement among them. This part of the technique of Matched Agreements appears vague at several points, although it is buttressed by much statistical evidence. To begin with, we are not told *how* the ten informants who supplied this information about Jonesville residents were selected.[26] Inasmuch as three were professional men, two were merchants, one a politician, and another was a "farm expert,"

---

[26] The use of a few selected informants to study a small community is part of what one reviewer of Warner's works calls his "tribal analogy." In other words, the same methods which are used to study a small, isolated tribe, which in many cases, constitutes the population universe, are employed in the study of a modern community. Walter Goldschmidt, "Social Class in America...A Critical Review," *American Anthropologist*, 52 (October-December, 1950), pp. 483-498.

whereas still another was "the daughter of a substantial citizen of Jonesville," it is doubtful that the informants are representative of a "typical" community.

The number of *different* names on the combined lists of the informants was not indicated, but by analyzing the table presented by Warner it seems that the greatest number of different individuals mathematically possible is 125.[27] How these residents were selected, we were not told. Thus ten informants, more socially similar than dissimilar, were found to "agree" on the class placement of probably no more than 125 Jonesville (population 6000) residents. Would they agree on the remainder? How many informants should we use in a city the size of, say, St. Louis? It would seem that the odds would be against our finding any duplication of names on the lists of people belonging to various social classes that would be presented by ten randomly selected St. Louis residents.

The problems we have indicated constitute some of the reasons why the technique of Matched Agreements seems to fall far short of being a precise method of determining the number of social classes in "any kind of a community."

Several of the other techniques that comprise the method of Evaluated Participation are quite dependent on the technique of Matched Agreements. Simple Assignment, for example, amounts to the informant stating that a certain person is a member of a specific class that was previously determined. The technique of Comparison consists of the statement by an informant that the social status of one person is the same, is higher, or is lower than that of another who had previously been placed in one of the classes.

The techniques of Status Reputation, Symbolic Placement, and Institutional Membership scarcely require further elaboration. In each case, the characteristic under investigation is undoubtedly important as far as the social status of community members is concerned. In each case, too, precise instructions for translating

[27] Warner, *op. cit.*, p. 64.

the behavior patterns in question into terms of membership in one of Jonesville's (or some other community's) five social classes were notably lacking.[28]

All in all, then, the chief difficulty with the method of Evaluated Participation is that it does not seem to live up to its originator's definition as a method of "determining the social stratification of a community or determining the status of an individual or family." [29] The six techniques that comprise this method can be considered as six convenient categories for classifying information obtained in rather lengthy interviews with members of a community. After a researcher has performed this operation, particularly in a small town, he is undoubtedly in a better position to understand how social status operates in the lives of the community members. Without more precise directions for categorizing and analyzing the interview data, it would seem difficult to expect two or more researchers to study a community, particularly a large city, by the method of Evaluated Participation and arrive at the same conclusions regarding the stratification system in the community and the placement of each individual in the hierarchy.

The Index of Status Characteristics

The Index of Status Characteristics, we will recall, measures the socio-economic level of the community by scoring individuals on four scales: occupation, house type, dwelling area, and source of income. The scores on the four sub-indices of the Index were manipulated statistically until weights were discovered

---

[28] The lack of precise instructions for using the several techniques of Evaluated Participation was also mentioned in various reviews of *Social Class in America*. See G. E. Swanson, *American Sociological Review*, 14 (December, 1949), p. 823; Harold W. Pfautz and Otis Dudley, "A Critical Evaluation of Warner's Work in Community Stratification," *American Sociological Review*, 15 (April, 1950), pp. 205-215; Ely Chinoy, "Research in Class Structure," *Canadian Journal of Economic and Political Science*, 16 (May, 1950), pp. 258-259; and Oswald Hall, review of W. Lloyd Warner, Marchia Meeker, and Kenneth Eells, *Social Class in America*, *American Journal of Sociology*, 16 (January, 1951), p. 368.

[29] Warner, *op. cit.*, pp. 36-37.

whereby an Index of Status Characteristic score would place a person in the same class as would an Evaluated Participation interview. In other words, the validity of the method of Evaluated Participation for determining the number of social classes in a community has been assumed. It should be noted that the relationship between the two methods of determining social status has certain spurious aspects. This is particularly clear in the case of the dwelling-area and house-type scales. Dwelling areas and house types are rated partly by discovering (through use of Evaluated Participation) the class position of persons living therein; thus, persons placed in a high class by Evaluated Participation would tend to receive a high score for their house and dwelling area. This interconnectedness of the two methods partially explains the similarity of their results.[30] In other words, there seems to be no *objective* reason why Index of Status Characteristics scores of certain magnitudes are indicative of placement in a given social class. We are not told of any cluster or grouping of the various score values on the Index of Status Characteristics which would lead one to conclude that there were "natural breaks" in the series or that certain score values, for some reason, "belong together."

Besides this basic difficulty with the Index of Status Characteristics, that is, that it depends for its validity upon the method of Evaluated Participation, there are some methodological difficulties with its constituent scales. The occupational scale, it seems, attempts to measure various dimensions of occupations. At one point it seems that it is the *prestige* of occupations that is involved; high school superintendents, for example, are rated higher than the proprietors of businesses valued at $75,000. In making changes on his occupational scale, furthermore, Warner mentions that "the primary criteria were *level of skill* that a job required and *prestige value* attached to a job." [31] Admittedly, then, the

[30] The interconnectedness of the two supposedly independent methods has also been noted by others. See especially: Hall, *op. cit.*, pp. 367-368; Pfautz and Duncan, *op. cit.*, p. 207.

[31] Warner, *op. cit.*, p. 133. Italics not in original.

same scale attempts to measure two separate dimensions. In addition, it seems that sometimes a third dimension is measured, inasmuch as we learn that when difficulty arose in rating factory jobs in Jonesville, "the ratings were finally based on the *hourly wage* paid for the job." [32] A fourth dimension is introduced by Warner's statement, "Whether a professional man received a rating of 1 or 2 on occupation depended primarily on the amount of *training* he needed for his particular profession." [33]

Thus, we cannot be at all certain why certain occupations are rated higher than others. Is a minister, for example, rated higher than a postal clerk because it takes more skill to become a minister, because there is more skill in being a minister, because there is more prestige attached to being a minister, or because a minister draws a larger salary? Admittedly it is not an easy matter to isolate these various dimensions of occupations, but certainly the task of rating occupations *not* contained on Warner's scale would be simplified if we knew on what basis they should be judged.

Two of the scales, the house-type and dwelling-area scales, seem to require a large amount of "artistic" interpretation on the part of the scale administrator. When using the house-type scale, for example, the researcher is not told what to do if to the best of his ability he cannot place a given house into one of the seven categories. It is conceivable that some houses would logically seem to fall between two of the house types or would otherwise seem not to fit any of the seven categories.

In addition, the descriptions of the various categories do not always lend themselves for use as criteria for judging the houses. What, for example, does the phrase "larger than utility demands for the average family" [34] mean? According to this criterion, would a house with five bedrooms, all of which are occupied by a four-child family, be ranked higher or lower than a four-bedroom home owned by a two-child family, with one bedroom

[32] *Ibid.*, p. 138. Italics not in original.
[33] *Ibid.*, p. 135. Italics not in original.
[34] *Ibid.*, p. 150.

unoccupied, if all other factors were equal? The point is, of course, that considerable interpretation is necessary on the part of the researcher. There can be reasonable doubt that two or more researchers would arrive at the same ranking of, let us say, a hundred houses.

A final point should be recalled. Any errors that may have been present in the Evaluated Participation method of ranking individuals would be reflected in the house-type scale, since houses were classified on the basis of the social-class placement of individuals occupying them most frequently. Since so few cases (from one to twenty-one) were involved in the house-type social-class breakdown, an error in the social-class placement of only a few individuals would affect the rating of the house types. The errors, of course, would be perpetuated and intensified in the social-class placement of other citizens when the Index of Status Characteristics was used alone.

There are other refinements that seem to be warranted in the interest of making the four scales that comprise the Index of Status Characteristics more objective. In the present state, however, the Index of Status Characteristics seems to furnish a relatively objective means of ranking the members of a community on the basis of their socio-economic status. The Index is assuredly a simplified scale and can be used with a minimum of interviewing unless, of course, the researcher is interested in translating the ISC scores into terms of social class placement. For many purposes, the raw ISC scores would seem to be an adequate manner of expressing relative socio-economic differences.

Throughout the foregoing section various criticisms have been levied against Warner's methods and the results of these methods. Some of these comments have been quite general, others have been concerned with procedural refinements of a specific and technical nature. It is time to summarize our appraisal.

SUMMARY

1. The Method of Evaluated Participation

Directions furnished the reader seem to lack the detail and precision necessary for them to qualify as "a manual of procedure for the measurement of social status." This is illustrated by the following: (*a*) directions for chosing judges or "informants" are not given; (*b*) instructions for analyzing the interview data seem to lack clarity; (*c*) instructions for comparing and equating the different status levels that were recognized by various judges are not furnished; and (*d*) the method of choosing a sample of persons to be rated is not specified. In view of the foregoing, the reliability and validity of Evaluated Participation has been seriously questioned.[35] Attention is also drawn to the fact that it is doubtful that this method can be used in "any type of community," particularly large cities.

2. The Index of Status Characteristics

This method, although resulting in a quantitative rating and fortified by many statistics, seems to lack objectivity. Dwelling areas are rated by the researcher on not-too-clearly stated subjective bases, residences are judged on similar terms and partly by the previously determined status of their occupants, and, in the last analysis, some occupations are simply assigned a score value on the basis of the opinion of the status-analyst alone. The valid-

[35] Chinoy suggests that the five (or six) classes do not constitute the *one* system that is recognized by all or most of the community members. "It would seem," he states, "that the status order in the community as it is described by Warner is actually a composite version of the prestige hierarchy which is built from the varied perspectives of local residents. It is basically a construction of the researcher rather than the consensus of the community." (Chinoy, *op. cit.*, p. 259.) In addition, two researchers reported they were unsuccessful in their attempts to study the social-status system of a small city according to Warner's scheme. See Gregory P. Stone and William H. Form, "Instabilities in Status: The Problems of Hierarchy in the Community Study of Status Arrangements," *American Sociological Review*, 18 (April, 1953), pp. 154-156.

ity of the Index of Status Characteristics is inferred from the
relationship of its results to those of the method of Evaluated
Participation which, it is assumed only, does measure the social-
class placement of individuals. In addition, the relationship between the two methods has some spurious aspects; their interconnectedness partially explains the similarity of results obtained
through their use.

3. The Six Social Classes—Products of the Method

There seems to be insufficient evidence that the social classes
described by Warner have a real existence in Jonesville. Informants do not agree on their presence, and the methods through
which they were "discovered" lack the definiteness necessary to
allow us to reach this conclusion. There is reason to doubt, as
others have doubted, that such a neat system of stratification (five
social classes in some small towns, six in others and in large cities)
accurately portrays the status situation in most localities.

SELECTED READINGS

DAVIES, A. F., "Prestige of Occupations," *British Journal of Sociology,*
3 (June, 1952), pp. 134-147.

HATT, Paul K., "Occupation and Social Stratification," *American Journal of Sociology,* 55 (May, 1950), pp. 533-544.

MACK, Raymond W., "Housing as an Index of Social Class," *Social
Forces,* 29 (May, 1951), pp. 391-400.

SMITH, Mapheus, "An Empirical Scale of Prestige Status of Occupations," *American Sociological Review,* 8 (April, 1943), pp. 185-192.

TWITCHELL, Alan, "An Appraisal Method for Measuring the Quality
of Housing," *American Sociological Review,* 13 (June, 1948), pp.
278-287.

7

Social Stratification in Columbus, Ohio[1]

THE SOCIAL-STRATIFICATION studies conducted within the past several decades have, by and large, utilized the traditional concept of social class. Although the concept has been employed somewhat differently, it seems that in most cases a social class was considered to be a group of individuals who were clearly set apart from the rest of their community by virtue of their social status.[2] Various stratification studies have discovered different numbers of these "clearly delineated" status groups. Apparently the American social-status scene is typified by two, three, four, five, or six social classes, depending on whose "study" one reads!

The present study arose because of a doubt, a question, and a theory. We doubted, first of all, whether there was so little repetitiveness about the social-stratification system of the United States as this diversity of research findings implies. We questioned, then, if the traditional methods of viewing the stratification system in terms of "true" social classes were fruitful and accurate ones for our present society. If not, how better might social stratification be studied?

[1] Adapted from William F. Kenkel, *An Experimental Analysis of Social Stratification in Columbus, Ohio* (unpublished Ph.D. dissertation, Department of Sociology, The Ohio State University, 1952).

[2] For an extensive treatment of the concept of social class see pp. 3-30. See also Milton Gordon, "Social Class in American Sociology," *American Journal of Sociology*, 55 (November, 1949), p. 262; Llewellyn Gross, "The Use of Class Concepts in Sociological Research," *American Journal of Sociology*, 54 (March, 1949), p. 409; Charles Page, *Class and American Sociology* (New York, Dial Press, 1940).

The hypothesis that grew out of these doubts and questions was phrased in a way that would lend itself to testing by empirical research in one particular city. It read: *The social-stratification system manifested in Columbus, Ohio, is represented by a continuous status series.*[3] According to this hypothesis, social status is a non-clustering, gradient variable. It would follow from the hypothesis that when people are ranked according to the usual criteria of social status, there would be no points in the resulting series where one could logically and *empirically* state that here one class ends and another begins.

Thus the Columbus project, rather than representing a broad investigation of social stratification in this city, was designed to test a specific hypothesis. It did not purport, furthermore, to establish new field procedures for the measurement of differential social status. The design of the project and the methods used to test the hypothesis are felt to be important, however, largely because they *were* applicable in a large city.

Columbus, Ohio

Columbus, Ohio, is the twenty-eighth largest city in the United States. With a population of over 375,000 in the central city alone, it ranks third in the state. Since it is the state capital and the home of a large university, Columbus can be considered atypical. But its diversified industries, its host of services, and the make-up of its population would also suggest that it probably is not radically different from many other United States cities.

[3] The junior author acknowledges, with pleasure, that it was Professor Cuber who first introduced him to the "continuum theory of stratification" from which the hypotheses tested in this study grew. The senior author, in addition, expended considerable effort in sharpening and clarifying the concept, formulating the problem in a testable form, and helping in the development of field procedures for testing the hypotheses in Columbus. *Social Stratification in Columbus* in some respects, therefore, represents a co-operative venture despite the sole appearance of the junior author's name. The final decision to use certain procedures, to draw specific conclusions, and the like, rested with the junior author.

METHODOLOGY

In order to test our hypothesis, the first task was to determine how the data would be obtained. It should be apparent that methods such as participant observation and "judges' rating" could scarcely be used in a universe of over 400,000 people.[4] In this situation, the data could be gathered either through use of mailed questionnaires, or by personal interviews. Although personal interviews are costly and time-consuming, the advantages in uniformity and completeness of the data, clarity of meanings, and the more tangible opportunities for keeping refusals at a minimum seemed to justify this method.

Sampling Procedure

There are, of course, many ways in which a sample can be drawn. Random sampling, area sampling, and stratified or quota-control sampling immediately came to mind as feasible and recognized means of obtaining the necessary number of cases. For this particular study, it was thought best to employ the random-sampling technique for these reasons: (1) it is difficult to estimate all of the variables that would need to be controlled for a stratified type of sampling; (2) data on population density and other characteristics of city blocks or census tracts were not recent for this population; and (3) most important, random sampling is usually considered the most accurate type and its use is recommended whenever feasible from the standpoint of time, expense, and other considerations.

Having decided upon this sampling procedure, it was then necessary to secure a listing of the population universe. As in practically every large American city, there is available in Colum-

---

[4] The city of Columbus has a population of about 375,000. The universe for this study, however, was "Greater Columbus," an area including the City of Columbus and several contiguous suburbs.

bus a city directory listing the name, occupation, and marital status of presumably every resident.[5]

A problem closely related to the type of sampling to be employed is the determination of the number of cases to be contained within the sample. Especially when, as in this study, the data were to be obtained through personal interviews, the smallest number of cases which would be representative to the degree required would be the best sample size.

Standard statistical measures were used to estimate the size of random sample needed. It was discovered that a sample of 300 would be sufficiently large to yield a fairly accurate picture of the residents of Greater Columbus, at least with regard to those characteristics in which we were interested.[6]

Two samples of 300 cases were randomly selected from the city directory. One was considered the study sample; the other was used for statistical comparison and as a source of replacements. Not all 300 of the original sample were interviewed. Completed interviews, however, were obtained from over two thirds of the original sample. Not-at-home's, moves, and refusals accounted for the remainder. Whenever a replacement was needed it was secured from the second random sample. Replacements were matched with the original respondent with respect to occupation, estimated value of dwelling, and dwelling area, or at least dwelling-area desirability rating.

[5] In the interest of accuracy, it must be pointed out that for several reasons a sample drawn from this source would not be a strictly random sample of Greater Columbus residents. In the first place, the directory was somewhat over a year old. People have moved from Columbus, into Columbus, and within Columbus during this time. In addition, when the census was made, dwellings may have been missed, individuals may have refused to tell their names, and other factors may have intervened to make the enumeration incomplete. Similar and perhaps additional difficulties would be met regardless of the sampling procedure employed.

[6] Margaret Hagood, *Statistics for Sociologists* (New York, Henry Holt and Co., 1941), pp. 417-418. The formulas used were taken from this source.

Interviewing

Previous to the interviewing, the name, address, and occupation of each respondent were placed on a 3 x 5 card. These cards were then sorted by sections of the city, thereby allowing consecutive interviewing of respondents in each area.

Since it was discovered during the pretest that the respondents appeared to be more at ease and willing to co-operate when convinced of their anonymity, the fact that their names were known to the interviewer was not disclosed. The interview introduction attempted to get across the following points: (1) it was an important, worth-while and interesting venture; (2) the process would be easy and of short duration; (3) it would be non-personal and anonymous.

It should be noted, at this point, that although the interviewer's introduction varied, the factual questions were all asked in the same way. All status data reported in this summary were systematically recorded on a pretested interview schedule.

Despite introductory assurances to the contrary, some of the questions could be construed as being personal. Since most had to do with an individual's social position, occupation, friendship pattern, and to a certain extent, financial position, a degree of rapport had to be reached and held. Often, in the interest of gaining or re-establishing rapport, irrelevant matters were discussed at some length. To some, it must be admitted, the interviewer played the role of willing listener. Many quite personal happenings were mentioned to the interviewer, who in turn supplied more than a few rationalizations. A list of the items not bearing on the subject at hand that were told the interviewer would be quite impressive, both in nature and length. A mother told of her son in prison; a wife told of her husband in a mental hospital; a woman, obviously pregnant, admitted that she had been divorced before the child was conceived, but added, "Now don't put that down." Another respondent talked of his own stay in an "institution," and complaints of unfaithful husbands and wives were registered. Regardless of the behavior or situation mentioned, the interviewer attempted to rationalize the behavior of the respondent and to give the impression that he both understood and accepted.

All this, of course, lengthened the interview, but the time was not considered ill-spent. Certainly we can assume a degree of rapport was present. And, having attained this rapport, the interviewer feels reasonably sure that he was receiving a minimum of "ideal" responses to his questions. If the respondents were willing to volunteer such intimate and personal items as cited above, it is reasonable to assume that they would also be willing to tell their real rent, their actual occupation, the highest grade in school completed, and the like.

It should be noted that the entire job of interviewing was done by one person. This should remove at least one difficulty sometimes thought to be associated with interview-type studies; the questions were all asked the same way and the necessary subjective ratings were made by the same person. Each interview usually lasted one half hour or more, making it possible to obtain up to five interviews a day. The entire field work covered a span of about four months.

MEASUREMENT OF SOCIAL STATUS

There are, of course, many personal and social characteristics that reflect an individual's social position in a community. This study restricted itself to the measurement of some of the more objectively verifiable, and perhaps more important indices of social status. Data were obtained on the following characteristics: (1) prestige of occupation, (2) rental value of dwelling, and (3) desirability of dwelling area. The manner in which data on these characteristics were obtained will be presented in the later sections where each status characteristic is analyzed.

The method by which the basic hypothesis was tested can be divided into two operations: (1) respondents were ranked according to their scores on each status-characteristic scale; and (2) the resulting series were inspected for the presence or absence of modes, clusters, or any other objective evidence of the existence of clearly demarcated groups of more or less similar-status individuals. If, for example, the status scores were grouped about four points, the hypothesis that social status is a continuous, non-modal variable would scarcely be substantiated. But first let us investigate the various status series.

OCCUPATIONAL PRESTIGE

A person's position in the system of producing and distributing goods and services, the way in which he earns his living, or, more simply, his "occupation," is generally thought to be a reasonably accurate manifestation of his generalized social status.

For various reasons the many different occupations in our society have varying amounts of prestige attached to them.[7] Some jobs or occupations are considered by the members of our society to be better than others, irrespective of objective or intrinsic differences, and invidious distinctions are made between and among the job incumbents. There are, of course, many factors that contribute to differential occupational prestige. The actual duties performed, the prerequisites for performing them, the rewards, both financial and psychic, that are received, and the working conditions all combine to account for the fact of differential occupational prestige.

Selection of a Suitable Occupational-Prestige Scale

From the various available measures of occupational prestige which attempt to measure one or more of its dimensions, it was necessary to select one scale best suited to the present study.

The North-Hatt Occupational Prestige Scale was thought to

[7] Various dimensions and types of classifications of occupations have been utilized by different researchers in an effort to measure the differences between occupations. For a summary analysis of the different attempts see Paul K. Hatt, "Occupation and Social Stratification," *American Journal of Sociology*, 55 (May, 1950), pp. 533-544.

fill this bill. This scale, based on a nation-wide cross section of 2290 Americans, contains the prestige scores of ninety different occupations.[8] Thus the scores of these occupations, ranging from 32 to 96, represent "the people's" opinion of the relative prestige of various occupations.

Of course, not all of the occupations of the Columbus respondents were contained on the North-Hatt scale. A list of all occupations not mentioned on the scale was submitted to five sociologist-judges who were asked to compare and equate them with occupational titles on the scale and assign to each the corresponding numerical score. In this way, a numerical definition of prestige was made available for the occupation of each of the 300 respondents.

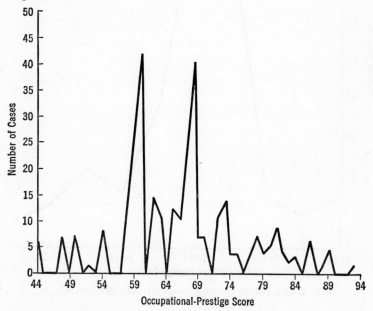

FIG. 5. Occupational-prestige scores by one-point intervals.

[8] The scale used in this study was Cecil C. North and Paul K. Hatt, *Occupations Ranked According to Prestige* (unpublished manuscript). A partial reproduction of this scale appears in Logan Wilson and William L. Kolb, *Sociological Analysis* (New York, Harcourt, Brace and Co., 1949), p. 464.

The Occupational-Prestige Series

Members of the sample were then ranked according to their occupational-prestige scores and the series was inspected for the presence or absence of clusters, modes, or cleavages. As is evident

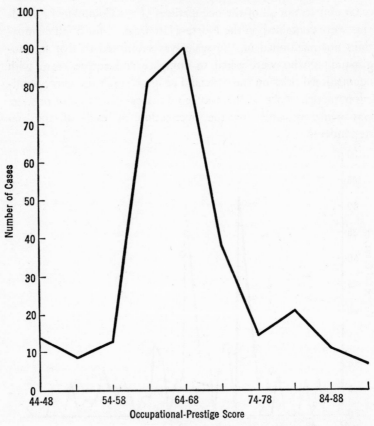

FIG. 6. Occupational-prestige scores by five-point intervals.

from the ungrouped data, Figure 5, the prestige scores exhibit a relatively non-clustering pattern. Extreme differences in occupational prestige are quite evident, but the hierarchal arrangement of individuals according to the prestige of their occupation shows no one or several places where one could legitimately say that here a definitive part of the population ends and here another begins; here "Class *A*" ends and "Class *B*" begins.

The data were combined in different ways, grouping the scores into thirty-two, twenty-five, and finally, as shown in Figure 6, ten categories. The fewer categories that were employed the smoother the curve became. The complete analysis led to the conclusion that there was no "natural" or inherent way to divide the occupational-prestige continuum. Differential occupational prestige is a striking fact. We can separate those of high prestige from those of low prestige; we can subdivide a group into high-prestige individuals, middle-prestige individuals, and low-prestige individuals. In other words, we can make our arbitrary divisions of the continuum at different points and at a different *number* of points to suit our specific purposes. We can thereby *create* statistical categories or statistical classes. This is not the same as *discovering* that a certain fixed number of "classes" inhere in the data.

RENTAL VALUE OF DWELLING

Where an individual lives—his physical place in the community —is thought to contribute to his social status. We judge, and are judged, by where we live. This characteristic has been measured in this study by two separate, but related methods: (1) according to the financial value of the individual's dwelling, and (2) according to the general condition of his neighborhood of residence. First, we will investigate the nature of the series that resulted when members of the sample were ranked according to the rental values of their dwellings.

For renters, the rental value of the dwelling is defined as the monthly rent paid. For those who are buying their homes, one tenth of the estimated sale price [9] was considered equivalent to

[9] Home-owners appeared to have a fairly accurate idea of the selling prices of their homes. Some had received unsolicited professional appraisals, others equated their homes with ones in the neighborhood that were recently sold, still others claimed simply to have "kept abreast" of the real estate market.

one year's rent.[10] One twelfth of this figure, of course, was used as the monthly rental value of the dwelling.

The Rental-Value Series

When the 300 respondents were ranked according to the rental value of their dwellings, the resulting series was found to encompass a range of $358 with sixty-five separate rental values. There was no tendency for the values to cluster about a few points on the scale.

In general, the rental values were distributed in a gradient manner. As is evident from Table 3, the gradualness in the rise and decline of the frequencies could quite easily have been missed by overgrouping. From Column III of this table it is clear that there is a relatively continuous progression and regression of rents manifested that cuts across any larger-grouping lines. Thus, if each of the largest groupings (A, B, C, D) were labeled a "class," we would see by inspection of Columns II and III that these "classes" could not be demarcated or distinguished from one another. The progression-regression is not strictly within these, or any other hypothesized divisions, but occurs over the entire series. To be sure, for specific purposes there may be one rental grouping better suited than the rest, but any and all must be recognized as being arbitrary divisions of the series, rather than inherent clusters.

In summary, that part of the social-status system that is reflected in the hierarchal arrangement of individuals according to the rental values of their dwellings does not allow us to impute to the system a given number of social classes in the sense of distinct population units, distinguished and differentiated by their social status.

---

[10] The relationship between the sale value of a house and its rental value was discussed at some length with an individual who teaches a university course in Real Estate Appraisal and also operates his own agency. The relationship used was that suggested by this instructor as being most appropriate for use in Columbus at the time.

TABLE 3. Distribution of the Rental Values of 252 Columbus Dwellings *

Category	Rental Value	No. of Dwellings	Category	Rental Value	No. of Dwellings	Category	Rental Value	No. of Dwellings
A	$90-119	49	A_1	$105-119	15	A-1	$110-119	8
			A_2	90-104	34	A-2	100-109	23
						A-3	90- 99	18
B	60- 89	97	B_1	75- 89	51	B-1	80- 89	30
			B_2	69- 74	46	B-2	70- 79	36
						B-3	60- 69	31
C	30- 59	93	C_1	45- 59	49	C-1	50- 59	38
			C_2	30- 44	44	C-2	40- 49	28
						C-3	30- 39	27
D	0- 29	13	D_1	15- 29	13	D-1	20- 29	12
			D_2	0- 14	0	D-2	10- 19	1
						D-3	0- 9	0

* Forty-eight cases with a rental value over $119 have been excluded due to the fewness of cases in each category.

DWELLING-AREA PRESTIGE

Just as individuals within a community can be ranked on the basis of the value of the dwellings in which they live, so also can they be ranked according to the desirability of the neighborhood or area in which this dwelling is located. There is, moreover, a whole cluster of traits that contribute to the differential prestige value of the various dwelling areas. Dwelling areas and the individual dwellings therein are, of course, intricately bound together. Certain areas are considered better partly because of the kind and type of houses that are there; houses are considered more valuable partly because they are located in certain areas. When rating dwelling areas, therefore, we must take into account the size, monetary value, and condition of the individual dwellings. Moreover, the general condition, appearance and aesthetic appeal of the areas, manifested by such things as cleanliness of the yards and streets, presence of trees, shrubs and lawns, and over-all order and quietness, all contribute to the amount of prestige attached to different neighborhoods.

Measurement of Dwelling-Area Prestige

Before attempting to rate the various sections of Columbus, considerable time was spent exploring and investigating the many different sections of the city. Finally, when a fairly clear conception of the total situation was formed, ratings of the different areas were attempted. The rating a given area receives should reflect its relative position to all the other areas of the city studied. In other words, although a certain section may appear, for many reasons, to be a "slum" or to be "very low," it cannot receive the lowest rating if more deteriorated areas are found. This illustrates the need for a clear conception of the total picture. The symbolic titles attached to the various ratings need not conform to a definition or stereotype of the kind of area in question; they are merely convenient labels for the condition of a given area, relative to the remaining areas.

It was at first thought that Warner's neighborhood-rating system could be employed in Columbus with sufficient accuracy.[11, 12] His seven types were distinguishable in Columbus and the titles he attached to the seven rates proved meaningful and helpful with respect to rating a specific section of the city. The terms *slum*, *average*, and *very high*, for example, make a rough classification readily possible. However, it was soon discovered that there was as much difference *within* any one of the seven categories as there was *between* some areas in different categories. Briefly, there appeared to be more than only seven different kinds of dwelling areas in Columbus. In small towns, perhaps, seven area-types may be sufficient, but in Columbus, and probably in other large cities, at least twice this number seems advisable. Any other number of

[11] For a brief description of Warner's dwelling-area rating system, see Chapter 6, pp. 119-120.

[12] Mack's housing scale was investigated for possibility of its use in Columbus. Since it combines the factors of "housing" per se and neighborhood and especially since it contains but three possible ranks (I, II, or III), its use was not considered feasible. See Raymond W. Mack, "Housing as an Index of Social Class," *Social Forces*, 29 (May, 1951), pp. 391-400.

categories could have been used. Fourteen was selected because
it was felt that this number combined a certain degree of precision with an ease of classification.

With these limitations in mind, we will turn to a description of
the various area-types differentiated in Columbus. The purpose
of the descriptions is to point out the nature and extent of the
differences between dwelling areas. Much of this difference, it is
thought, cannot be expressed in wholly quantitative terms.

Areas 1 and 2

At the southern edge of Columbus stands a small group of
dwellings that are referred to individually as shacks and collectively as "shanty-town." The streets are unnamed, unpaved, and
almost impassable. The shacks themselves have been constructed,
in most cases, by their occupants. The roofs and sides were at one
time completely covered with tar paper, but the wind and other
elements have taken their toll and the undisguised building material now gives mute and unsolicited advertisement to the citrus
growers of America. Along the road that leads a block or two to
the railroad track, men are seen carrying buckets, large cans, or
gunny sacks. Another train has passed and perhaps another
thoughtful tender has scattered a few lumps of coal along the
track. Each little shack has its lesser shack behind it. Kerosene is
the sole light-providing substance for the little community. This
is a "slum." For our purposes, areas such as this were labeled low
slums or simply, "slum minus."

In the vicinity of West Goodale Street there is an area even
now slated for razing. A committee has been appointed and a
program for "urban redevelopment" (slum clearance) is in the
process of formation.

The dwellings in this area are made of both wood and brick,
but in either case are in an extreme state of disrepair. Roofs are
buckled, steps are sagging, and often enough entire buildings list.
The streets, which seem to be alleys dignified with names, offer
no contrast to the buildings. Tin cans, trash, a dead dog or cat,

and other debris somehow make it unimportant to distinguish the paved from the unpaved streets. But yet this area is somehow different, some degree better, than shanty-town. Its dwellings, unsturdy structures themselves, are sturdier than the self-constructed shacks. Definitely they seem to offer more protection to their inhabitants from the cold and the wind. But by definition of the Columbus Urban Redevelopment Authority, Goodale is a slum area. The distinguishing eye, however, can differentiate between slums. Even the "masses" would probably not be hardpressed to decide which of several slums was the most (or least) desirable. Something would be lost if we failed to record these differentiations. Areas similar to the Goodale section, therefore, are labeled "slum plus."

Areas 3 and 4

Progressing up the dwelling-area-prestige scale we come to areas that would probably best fit what Warner has called "low." Warner says this about them: "These areas are run-down and semi-slums. The houses are set close together. The streets and yards are often filled with debris, and in some smaller towns, like Jonesville, some of the streets are not paved." [13]

In large metropolitan districts, however, there seems to the author to be a difference between "semi-slums" of sufficient magnitude to warrant at least a twofold separation into "semi-slum plus," and "semi-slum minus." Although both of the subcategories are characterized by multiple dwelling units, in varying stages of disrepair, a certain amount of litter and debris, they are sufficiently different in the amount of deterioration, general unkempt appearances, and all of the other characteristics that combine to make some dwelling areas more desirable than others.

[13] W. Lloyd Warner, Marchia Meeker, and Kenneth Eells, *Social Class in America* (Chicago, Science Research Associates, Inc., 1949), pp. 153-154.

Areas 5 and 6

So it is also with areas loosely described as "below average." Areas thus classified, to use Warner's description, are "not quite holding their own." Some, it seems, are holding it better than others. Areas nearer the business district of the city, those that started to decline at a somewhat earlier date, or that have for some reason made the descent more rapidly can be thought of as "below average minus." They are not semi-slums, if the areas previously described are semi-slums; they differ in degree, from what we shall call "below average plus."

Areas 7 and 8

What are average residential areas? In Jonesville, "these are areas of working-men's homes which are small and unpretentious, but neat in appearance." [14] Almost one third of the Columbus sample lives in areas that fit into this description. Average areas that are characterized by somewhat smaller dwellings that are not quite as well-kept, or that are nearer factories or closer to less desirable areas, were called "average minus." Homes in these areas would generally sell from between $7500 and $9500, while apartments would rent for about $70 per month. "Average plus" areas for various reasons seem more desirable. Not only are homes larger and somewhat more valuable, but the areas themselves are cleaner, tidier, and more appealing to the eye. Then too, there is not quite the same degree of similarity of dwellings that one sees in the "cheese-box villages."

About 20 per cent of the sample live in areas classified as "average minus," while 11 per cent live in "average plus" areas. In either case, the people themselves believe that they are "doing all right" but would like to "get ahead." They "believe in God, work at Timken, and do their shopping at the A & P."

[14] *Ibid.*, p. 153.

Areas 9 and 10

Next we come to the areas of "nice but not pretentious houses" or "above average" areas. Thirteen per cent of the Columbus sample live in this kind of an area. As in Warner's Jonesville, "the streets are kept clean and the houses are well-cared for." [15] The houses in these areas would generally sell from about $12,000 to $16,000. Better apartments, renting for $100 or more per month, are found in these areas. Chiefly, however, these areas are comprised of single dwellings. The homes give the impression of more individual architecture and some were built by the owners. In addition, the larger lots, as compared to "average" areas, give evidence of care and attention, usually performed by the occupant. The streets are clean and repaired and the lack of through traffic and bus lines contributes to the general quietness of the area.

It is probably already apparent that the various areas that fit this general description differ among themselves with respect to status-bearing characteristics. The same procedure was followed as with the other area types; the general category was divided into two subcategories, "above average plus," and "above average minus."

Areas 11 and 12

High dwelling areas house about 4 per cent of the Columbus sample. The dwellings in "high" areas are well spaced, large, and in very good condition. In price they range from $18,000 to $30,000. Most of the lots are large and give evidence of professional landscaping, but full-time gardeners are not usually employed. The homes are largely of natural stone or better-grade brick construction, or at least "fronted" with these materials. Individual architecture is the rule, not the exception. However, the over-all status appeal of these areas is not as great as that of

[15] *Ibid.*

the best sections of the city, to which incidentally, they are sometimes contiguous.

Areas 13 and 14

Only 2 per cent of the respondents live in the highest dwelling areas, characterized by large spacious mansions, private estates, and the very best that Columbus can offer in status-appeal. The homes are widely separated and, placed deep on professionally landscaped lots, offer a degree of seclusion not found in areas of lower categories. Multiple-car garages are the rule and quarters for the help are found. Despite the observable differences that are revealed to the trained and objective eye, individuals who fall in the middle range of the status continuum, and lower, often fail to distinguish between the "high" and the "very high" areas, and are even less likely to differentiate subcategories of each. All are interfused and referred to by such picturesque descriptions as "mortgage row" and "snob hill" which tend to reveal more about the namer than the named. But people who actually live in these "very high" dwelling areas apparently do recognize subtypes. In fact, respondents living in areas classified as "very high" seemed both willing and ready to acknowledge prestige differences between their own and friends' neighborhoods. It is not that they enjoyed making distinctions, or made them significantly more frequently than others, but that they made them more easily. Apparently, they found it less ego-shattering to grant that a certain friend lived in a more desirable neighborhood and derived less gratification when the reverse was true.

It should be apparent from the foregoing description that desirability of dwelling areas is a matter of degree. Even when the areas were rated on a fourteenfold scale there were still areas that fell between two categories. Great differences were noted between areas in the extreme categories, between areas 1 and 14, but the entire series was relatively continuous. As we progress up the neighborhood desirability series we find that one area is "a little better" than the last. Because of the continuous nature of this variable, it would not be realistic to "type" the various dwelling areas according to a specific number of "classes."

THE CONTINUOUS NATURE OF SOCIAL STATUS

The basic hypothesis of this study seems to be fully substantiated by the data: *the social-stratification system manifested in Columbus, Ohio, is represented by a continuous status series.* Apparently, it would not be realistic to speak of social classes in this city in the sense of a *fixed number* of clearly demarcated groups of similar-status individuals logically and empirically distinguished from the rest of the society on the basis of social status. The evidence would not allow such an assertion.

It will be recalled that all three of the particularized status series—the occupational-prestige, rental-value, and neighborhood-prestige series—formed continua. In addition, these three variables were combined and, by means of a differential weighting system, composite social-status scores were obtained.[16] These scores were hierarchically arranged and the resulting series unmistakably formed a continuum. Thus, social status, as inferred from any one of the three particularized indices or from the composite social-status scores, is a matter of degree and not of kind. It was discovered, by ranking the sample on the basis of their social statuses, that the difference between hierarchically contiguous statuses is usually slight indeed. One could, of course, divide the social-status continuum into as many arbitrary divisions as desired in a manner somewhat analogous to the age continuum. Just as the

[16] The occupational-prestige and rental-value scales were each reworked into a fourteenfold scale, since this was the nature of the dwelling-area-prestige scale. The weights for the three variables were as follows: occupational prestige, 5; rental value of dwelling, 4; and dwelling-area desirability, 3. Further analysis revealed that it is highly improbable that any other system of weighting would destroy the continuous nature of the composite social-status series.

age continuum is sometimes divided in such a manner as to produce three statistically defined age categories as youth, middle
age, and old age, so also can the social-status continuum be tri-
sected into lower-status, middle-status, and upper-status groups.
It is generally recognized, to continue the analogy, that there is
no inherent basis for defining middle age, for example, as ranging
from thirty-five to fifty years of age, or even for employing three
age groups instead of two, four, five, or any other number. On the
basis of the evidence furnished by the Columbus study, it seems
that there is no one number of status groupings inhering in the
stratification system and that, therefore, it would not be realistic
to speak of a definite number of social classes in Columbus, in
the objective sense of the term.

SOCIAL CLASSES AS ASSOCIATIONAL GROUPS

Although the various status-characteristics are largely continuous, could there be large groups of individuals who restrict
their serious associations to others within a definite portion of the
social-status continuum? If this could be demonstrated, we would
then be able to speak of social classes in Columbus in the sense of
broad segments of the society that are *socially set apart* from one
another.

Each of the 300 respondents was asked to name his five most
intimate associates, defined as being the five persons with whom
his most frequent and most serious social interactions occur. They
also supplied the information necessary to assign these associates
their places on the various status continua. It was then a matter
of determining how the social status of respondents related to
that of their closest friends.

The Status Range of Acceptance

It was discovered that the majority of Columbus respondents
do not choose as close associates individuals whose social status is

quite similar to their own.[17] But neither do people usually associate, on an intimate level, with those whose social status is very much higher or very much lower than their own.[18] Each person, in a sense, marks off on the status continuum *his own* loosely defined "range of acceptance" and chooses his friends within this range.

The Columbus respondents did not speak of restricting their associations to their own "class," and there was no objective evidence that they did remain within any hypothesized class boundaries. There were as many different ranges of acceptance as there were respondents of different statuses; the inclusiveness of the ranges was dependent upon the individuals' own position in the status hierarchy.

Perhaps the situation can most clearly be demonstrated by considering the case of two Columbus respondents. One fell near the top, the other near the bottom of an arbitrarily defined "middle class." Each named some friends whose social status was lower and some whose status was higher than his own. This meant, it turned out, that each had to cross the arbitrarily established boundaries of the "middle class," the one crossing the upper, the other crossing the lower boundary. And so it was, regardless of where the class lines were drawn or how many lines were established. Each person was found to operate within his own range of social

[17] Similarity of social status was reckoned in terms of points on the three status-characteristics scales. Scores within 5 points above or below one another on the North-Hatt Occupational Prestige Scale were considered "similar." "Similar" monthly rents were defined as those within $15 above or below one another. Similarity of desirability of respondents' dwelling area to that of their friends was determined by asking respondents to compare each of their friends' neighborhoods with that of their own. The choices were: the friend's neighborhood is about the same as their own, somewhat more desirable, somewhat less desirable, a lot more desirable, or a lot less desirable.

[18] Loomis *et al.* discovered a somewhat similar associational relationship pattern in Klamath Falls, Oregon, and summarized their findings by stating that, "In this neighborhood, a clustering of visiting relationships by income does not appear." See C. P. Loomis, J. H. Beegle, and T. W. Longmore, "Critique of Class as Related to Social Stratification," *Sociometry*, 10 (November, 1947), pp. 319-337.

acceptance, regardless of what arbitrary categories he was thereby forced to cross. *It was not possible to divide the social-status continuum in such a way that most people would remain within their "class" for most of their intimate associations.* Thus we have additional evidence that it is not realistic to speak of the stratification system of Columbus in terms of a specific number of clearly defined social classes.

EVALUATION

The Columbus study was designed to test the hypothesis that social status is distributed in that city in such a way that there is no objective evidence of clearly delineated social classes. We will restrict our remarks, then, largely to the adequacy of the methods used to test this hypothesis and to the extent to which the hypothesis has, in fact, been substantiated.

The hypothesis was tested by examining the series that resulted when the Columbus residents were ranked according to (1) the prestige of their occupations, (2) the desirability of the dwelling area in which they were living, and (3) the amount of rent they were paying. The results of this study, therefore, are to a large extent dependent on the manner in which these characteristics were measured.

The prestige of occupations was measured, it will be recalled, through use of North-Hatt Occupational Prestige Scale. It should be noted that data from which this scale was developed were collected about five years before the Columbus study was made. The prestige of occupations may have undergone some changes in the interim. The prestige attached to the position of "nuclear physicist," for example, may have increased, due to the continued recognition of the undertakings and accomplishments of individuals in such positions.

The scores on the North-Hatt scale, in addition, represent an average of the ratings of occupations made by a nation-wide cross section of Americans. Inasmuch as some regional differences in the evaluations of some occupations were noted, the nation-wide average scores may not be the most accurate way to express the job evaluations of Columbus residents.[19]

All in all, then, it is thought that a more precise measurement of the prestige that Columbus residents attach to various occupations could have been obtained. A survey in Columbus might have met with interesting results. It is thought, however, that the refinements that may have resulted from a retest of the North-Hatt study would not seriously affect the results of the Columbus study. In other words, it is doubtful whether the continuous nature of the occupational-prestige series would have been "upset" by relocation or transposition of several occupations.

The differences in the desirability of the sections of Columbus as dwelling areas were determined by a subjective evaluation by the author. The fact that he recognized the nature of these evaluations makes them no less subjective. It is still true that the gradient differences that are purported to exist between the neighborhoods of Columbus are based on the judgment of the author. The descriptions of the various areas furnished by Kenkel would seem to support his conclusions regarding the unbroken and progressive series that is formed when dwelling areas are rated for desirability and the resulting series is ranked. Could another researcher, however, repeat his "rating and ranking" process utilizing the same methods? More important, perhaps, would a retest of this section of the Columbus study yield the same conclusions? Since it would seem to be difficult to perform an exact repetition of this part of Kenkel's study, we are scarcely able to conjecture on the results of a proposed retest.

There would seem to be some technical difficulties connected with Kenkel's rental-value scale. In the first place, the question could be raised, "Is the scale attempting to measure the prestige that is afforded individuals by virtue of the dwelling in which they live, or is the scale a partial index of the respondent's wealth?" If the scale is to be thought of as a prestige-index, the

[19] North, *op. cit.*, pp. 467-468.

procedure of converting selling price of a home-owner's dwelling into its rental value may not have been advisable. It would seem that ownership of a dwelling would, in itself, carry greater prestige than tenancy in the same or comparable house.

If, on the other hand, the scale was intended to differentiate between the relative wealth of Columbus residents, the prestige attached to home-ownership need not be considered. Converting the selling price of a house into its rental value would then seem to result in an objective manner of comparing the financial value of the respondents' dwellings, if, of course, the conversion factor used was actually "the most appropriate for use in Columbus at the time the study was made."

In summary, then, certain technical refinements would seem to be necessary in the interest of producing a more objective and precise measurement of socio-economic characteristics. On the basis of the evidence presented, however, there seems no reason to doubt that the "social-stratification system manifested in Columbus, Ohio, is represented by a continuous status series." But is this *all* the evidence we need in order to conclude that there is no specific number of true social classes in Columbus?

Several sources of data were apparently left untapped in the Columbus study. "One of the most often demonstrated local effects of the class structure," says one student, "is a barrier to intimate social intercourse." [20] Although the Columbus study investigated the friendship patterns of the respondents, no mention was made, for example, of a study of the formal associations to which individuals belonged. Are there clubs and organizations, perhaps, that restrict their membership on a class-basis? This is the type of information we would like to have not only to shed some light on the author's hypothesis but to show how social status operates in the everyday life of Columbus residents.

[20] Harold W. Pfautz, "The Current Literature on Social Stratification," *American Journal of Sociology*, 58 (January, 1953), p. 401.

SELECTED READINGS

DAVIES, A. F., "Prestige of Occupations." (See bibliographic note, p. 131.)

HETZLER, Stanley A., "An Investigation of the Distinctiveness of Social Classes." (See bibliographic note, p. 107.)

MACK, Raymond W., "Housing as an Index of Social Class." (See bibliographic note, p. 131.)

NORTH, Cecil C., and HATT, Paul K., "Jobs and Occupations: A Popular Evaluation," in Logan Wilson and William L. Kolb, *Sociological Analysis* (New York, Harcourt, Brace and Co., 1949), pp. 464-473.

SMITH, Mapheus, "An Empirical Scale of Prestige Status of Occupations." (See bibliographic note, p. 131.)

8

"Elmtown's Youth" [1]

DURING THE LAST DECADE or so considerable emphasis has been placed on the problems of adolescents. The "teenager" (an expression that arose within this period) has been featured in popular magazines and catered to by fashion designers. Ministers preach about him and speakers lecture about him; columnists write to him and about him. The teenager's behavior receives as much attention as does his vocabulary, his record collection, and his "hot rod."

In 1941 August B. Hollingshead, a sociologist, instituted a study of adolescents which proved to be as rich in its findings as it was new in its approach. After a few months in "Elmtown," Hollingshead phrased his working hypothesis as follows: [2] "The social behavior of adolescents appears to be related functionally to the positions their families occupy in the social structure of the community." The problems involved in testing this hypothesis would seem to lie in three areas: (1) Elmtown and its social-stratification system, (2) the social status of families with adolescents, and (3) adolescent behavior.

THE COMMUNITY SETTING

In the heart of the Corn Belt lies "Elmtown," the county seat of "Home County." Six thousand people live in the town and

---

[1] August B. Hollingshead, *Elmtown's Youth* (New York, John Wiley and Sons, 1949).

[2] *Ibid.*, p. 9. Original italicized.

4000 live in the surrounding "country." In 1940 the average acre-value of farm land in the county was considerably higher than the state average. Home County's farms are larger than the average for the state and their tenancy rate is higher. In general, however, the Elmtown farmer runs a "mechanized" farm fairly typical of those in Corn Belt regions. In the town itself a man may work at the mill, the foundry, or the factory, or at any of about twenty small manufacturing plants. Others, of course, work at trades or professions or are employed by various maintenance and service industries.

ELMTOWNERS

When Hollingshead came to Elmtown it was celebrating its centennial. Since the days when the "real Americans" first drove the Indian westward, Elmtown has received four waves of European immigrants. First came the Irish "canal diggers." Many moved on when the job was completed but as a result of those who did not, Elmtown now has a Catholic church and school and an "Irish element." A few Germans began to arrive in Elmtown about 1850. Their numbers were never large and today they are scattered about the town. The largest "foreign group," the Norwegians, first came to Elmtown in the late 1860's. First, as farmers, they successfully cultivated the very worst land in the Elmtown area. Gradually they are moving to the town, since fewer men are now needed on the farms and acreage expansion is limited.

The last group of immigrants arrived under something less than pleasant circumstances. In 1906 Polish laborers were brought in to break the strike at the tannery and the foundry. They remained in the employ of these concerns and in 1941 their numbers had swelled to eighty-five families. Most Poles now work at the factory, the foundry, or the mill.

METHODOLOGY

Hollingshead used several methods to gather data on the adolescents, their parents, and other Elmtowners. Participant observation, formal and informal interviews, official records, tests, and autobiographies all were utilized to supply the information which he sought.

Shortly after Elmtown was selected as the town in which the studies were to be carried out, Hollingshead, his wife, and their two young daughters moved into the small town. There they took an active part in community activities. Hollingshead was invited into the Rotary Club and faithfully attended its meetings. For several months he also taught the adult Bible Class in the Federated Sunday School. He served on the rationing board and was made County Rationing Director. Mrs. Hollingshead was invited into the Women's Club and other social clubs.

With his wife, or alone, Hollingshead spent a great deal of time frequenting those places at which adolescents were likely to be found. He would be found at the high school during lunch period, at the drugstore "hangout," the pool hall, the roller skating rink, and the tavern. Gradually he began to know the high school students and many of their out-of-school peers. Informally, then, these adolescents were interviewed, and they supplied much information about their activities, their ideas, and their friends.

On a more formal level Hollingshead completed schedules for each adolescent and his family, with their assistance and that of other Elmtowners. The nonfamily members supplied information concerning how the families of adolescents fitted into the social structure. Factual material as well as further insights were obtained from town and school records as well as from the autobiographies written by the high school freshmen and seniors.

Hollingshead recognized one factor connected with his study that put a strain on his relations with the adolescents. The Committee on Human Development of the University of Chicago was the agency which planned the larger study of which Hollingshead's was a part. This committee had conferred with leading Elmtowners and explained the purpose of the broader study. The point was stressed that it was concerned with "the development of character in boys and girls." [3] It is understandable that "Elmtown's youth" did not "take well" to this sort of study. Recognizing this condition, Hollingshead planned his relations with the adolescents carefully. He tells us: "The observational technique of being with them as often as possible and not criticizing their activities, carrying tales, or 'interfering' overcame the original suspicion in a few weeks." [4]

THE SAMPLE

Since Hollingshead was interested in the behavior of adolescents, he was concerned with a social definition of this stage of life. He was concerned not so much with what an adolescent *is* physically or psychologically, but with the role he is expected to play in society and the roles he should not play. Formally defined, Hollingshead considers adolescence as ". . . the period in the life of a person when the society in which he functions ceases to regard him (male or female) as a child and does not accord to him full adult status, roles, and functions." [5]

In an effort to get a sample of workable size, Hollingshead focused his attention on those adolescents who either were in high school during the academic year 1941-1942, or were "supposed to be" in high school by virtue of having graduated from the eighth grade between 1938 and 1941. Those who left grade school before graduation, but who were old enough to have graduated between these years, were also included. In short, we can say that the sample consisted of one "high school generation," if we remember that it included not only actual students but those who "should" have been students.

[3] *Ibid.*, p. 8.
[4] *Ibid.*, p. 20.
[5] *Ibid.*, p. 6. Original italicized.

Three hundred and sixty-nine boys and 366 girls comprised the final sample. They ranged in age from thirteen to nineteen years. Slightly over half, or 390 of the adolescents, were in high school at the time of the study.

ELMTOWN'S STATUS SYSTEM

Since the major hypothesis of this study posited a relationship between adolescents' behavior and their parents' social status, it is important to understand how Hollingshead investigated the status system of this town and determined the statuses of the adolescents' families.

Hollingshead employed what we have earlier referred to as the "judges' rating" technique.[6] His use of this technique, however, had certain unique features.

The stratification procedures were instituted after a considerable number of interview schedules had been completed. Hollingshead selected fifty of these schedules and from them abstracted status data on thirty families. These thirty families, he discovered, had been placed "in similar, if not identical, positions by different interviewees...."[7]

Next, cards with the names of these thirty families were shown to twenty-five residents of Elmtown. They were asked to do two things: "(1) to tell how representative they believed these people were of the different positions ('station,' 'pegs people belonged on,' 'classes'—in local usage) in the community, and (2) to place each family where they believed it belonged in terms of its 'station,' 'peg,' or 'standing.'"[8]

Nineteen of the interviewees ranked the thirty families by placing the cards into five piles; three placed them into three

---

[6] Compare Hollingshead's use of the "judges' rating" technique with that used by Lenski. See pp. 87-92. See also Harold F. Kaufman, "Members of Rural Community as Judges of Prestige Rank," *Sociometry*, 9 (February, 1946), pp. 71-85.

[7] Hollingshead, *op. cit.*, p. 29.

[8] *Ibid.*, p. 30.

piles; two used four; and one rater used two groups. The raters disagreed on the ranking of *one third* of the families, consistently so on nine of them and to a lesser extent on the tenth. These ten families were dropped and the remaining twenty were considered the "control list" of families.[9] Since nineteen of the twenty-five interviewees had used five categories in ranking the families, Hollingshead considered that Elmtown was apparently characterized by five "classes or strata." The twenty families were distributed in the "classes" as follows: Class I, two families; Class II, three; Class III, four; Class IV, six; and Class V (lowest), five.

Hollingshead then tested whether the twenty families could be considered representative of the five strata. Twelve additional adults were asked to classify the names on the control list. Ten of these twelve persons also used five groups for their classification of these twenty families. They seemed to agree with the original raters with regard to which family belonged in each category.[10]

The Rating Procedure

The next major problem was the actual rating of the 535 families of adolescents.[11] Hollingshead selected a panel of thirty-one raters, assuring that as a group they were as representative of the community as possible. The raters were instructed to compare and equate as many of the 535 families as they could with the

---

[9] The one third of the families who were dropped from the study were so treated because they were adjudged to be unstable in their own social position or because one of the adult members of the family differed so significantly in his prestige from the other.

[10] Hollingshead tells us that the ten raters in the second group were compared with ten of the original nineteen who had also used a fivefold classification. The two groups of raters agreed substantially on the position of the twenty families (coefficient of correlation between +.84 and +.97). However, we were not told how the ten raters in the second group agreed with the remaining nine in the first group of raters.

[11] This step was preceded by a test of whether the proposed technique was feasible. Fifty-three adolescent families were rated by eight of the original raters who were told to equate them with the names on the control list. Since they were able to do this, it was assumed that another group of judges could also compare the entire list of families with the control list in a similar manner.

twenty names on the control list. In this way, then, he avoided the possible confusion that could result from the raters using a different number of categories in the course of rating the families. The number of ratings thus obtained for the families ranged from seven to twenty-two. The ratings a given family received were translated into terms of class position by assigning a score value of 1 for each time the family was equated with a Class I family, 2 for each time it was equated with a Class II name on the control list, and so on. The average score for each family was then converted into class position.[12]

Agreement and Disagreement Among the Raters

Although all of the 535 families could be placed in one of the previously described classes, several interesting facts were discovered concerning the amount of agreement and disagreement connected with the class placement of the families.

Raters were most likely to agree among themselves concerning a given family's position if four conditions were present: (1) the raters and the family rated were of similar status; (2) the family being rated was well known to each of the raters; (3) the family being rated was stable in its position; and (4) the family being rated was at either extreme of the prestige hierarchy. The converse of these conditions, plus two additional factors, were generally associated with disagreement among the raters: (1) one or more of the raters were in a *lower* position than the family rated; and (2) the family being rated was near, but not at, the bottom of the social structure.

From the average (mean) scores of all people within a class, and from the extent to which the various scores centered about the averages, Hollingshead seemed to conclude that there was good agreement between raters concerning the class placement of the 535 families.

[12] A family with an average score between .51 and 1.50 was considered in Class I; families with a score between 1.51 and 2.50 were placed in Class II; and so on.

ANOTHER GROUP STUDIES ELMTOWN

Shortly after Hollingshead left Elmtown another group of social scientists class-typed a number of sixteen-year-old Elmtowners as part of a different study. Although this study, too, was one of the series under the auspices of the Committee of Human Development, the class-typing was conducted independently. This later group used Warner's Evaluated Participation technique.[13]

One hundred and thirty-four families were rated by both Warner's and Hollingshead's techniques. Since Warner also used a five-class breakdown in this town it was relatively easy to compare the results of the two studies. In general, the agreement between the studies was good; at least 72 per cent of the families were placed in the same class by both techniques. Less disagreement between the two methods was found in the placement of families in the higher classes than the lower ones. The fewness of individuals in Class I (two cases) and Class II (nine cases) limits the conclusions that can be drawn about this tendency.

CHARACTERISTICS OF THE FIVE CLASSES

As the news of Hollingshead's proposed study reached the Elmtowners, many were quick to offer the advice that it would be useless to try to understand adolescents' behavior without first learning "how their families live," and "how the town is organized." Perhaps, then, if we turn to a brief description of the five classes and see "how things work around Elmtown," we will be better able to understand how adolescent behavior is related to their families' social status.

Class I

On the top of Elmtown's "social heap" is the "exclusive two per cent." Particularly at first glance, the most noticeable charac-

[13] For a description of this technique see p. 110.

teristic of this class is its possession of things that money *can* buy. We would include here their large homes, concentrated mostly in one area. Most families have two or three cars; the "family car," a late model Buick or "Caddy," the "business car," and the "youngster's coupe." Money is also spent on a Country Club membership, a cottage at "the lake," and a yearly trip to Florida or the Gulf Coast.

Much of the money thus spent is derived with a minimum of daily effort, since it represents a return on wealth previously invested in lands, securities, and businesses. Class I families own the two banks, the large industries and practically all of Elmtown's business buildings. They also have extensive holdings in farm lands.

A closer look at Class I makes it apparent that it is not "just money" that places an individual among the highest-status people of Elmtown. Almost all members of Class I were born of Class I parents. As a result of strong social and parental pressure, in four out of five cases the present Class I youths will marry their "equals." Usually Class I parents have only one or two children to inherit the "good blood" and "natural ability" that Class I families are said to possess. Inasmuch as they will probably also inherit large businesses, industries, or other means of production, they will undoubtedly have an opportunity to demonstrate their "natural ability."

All Class I families belong to a church; almost all are members of the Federated Church. They give most generously of their wealth but are not noted for their regular attendance at services. One family, for example, donated $1600 for church parlors; the family was represented at services three or four times during the year by one member.

From Hollingshead's description of this class it seems that "family name" is the most important characteristic that puts an individual in Class I. Once there, how he manages his personal life and his inherited wealth will determine whether or not he retains the position. "Choose your parents carefully," would seem to be the best advice to offer a yet unborn Elmtowner who was desirous of high social status!

Class II

To belong in Class II an individual must possess some, but not all, of the same traits that are prevalent in Class I. Half of the members of Class II live in the "best" (Class I) residential area of Elmtown. All but 10 per cent own their homes. A late model family car is practically a must; it "should" be one of the larger models. Only a handful of Class II's, however, have more than one automobile.

Like the members of Class I, almost all families in Class II are affiliated with a church. About 60 per cent belong to the one, the Federated Church, to which the highest-status group belongs. But Class II appears to be the more active class in church work and many of them are "leaders," at least on the surface, in their respective churches.

A big difference between the highest two classes lies in their wealth and the way in which it was acquired. The Class II male typically earns his living from his independent profession (medicine, law, engineering), from operating a business, or from his executive position in a large business owned by a Class I family. This income may be supplemented by that from small holdings in real estate or securities. Thus, a member of Class II is able to "live well" but most of his income is spent on daily living.

Class II could also be called "the class of the community leaders." A man is likely to be an active member in such "power-wielding associations" (to use Hollingshead's terminology) as the major political parties, the Chamber of Commerce, the Rotary Club, the Country Club, and the Masonic Lodge. Class II women "lead" the Women's Club, the D.A.R., the Country Club, the Home and Garden Club, and others. Community improvement committees of various sorts are headed by members of Class II. The rank and file of Elmtown respect these people for their interest and activity in "community affairs"; few realize that behind the scenes a quiet but powerful Class I family is probably "pulling the strings."

Perhaps the greatest difference between Class I and Class II families lies in their respective members who had their origin in a lower class. Most Class I's were the children of Class I parents; about half of the present members of Class II have achieved their positions through their own efforts.

Class III

A few Class I traits are still in evidence as we drop farther down the "social ladder." A fourth of Class III families live in the "best" residential area, but not on the best streets. Two thirds of the families own their homes, as opposed to 90 per cent home ownership in Class II and 100 per cent home ownership in Class I. Seven out of eight Class III families own automobiles. They are likely to be light- or medium-weight vehicles, and they are most often late models.

Most Class III families claim membership in one of Elmtown's churches. About 16 per cent affiliate with the Federated Church as contrasted with almost 60 per cent of Class II's and most of Class I's. The fact that the Lutheran and Catholic churches jointly claim half of Class III families reflects, in part, the ethnic origins of these people. Almost two thirds of them trace their ancestry to European rather than "American" stock.

Fifteen per cent of the much coveted Country Club memberships go to Class III families; the rest are bought by families in the higher classes. Only 10 per cent of the names on the Rotary Club rolls are Class III's. Although members of this class are "true joiners," only a small number belong to Elmtown's high-prestige organizations.

Family income is largely earned by the male head, but one sixth of the mothers are gainfully employed outside the home. There is no stigma attached to an employed mother. Fifteen per cent of the occupations of Class III families fall in the categories "farm tenants" or "service workers and laborers"; about one fourth fall in the category "professional workers and proprietors." Another fourth of the males are "craftsmen and machine opera- tors" in the mills and factories; the rest (about 35 per cent) in almost equal numbers either own farms or perform "clerical and saleswork." Occupationally this is a quite varied class.

Members of Class III, we learn, are outwardly quite "moral" and conservative, but Hollingshead found that some evidence "indicated a wider departure from professed moral standards among the Class III's than among the Class II's." [14]

The trend with regard to criminal charges and conviction is consistent as we progress down the status range. In a seven-year period, no one in Class I or II was even charged with a crime, but 4 per cent of Class III fathers, 14 per cent of Class IV fathers, and 46 per cent of those in Class V were convicted of crimes. Other studies have indicated, however, that this trend is not en- tirely due to the avoidance of criminal activities by higher-status persons.[15] Rather, such persons may commit different types of crimes; in addition, they are more likely to avoid charges for offenses they may commit.

Class IV

Class IV's consider themselves "the backbone of the commu- nity"; [16] their backbones receive recognition from the higher classes, but only to the extent that they are strong enough to carry the weight of Elmtown's physical labor. About 90 per cent of the Class IV males were classified as "craftsmen and machine operators," "farm tenants," and "service workers and laborers." Not quite twice as many Class IV mothers are gainfully em- ployed outside the home as are those in Class III. The annual

---

[14] Hollingshead, *op. cit.*, p. 102.

[15] A leading criminologist holds that what he terms "White-Collar Crimi- nals" are the most dangerous to society of any type of criminal from the point of view of the pervasive nature of their crimes and their effect upon society. See Edwin H. Sutherland, *Principles of Criminology* (Philadelphia, J. B. Lippincott Co., 1947), pp. 36-43.

[16] Hollingshead, *op. cit.*, p. 103.

income of a Class IV family, however, usually provides more than the necessities of life.

Marriages in Class IV take place earlier, are more fertile, but less stable than those in higher classes. Neither husbands nor wives participate in organized religious, social, or civic associations in any large numbers. The concentration of Class IV's in the Eagles, Redmen, Woodmen, and their auxiliaries is the major exception to this tendency.

Members of Class IV appear to realize where they "stand" in Elmtown. Apparently, however, they can derive comfort from knowing that they are not afforded the lowest status in the community.

Class V

"Behind the tannery," "down by the garbage dump," in "Ixnay," and in "Frog Hollow" stand small, dilapidated shacks and huts. It is in areas with such descriptive labels and in dwellings whose conditions almost defy description that the members of Class V live.

City water is piped into or near less than three fourths of the homes within the city limits. About one home in seven has bath and toilet facilities. The wood and coal stoves or kerosene burner that is used for cooking is almost always the only heating device in the home. The homes are sparsely furnished but the condition of the furnishings is probably more noticeable than its poverty. None-too-clean, stringy curtains hang in the place of freshly-starched priscillas or soft, flowing draperies. A sagging iron bunk-type bed and a chest of drawers may make up the "bedroom suite." Floors are either uncovered or incompletely covered by well-worn linoleum or strips of roofing.

If Class V's physical plight is unenviable, so much more is its social position. The members realize that they stand at the very bottom of the social structure. Apparently they are ranked here for many reasons including their poverty, their seeming lack of "success" goals, and their reputed disregard of morals. In the opinion of their social superiors, all members of Class V live biologically-oriented lives, with particular attention to the pleasures derived from sex and drink. They have a reputation for criminal behavior, laziness, and vulgarity. Special mention is usually made of their sexual promiscuity and incestuous relations. Not all of their notoriety is earned. The members of this class, however, are frequently involved in "trouble with the law." About half of the fathers had been convicted once or more within an eight-year period. The offenders averaged about four convictions apiece. During the same period, about 8 per cent of the women were charged with drinking, disorderly conduct, family neglect, and sex offenses.

Regardless of the factual basis for their unsavory reputations, the reputation persists and has its effect on the treatment afforded Class V members. Employers dislike to hire them, money lenders do not "trust" them, and the churches largely ignore them. A few "rough," low-ranking taverns and the Bright Star, a theater that "specializes in second-rate shows and sensational sex films" [17] cater to the presumed needs of this class.

HIGH SCHOOL STUDENTS

As Hollingshead continued his studies of adolescents it became more and more apparent that great differences were found between the in-school and the out-of-school adolescents. Whether or not an adolescent attended high school, moreover, was related to the social status of his parents; the higher a family's social status the more likely his high-school-age children were on the rolls of Elmtown High.

But regardless of the reasons for the differences in behavior, the distinction between students and nonstudents seemed compelling. In the following section, therefore, we will report on Hollingshead's findings regarding the relationship between the social position of the 390 students and the manner in which they

[17] *Ibid.*, p. 301.

participated in school activities, in social cliques, and in several types of recreational activities.

Elmtown High

Even before they reach the school building, striking differences can be noted between the students approaching from the several residential areas of Elmtown. From "across the canal," the lowest-status residential area, come small groups of boys and girls wearing not-too-clean and not-too-new looking clothes. Many carry a lunch wrapped in newspaper. The close observer will also notice that their hands are often dirty and their hair reveals the lack of professional care. The girls who come to school from this area outnumber the boys by three to one.

The students who come from Frog Hollow appear only a little better dressed and groomed than those from across the canal. Again, more girls are noticed than boys. Those who are approaching the school from Ixnay present still better appearances but could scarcely be called well groomed or well dressed. Close inspection would probably reveal that their hands are clean and that the boys' hair had been cut in a barber shop. Lunches are packed in a bag rather than wrapped in newspaper.

By way of contrast, we can observe briefly a student coming from the best residential area of Elmtown. We notice him coming out of his father's near-mansion and walking to the two-car garage. As he backs out in his convertible we see that he is wearing a soft leather jacket. Since it is open at the neck, we get a glimpse of his bright tie and his starched white shirt. His "crew cut" is neat and becoming. On his four or five block drive to the high school he will stop for several friends. It may seem hard to believe that their destination is the same as that of the boys and girls from across the canal or from Frog Hollow.

The Curriculum

Once inside the high school, small groups of either boys or girls, of about the same age and "year" in school, are seen going into the different classrooms. Some are headed for an hour's instruction in a foreign language, others are going to a bookkeeping, typing, or commercial law class. Still others may be completing their third and last year of English as required in the General Course.

The three basic courses offered at Elmtown, the college preparatory, the general, and the commercial, can be ranked both according to the social status of the students enrolled in them and the prestige the courses carry among the students. The commercial course carries the least prestige of the three, while to "really rate" a student should enroll in the academic (college preparatory) course.

Almost two thirds of Class I and II adolescents enroll in the academic; one girl took the commercial course. About half of the Class III's are found in the general course; the remainder show a slight preference for the academic. Only 9 per cent of Class IV's take the academic course; 58 per cent enter the general, and one third take the commercial one. The percentage of Class V's who take academic studies drops to 4 per cent while somewhat more V's than IV's start in the commercial course.

Grades, Awards, and Punishments

A definite status-bias is noted in the grades that students receive for their work, the awards that they attain, and the disciplinary action that is taken against them for infraction of rules.[18]

Students in Class I and Class II receive about twice as many grades between 85 and 100 as they would if chance factors alone were operating. On the other hand, if the grades were distributed randomly among the students regardless of their social status, Class V children would receive *three times* as many grades between 85 and 100 as they do now. Thus, the higher an adolescent's social status, the more likely he is to receive high grades.

---

[18] For a more comprehensive description of the relationship between social status and grades, rewards, and punishments see Chapter 11, pp. 267-268, and the references cited in that chapter.

In addition, course failure was more prevalent among the Class IV and V students.

Merely indicating the direct relationship between high school grades and high social status does not explain the bias. The most common "reason" offered to account for the phenomenon is that the higher-status adolescents are more intelligent than the lower-status ones. Hollingshead investigated this belief by comparing the scores students made on an intelligence test with their social-class position.[19] From his statistical analyses he concluded the following:[20] "Although intelligence was associated significantly with class position, the degree of association was not high enough to account for the concentration of failures in Class V. Neither was it great enough to attribute the high grades in Classes I and II to the intellectual capacity of this prestige level." Factors other than intelligence, therefore, are operating to produce the relationship in question. According to Hollingshead, these "other factors" included (1) home training and influence, and (2) teachers' expectations that the Class I and II students will do better.

Apparently the higher-status families are the ones who stress academic success and instill in their children the desire to "make good" in school. Not to be dismissed, however, are the greater ability of the Class I and II family to "cause trouble" if a child is treated "unfairly," and the expectations of teachers concerning the grades of their students. The adolescents themselves stress this last point and some claim that a student is "rated" by his teachers as soon as he enrolls in high school and particularly after it is noted whether he takes the academic, the general, or the commercial course.

On a subject such as this it is difficult to draw specific conclusions on the importance of the several variables. Suffice it to say,

[19] The *Otis Group Intelligence Test, Advanced Examination: Form A* was administered to all students shortly after they enrolled in Elmtown High. It is held by some that such verbal intelligence tests are unwittingly status-biased; the language used and the problems cited are often most typical of life at middle-status levels.

[20] Hollingshead, *op. cit.*, p. 175.

then that intelligence, to some extent, and other factors, to a greater extent, account for the direct relationship between academic grades of students and their social standing in the community.

Various awards by the school follow the same pattern as grades. Two examples particularly were mentioned by both students and adults to illustrate "how the school works." Both involved the award of a college scholarship to a student who was supposedly academically less qualified than the next contender. In both cases, the person said to have deserved the scholarship, from the standpoint of scholastic achievements, was a lower-status adolescent.

It was said in Elmtown that grades have been changed, teachers have been threatened with dismissal, and examinations have been rigged in order that the children of "prominent" families may receive various awards. The high school principal indicated that "in a few cases" grades of Class I and II children were changed after graduation so the children could enter college. He did not admit to the other charges.

"The administration of discipline laid bare the class system in a way that is directly observable but difficult to quantify." [21] Most of Elmtown High's disciplinary problems centered about lateness. Any student who was late for class had to go to the principal's office, explain his tardiness, and obtain a slip admitting him to class. If his explanation was not acceptable, he was required to spend an hour in the detention room.

It so "happened" that the excuses given by Class I and II children were usually acceptable. The teachers recognized the unfairness of the system that made it virtually impossible to send an adolescent from a prominent family to detention and once they voted that "no excuses" were to be accepted from any child. While this rule was in effect a Class I girl failed to report to detention but went instead to the hairdresser in preparation for a Country Club dance. She reported to the principal the next morning, "dressed neatly in a brushed wool sweater and tweed

[21] *Ibid.*, p. 185.

skirt," [22] and was told "don't let this happen again." [23] Previous to her arrival in his office, the principal had been "talked to" by the superintendent whose wife, in turn, had received a call from the girl's mother. A few other such instances and Elmtown High was back to normal; excuses could be accepted in lieu of detention and such excuses were more often accepted from the students from "prominent families."

Extracurricular Activities

At Elmtown High there are eleven organizations to which boys can belong and twelve for girls. Other extracurricular activities include school dances, plays, parties, athletic events, and memberships on the Student Council. In all cases, there is a strong relationship between social status and participation or nonparticipation in these organizations and events. All adolescents in Class I and II belong to "something" as do also three fourths of Class III's. Only one fourth of Class V's belong to any organization. In addition, students from the higher classes belong to *more* organizations and participate *more frequently* in school dances, plays, and parties.

The students themselves apparently recognize the status-bias that operates with regard to all extracurricular activities except boys' athletics. They talk of being "pushed out" of clubs, of being snubbed and ignored, and of being made to feel "out of place." The truth in such statements is hard to ascertain but the fact remains that lower-status adolescents do participate in extracurricular activities much less frequently than higher-status students.

And so we have a preliminary look at Elmtown High and "how it works." In the various phases of high school life a definite and persistent status-bias is readily discernible. The impact that social status has on the lives of these high school students will become even more apparent as we investigate their cliques, dating, and recreational behavior.

[22] *Ibid.*, p. 188.
[23] *Ibid.*

Cliques

One of the things that Hollingshead noticed about Elmtown's youth was that they were seldom alone. The adolescents themselves talked of "our bunch," "our gang," or sometimes simply an unmodified "we." Teachers and other adults commented on the "high school cliques" or "those high school bunches" and Hollingshead often observed small groups of boys and girls walking to school together, strolling in the halls, and eating lunch together.

Hollingshead considered as cliques those small, informal groups of either boys or girls (but not both) that had a certain amount of permanency about them. Membership in these cliques is strictly voluntary but can only be attained by unanimous consent of the existing members.

New cliques, like Topsy, seem to "just grow" but not in a completely unrestricted manner. Further study of the student cliques revealed that the odds are in favor of the members of a clique belonging in the same prestige class and same class in school. It is significant, however, that slightly over one third of the boys' and slightly under one third of the girls' clique relations are *outside* the limits of their own prestige class.

Clique relationships appear to have significant effects on the adolescents' behavior. Many of their waking hours are spent in the company of clique members. The opinion of the clique on school, recreational, and personal matters, is highly valued, more so, even, than that of parents. Seldom, it seems, will adolescents openly engage in behavior that is known to be contrary to the values of the clique. Thus, since cliques are definitely "status-bound," we see again the impact of social status.

Dates and Dating Behavior

Youths may begin to date as young as age twelve but most do not start until they are fifteen. By this time, about 93 per cent of both sexes date regularly. However, there are several factors that affect the dating pattern. The more important of these seem to be their class in school, their prestige class, and their cliques.

About half of the dates reported by students were with other students in the same year at Elmtown High. When dates are between members of different school classes, it is likely that the boy will be in a class above the girl. This is, of course, consistent with folkways of America which dictate that the male should be older than the female in such a relationship.

Students, as a rule, do not usually have dates with those whose social status is quite different from their own. Half or more of the dating occurs between members of the same class. The next most frequent type of dating involves adolescents in adjacent classes. The social distance between the members of Class II (with which were combined the few Class I's) and those of Class V was apparently so great that no dates were reported between adolescents at such opposite extremes of the prestige hierarchy. In all cases that involve interclass dating, the chances are greater that the boy belongs in a higher prestige class than the girl.

The clique to which an adolescent belongs also affects his dating pattern. Sometimes the members of a girls' clique will date only the members of a certain boys' clique. Other times the cliques function chiefly as the agencies which enforce the "rule" of no dating between those who are socially too dissimilar. In addition, cliques develop reputations which are applied to all their members and effectively limit dating possibilities. Bob's gang may be considered as "wild" and the G.W.G. (God We're Good) girls won't date any of them. A group of girls may collectively be known as "pretty fast"; fear of ostracization may prevent the members of certain male cliques from dating any of these girls.

Although many students date, during a given month, only 18 per cent of them (or fifty-four students) reported that they were "going steady." Fifteen of the high school steady daters were boys and thirty-nine were girls. Thus, much of the steady dating took place between students and nonstudents.

That so few students regularly dated only one person of the

opposite sex should please the parents, teachers, and other adults of Elmtown who generally disapproved of such practices. Their disapproval rests largely on their suspicions that steady daters are likely to become "too intimate." Their fears are not entirely ungrounded. Twenty-nine of the thirty-eight students "going steady" with nonstudents reported they were having sexual intercourse with their dates. Of the eight student couples who dated steadily, three reported having sex relations with their "steady" and four more were alleged to have had.

Comparable figures for students not dating one person exclusively are not available. Hollingshead stated that "the sex taboo is violated by many students, but the percentage was not ascertained, for even to talk of such things was tabooed." [24, 25] The amorous activities of Elmtown's youth, like other aspects of their behavior, are apparently related to their social status. Hollingshead gained the impression, from his analysis of the sexual behavior of the steady daters and the untabulated data on the remaining adolescents, that the sex mores were violated more frequently by Class IV and V adolescents than by those in Class III. Class III's, in turn, were more likely to have sex relations than were Class II's. This is consistent with Kinsey's findings.

Social status entered into the sexual behavior picture in still another way. In 82 per cent of the cases of steady daters who acknowledged having sex relations, the girl belonged to a *lower* class than the boy. Some of the boys reported that they were just "having fun" and that they had no conjugal intentions. Others were apparently "serious" at the time. Statistically, however, it is unlikely that the amorous affairs that involve partners of quite different social statuses will end in marriage unless strong social pressures, perhaps of the "shot-gun" variety, are applied.

[24] *Ibid.*, p. 238.

[25] If Kinsey's data are applicable in Elmtown, it would be estimated that almost half of the males who enter, but do not go beyond high school, have sexual intercourse with companions while of school age. See Alfred C. Kinsey, W. B. Pomeroy, and Clyde E. Martin, *Sexual Behavior in the Human Male* (Philadelphia, W. B. Saunders Co., 1948), p. 686.

Recreation and Pleasures

The higher an adolescent's social status, the more of his leisure time is spent with his clique in informal group activities as opposed to leisure spent at various organized clubs and organizations. In addition, the kind of activities in which adolescents engage is also status-linked.

Almost all boys and girls attend the "movies" with some regularity. Class II's and III's go more frequently than do those in the lower two classes and are far more likely to see them at the Elmtown Theater than the Bright Star or the Silver Bell.[26]

Dancing is very popular among the high school students, despite the fact that it is disapproved by several religious leaders, particularly the Lutherans. Students dance at high school sponsored dances, at the Country Club, and at various commercial dance halls. Most of the students who attend the Country Club dances are from the higher classes, but 21 per cent of Class III youths and 7 per cent of those in Class IV also go to one or more of these dances. Class II girls would *never* go to the commercial dance halls and boys from this class avoid them unless they are "on the prowl."

Bowling and roller skating are popular among the adolescents, but participation in these sports is definitely status-connected. The higher an adolescent's status, the more likely he is to prefer bowling to roller skating. The skating rink, because of its unsavory reputation, is avoided especially by the girls in the higher classes. "Pick-ups" are common, fights occur, and it is not unusual to observe couples engaged in "a little necking" in the darkened corners. One Class V girl, a member of a clique that frequented the rink four or five times a week, reported that all five girls in her clique would have sex relations with the "right fellow." All but one of the girls confirmed her story. Apparently, it is not

---

[26] *Ibid.*, p. 301. "Local values place the theaters in a hierarchy with the Elmtown at the top, followed at some distance by the Silver Bell, and the Bright Star a very low third."

only because roller skating is considered a "cheap sport" that it is avoided by the higher classes.

In various other situations the social status of an adolescent is related to his behavior. Where and how an adolescent drinks intoxicants (but not *if* he drinks them) are related to his prestige class. Students participate in religious activities in a manner similar to their parents; the influence of social status is noted strongly here.[27] Students from Classes III, IV, and V are far more likely to have a part-time job than those from the higher classes. The higher an adolescent's class the more likely he is to have a "desirable" job, often by parental arrangement.

Thus in almost every aspect of high school students' lives their social status plays a part. Next, let us investigate to what extent this is also true of the out-of-school adolescent.

THE OUT-OF-SCHOOL ADOLESCENT

According to the school law in effect in Elmtown, no youth can leave school before he is sixteen years of age, unless he has a work certificate. Employment certificates can be issued to adolescents fourteen years of age and older. Hollingshead, however, was able to contact 345 out-of-school adolescents; three fourths of them withdrew from school before they were sixteen and few had been issued work certificates prior to their withdrawal from school.

Who are these high-school-age youths who, to a large extent, extra-legally forsake the traditional adolescent life? How does social status fit into this withdrawal process? What is the relationship between the activities of *these* youths and their social status? These are the kinds of questions about the out-of-school adolescents that press for an answer.

[27] For the relationship between social status and the religious activities of Elmtown's adults, see pp. 165-170.

Social Status and Leaving School

Our own experiences, perhaps, would lead us to believe that there is "some" relationship between social status and the incidence of withdrawal from school. This relationship was found to be quite strong among the Elmtown adolescents. None of the thirty-five adolescents in Class I and II had dropped out of school but about 8 per cent of Class III's had entered the nonschool world. The percentage of Class IV and V adolescents who were not in school was 41 and 89 per cent respectively. Thus, the study of Elmtown's nonstudent youths is largely a study of Class IV and V adolescents; 333 of the 345 out-of-school adolescents were in either of the lower classes.

Even with this decided overrepresentation of lower-status Elmtowners in the out-of-school group, we can investigate further the relationships between social status and withdrawal from school.

Age. How old a youngster is when he leaves school, prior to graduation, is associated with his social status. If he (or she) is under sixteen the chances are great that his family is in Class IV or V; the odds are slightly higher that he is in the lower of these classes. Class V's may quit school as young as twelve years of age. Eleven of the twelve Class III's who dropped out of school, however, were sixteen or over.

Sex. Boys are somewhat more likely to leave school than girls. This is particularly true in Class IV but in Classes III and V only slightly more than half of the withdrawees are boys (58 and 53 per cent respectively). Apparently, there is no clear relationship between the sex of a withdrawee and his social status.

Grade completed. In view of the relationship between age at time of leaving school and social status, we would expect a similar pattern with respect to school grade completed. All Class III withdrawees finished the eighth grade and almost all started high school. Ninety-two per cent of Class IV's but only 57 per cent of Class V's completed the eighth grade. A member of Class V is a rarity in the graduating class of Elmtown High and there are not many diplomas given to Class IV's.

Hollingshead has indicated that there are many reasons for adolescents' leaving school. The withdrawee comes most frequently from the classes that receive lower scholastic grades, participate less in extracurricular functions, and are more likely to receive discipline for their infractions of school rules. Some lower-status adolescents point to these discriminations as their "reason" for leaving school. Hollingshead feels, however, that it is largely the family background of an adolescent—the values he is taught, the attitudes he learns, and the behavior patterns he "picks up" at home—that make him unwanted at school and, therefore, willing to drop out.

Withdrawees themselves also cite, as a reason for dropping out of school, their desire to "make money and have fun." In the next sections, we will investigate how the out-of-school youth "makes money" and how he spends his leisure.

Out-of-School Adolescents on the Job

In 1941-1942 it was not very difficult for a high-school-age youth to get a job. To get a "good job" was a different matter, however, for those in Elmtown that bear the most prestige generally did not go to the youths who failed to complete grade or high school.

The out-of-school adolescent is likely to work at a menial, dirty, low-skilled, and low-salaried job. Differences were found, however, between the occupations engaged in by Class IV and Class V out-of-school youths. Class V boys are more likely to be found doing general labor and janitorial work or working in the bowling alley and roller skating rink. More Class IV's than V's are clerking in stores, working on "the line" in the factory, and working in service stations or garages. Employers generally do not expect the boys from the lower classes to "make good" and especially dislike those whose families are known as "reliefers." In general, then, Class V boys get the occupations that bear the least prestige. Some IV's share their plight, whereas others can get somewhat more desirable jobs.

Among the withdrawee girls the employment picture is much the same. The Class IV adolescent girl is employed as a waitress or as a sales clerk more frequently than the Class V. Class V girls are more often employed as maids, laundresses, janitresses, and line employees at the factory. Girls from the lower of the two classes are somewhat more likely to be unemployed. Over a fourth of those unemployed are housewives (as opposed to less than 20 per cent of Class IV). A few more V's than IV's are "just living" at the parental home.

In general, then, the employment picture for the out-of-school adolescents could scarcely be called bright. There is little left of their meager earnings after they buy their clothing and pay their parents a few dollars a week for room and board. Much of what does remain is spent on recreation and leisure time pursuits.

Leisure Activities of the Nonstudent Adolescent

When a boy or girl drops out of school he generally leaves behind not only the "pencils and books" but also his school chums and his ties with school-centered youth organizations. Gradually he gets into a clique with other nonstudents. A few, about 5 per cent, will join formal associations such as a ping-pong club, or a church group, or a bowling league. Most of the adolescents' away-from-home leisure time is spent with their clique mates or on a date. Many of their activities, in either case, are related to their social status.

"The search for something exciting or novel is a major part of a clique's activity." [28] This usually means an automobile should be available and 83 per cent of withdrawee boys in Class IV and 65 per cent of those in Class V who have been out of school a year, do own an automobile.[29] On a typical night, the gang is

[28] Hollingshead, op. cit., p. 398.
[29] The automobiles owned by Class IV boys average seven years old; those owned by Class V's are slightly over nine years old. Hollingshead, op. cit., p. 398.

"rounded up" and a somewhat aimless trip is begun in response to the beckonings of Bacchus and Eros. Various "hangouts" are visited, including taverns, hamburger stands, and gambling places. A considerable amount of time is spent "cruising." The object of this activity is to "pick up a babe or two," if they were not to be found at the hangouts. If the mission is successful, the boys and girls ride around a bit, and stop at a roadhouse for something to eat and drink. Then they ride around some more and finally bring the car to a stop at the side of a lonely road or in some secluded spot where "the view is lovely." It is well understood that amorous activity is the object at this stage of the evening; sometimes they "just pet," sometimes they "go all the way."

On Saturday night almost all out-of-school adolescents "go out." Between 80 and 85 per cent of the unmarried boys and girls are found in the motion picture theaters, the roller rinks, or the public dance halls and taverns. Most Class V boys and girls can be found in the "disreputable" places, but a third go to the "respectable, but..." ones. Class IV's go more often to "respectable, but..." hangouts, but a third can be seen in the lowest-status ones. The kind of a place an adolescent frequents is related to his social status, but not in the sense that the places can be, strictly speaking, class-typed.

In the course of satisfying their desire for excitement and pleasure, the out-of-school youths sometimes run into conflict with the law. They are decidedly more likely to have "trouble with the law" than their age-mates in high school. This, in a sense, is indicative of the status-bias connected with criminal convictions, inasmuch as withdrawees are more likely to belong to the lower classes than students.[30] In addition, even among the withdrawees it was discovered that the incidence of conviction is related to the social status of the adolescents involved. Fifteen per cent of Class V adolescents were convicted of criminal offenses as opposed to 8 per cent fewer Class IV's.

[30] Sutherland, *loc. cit.*

Sex and Marriage

It is common knowledge that the sex taboo is violated by out-of-school adolescents. According to Hollingshead, "the sex mores are violated consistently by a considerable proportion of withdrawees." [31] Since the sex taboos include even the talking about "such things," the data were not sufficiently complete to compare the sexual behavior of students and nonstudents. However, it was discovered that among nonstudents there was some relationship between social status and sexual behavior. In general, more Class V boys than IV's visit Polish Paula's "house" and similar commercial establishments. The withdrawees in Class V also outnumbered those in Class IV who visited Myra's apartment on those evenings when she "entertained" for fifty cents or a dollar.

Both Class IV and V boys, however, prefer the casual pick-up, their "date," or their "steady," as a sex partner. The data are not sufficiently complete to allow a breakdown by class of this type of sexual behavior.

Somewhat more of the out-of-school boys and girls date than do students. Nonstudents, moreover, are decidedly more likely to be "going steady" than students. Like students, however, withdrawees generally date within their social class or in an adjacent class (less frequently). The higher a withdrawee's social status, the more likely he is to date a high school girl, although no more than about one quarter of all nonstudent males date students.

For 26 per cent of these school-age youths, dating led to going steady, going steady to engagement and marriage. [32] Engagements among the group were never found to be announced in the Elmtown *Bugle*. In addition, they are usually kept from families and friends. The engaged couple goes out together as often as five times a week. For those with a car, a generous portion of the evening is spent in the automobile, parked at "some quiet spot."

[31] Hollingshead, *op. cit.*, p. 418.
[32] Average age of married girls in the study was 17.1 years; the unmarried averaged 15.4 years of age. For boys the comparable figures are 18.0 and 16.8 years. Hollingshead, *op. cit.*, p. 427.

According to Hollingshead, "Heavy petting followed by sexual relations often occurs in the parked car, except in the very coldest weather." [33]

Soon the couple decides to marry, or, as tales will have it, many realize they "have to" marry. In a rather large percentage of the cases checked by Hollingshead, the inappropriate arrival of an "eight-month baby" led him to place some credence in the number of "shot-gun affairs" that were said to have taken place.

More Class V withdrawees were married than Class IV's. In both cases they chose partners from the same class far more frequently than they did from another class.[34] Apparently, however, there was no relationship between the percentage of "military weddings" and the social status of the adolescents involved. In fact, the three marriages involving a Class III adolescent were almost certainly performed after the conception of a child.

The adolescent couples begin their married lives, according to Hollingshead, much the same as their parents did a generation earlier. A sizable number, but more Class V's than IV's, live with one of the parental families for "awhile." Most of the remainder rent a place, perhaps above a store, in the same type of neighborhood in which they were reared. "All of the husbands held unskilled or semi-skilled, low-paid jobs." [35]

Thus the lives of these adolescents are quite different from those withdrawees who are not married. But the greatest differences, it is thought, are those drawn between all nonstudents and the adolescents who are still in school.

Picture, if you will, the boys and girls who stroll through the halls of Elmtown High, discussing the latest school play, the next Country Club dance, or the football game with their arch-rivals. Picture them too in their after-school hours; some are practicing

---

[33] *Ibid.*, p. 428.

[34] Sixty out of sixty-four Class V's married equals; three married a Class IV, and one a Class III person. Eighteen out of twenty-two Class IV youths married a Class IV, while three married a Class V and one Class III boy or girl. Hollingshead, *op. cit.*, p. 433.

[35] *Ibid.*, p. 435.

athletics, others are at a meeting of their favorite social club, a few are being coached for their parts in intramural debates, while a few more may be in the library thumbing through catalogs of colleges and universities.

Compare their life, then, with that of the boys and girls, of about the same age, who have dropped out of school. Watch this group as they daily "put in their eight hours" at their menial, low-paid jobs or as they cruise or walk the streets of Elmtown in search of excitement and escape from their work-a-day routine.

This is the social-status system in action; there is no escaping the fact that almost all of the withdrawees are lower-status youths.

EVALUATION

A division can be made between what this study has contributed to the broader field of social stratification and what it has contributed to an admittedly specific area—the relationship between social status and the behavior of adolescents. Contributions in both areas are important, but since those in the latter naturally build upon the knowledges and techniques in the former, somewhat greater emphasis will be given to the stratification techniques and procedures than what was discovered through their use.

The Stratification System of Elmtown

After reading Hollingshead's description of the stratification system in this "typical" Midwestern community one reviewer remarked, "If that kind of community has clearly demarcated 'classes,' then the United States does!" [36] Many of our remarks will concern the problems summarized by this statement, that is, we will be concerned with *how* the classes were discovered in Elmtown and how clearly demarcated they appear to be.

[36] Robert S. Lynd, *American Sociological Review,* 14 (August, 1949), pp. 560-561. (Review of *Elmtown's Youth.*)

The first reference to Elmtown's five classes concerned the fact that nineteen of the first twenty-five raters separated a total of thirty families into five categories. The raters felt that the most "natural" way to separate these people according to their social standing in Elmtown was to divide them into five categories. These raters, in addition, largely agreed on the ranks of twenty of these families. *The one third concerning whom there was considerable disagreement were eliminated from further tests!*

With reference to the original thirty, Hollingshead states that "Great care was taken to see that *several* families were selected from *each station* in the social structure."[37] Some would undoubtedly infer from this that Hollingshead was aware of a definite number of "stations" within the Elmtown prestige structure. From how many "stations" did he select families? He does not say, but, apparently, it could not have been from many. Since several families at each "station" were socially similar, there seems to be a definite limitation on the number of "stations" that could be used. Thus, it is not surprising that only five "stations" (categories, "classes," etc.) were found when the control group of *twenty* families was ranked.

It would appear, then, that if *fewer* families had been selected, (for example, nine, with several at each "station") the raters may have divided them into less than five groupings; if *more* families had been selected and with no attempt to choose several from a *few* "stations" (for example, a random sample of 250) the raters *may* have discovered that the families fell at more than five different "levels" in the prestige hierarchy.

A question may be raised concerning the agreement found between the first and second group of raters who ranked the same twenty families. *Their agreement was good.* Ten out of twelve of the second group also employed a fivefold classification and, for the most part, put the same people in each of the categories. This would seem to demonstrate that the twenty people did fall at five levels. Inasmuch as the twenty families were previously

[37] Hollingshead, *op. cit.*, p. 29. Italics not in original.

selected so that several would be representative of various "stations" in the prestige hierarchy, this is scarcely surprising. We can only ask, "At how many levels would a random sample of 250 families have fallen?"

The student should remain aware that the 535 families of adolescents used in the Elmtown study did not enter into the determination of the class structure of that town. They were ranked, it will be recalled, by comparison with the original twenty families who, in turn, had been previously placed in one of the five classes.

How Clearly Delineated Are the Five Classes?

The five classes which Hollingshead utilized in Elmtown are generally treated as discrete entities and clearly demarcated social classes. There is some evidence, however, that the classes are not as clearly delineated as we might assume from the many unmodified references to them.

Unfortunately, the average status-scores of the 535 families are not furnished. The mean score for each class is given as well as the average deviation from the mean.[38] In view of the magnitude of the average deviations, it seems that the cases *within* each class are not distributed normally. The cases within each class do not, then, cluster about the mean as they would be expected to do if the "classes" represented discrete categories;[39] rather the magnitude of the average deviation seems to indicate that *the scores are fairly well spread out within each class.* In other words, it

[38] Class I, Mean rating = 1.04 A.D. .04; Class II, M = 1.93 ± .16; Class III, M = 2.91 ± .25; Class IV, M = 4.17 ± .47; Class V, M = 4.71 ± .39. Hollingshead, *op. cit.*, p. 37.

[39] A crude estimate of the way the cases were distributed within each class interval was made by utilizing the relationship between the average deviation and the range when normally distributed data are involved. There is some question about the advisability of presenting average deviations for data such as these that quite obviously are not distributed "normally." Similar objections would arise concerning the use of the average deviation to estimate the spread within the class intervals. The crudeness of these estimates is well recognized; the lack of the raw scores precludes the possibility of better estimating the score ranges.

would appear that the five "classes" in Elmtown could better be described as constructed and convenient class intervals rather than clearly delineated social classes.

The cultural characteristics of the 535 families, as well as the behavior of their adolescents, leave no doubt about the fact of differential social status in Elmtown. But do the data indicate that there are lines of cleavage in the Elmtown social-status structure that separate the community into more or less distinct divisions along the lines of cultural characteristics and behavior patterns?

In most cases, the answer is negative. Great differences appear between the extreme groups but in many cases the intermediate groups form a gradient series between the extremes. More Class I's, for example, belong to the Country Club than do Class II's, but 15 per cent of Class III families also belong; in addition, a few Class IV adolescents have gone to Country Club dances. No father in Class I or II was charged with a crime, during a seven-year period; the statistics for Class III, IV, and V are 4 per cent, 14 per cent, and 46 per cent, respectively. Twenty-seven per cent of Class V adolescents participate in extracurricular activities at the high school as do also 57 per cent of Class IV's, 75 per cent of Class III's and 100 per cent of Classes I and II (collectively). Many other examples could be cited to show that although the presence or absence of traits and behavior patterns is related to differential social status, they are not related in a manner that would "prove" the existence of clearly defined social classes.

Adolescent Behavior and Social Status

There can be little doubt that Hollingshead was successful in analyzing the relationship between social status and many different types of adolescent behavior. The pervasive nature of Elmtown's social-status system was made all too clear.

It is particularly noteworthy that this study was not restricted to those adolescents who were in high school. The behavior and status differences between out-of-school and school youths constitute an important contribution of this study.

Some, perhaps, might feel that the role of status in the lives of adolescents has been overemphasized.[40] It is thought that this impression, where it is present, is due largely to the fact that the various types of behavior that are *not* related to social status are de-emphasized. If those areas in which status did not seem to affect the adolescents' behavior had been treated more fully, perhaps the criticism of "overemphasis" on status factors could not be levied. Social status *is* important, however, in the lives of children and adults. The purpose of this study was to indicate its role in the lives of adolescents. This purpose was remarkably achieved.

SELECTED READINGS

DUNCAN, Otis D., and ARTIS, Jay W., "Social Stratification in a Pennsylvania Rural Community." (See bibliographic note, p. 107.)

HIMMELWEIT, H. T., HALSEY, A. H., and OPPENHEIM, A. N., "The Views of Adolescents on Some Aspects of the Social Class Structure." (See bibliographic note, p. 83.)

JANKE, L. L., and HAVIGHURST, R. J., "Relations Between Ability and Social Status in a Midwestern Community II," *Journal of Educational Psychology*, 36 (November, 1945), pp. 499-509.

KAUFMAN, Harold F., "Members of a Rural Community as Judges of Prestige Rank." (See bibliographic note, p. 107.)

————, "Prestige Classes in a New York Rural Community." (See bibliographic note, p. 107.)

NEUGARTEN, Bernice L., "Social Class and Friendship Among School Children," *American Journal of Sociology*, 51 (January, 1946), pp. 305-313.

OYLER, Merton D., "Neighborhood Standing and Population Changes in Johnson and Robertson Counties, Kentucky." (See bibliographic note, p. 107.)

[40] Reser, for example, states that the "case is made a little too strong for class and its consequences." Richard M. Reser, *Social Forces*, 28 (December, 1949), p. 211. (Review of *Elmtown's Youth*.)

SCHULER, Edgar A., "Social and Economic Status in a Louisiana Hill Community." (See bibliographic note, p. 107.)

SIMS, Verner M., "Some Correlates of Social Class Identification Among High-School and College Students," *School Review*, 60 (March, 1952), pp. 160-163.

9

"Life, Liberty, and Property"[1]

ALL OF THE STUDIES summarized thus far have clearly indicated that differential status exists in American society. Whether occupation, possessions, or other objective criteria are utilized, or whether individuals are judged by their fellow citizens, it is clear that all of us can be (and are) ranked into socially superior and inferior positions. The study we are about to summarize deals with somewhat different aspects of social status than have been heretofore discussed. It is one of the earlier studies concerned with the broad question, "What is the relationship between a person's attitudes and opinions, and his 'position in life'?"

We have seen that the culture of the United States is replete with references to the fact that "everybody is equal." We have all heard, too, that worker-manager splits, "class struggles," and other expressions of ideological differences between persons in different economic positions belong to an era and a culture other than our own. Differences in opinion on political and economic issues are recognized, but some do not believe these differences are related to a person's own economic position. In professional circles, of course, this popular belief has often been questioned, but it is only within the last decades that sociological and psychological studies have been conducted to investigate this problem objectively.

In 1938 Alfred W. Jones initiated a study specifically designed

[1] Alfred W. Jones, *Life, Liberty, and Property* (Philadelphia, J. B. Lippincott Co., 1941).

to investigate the relationship between certain attitudes and opinions and the economic position of the persons involved. The results of this study were published under the title, *Life, Liberty, and Property*, which is indicative of the kind of attitudes and opinions with which Jones was concerned. Jones describes his field of study as follows: [2]

The issue that we have chosen revolves about the present characteristic device for the ownership of large aggregations of productive wealth, namely, the modern corporation. This is a form of organization that permits a great number of widely scattered individuals to own and benefit from the operation of factories, mines, railroads, and the like, while at the same time the enterprises enjoy centralized management. Social production is thus accompanied by a modified form of individual ownership permitting large aggregations of capital. It is generally recognized that corporate property is the important modern form of productive property in general. Individuals in the population are related to it in a variety of ways—as workers of various sorts, as managers, as owners, and more indirectly as independent producers. *Because it is at the center of things and because of the various different economic relations to it, we have chosen to investigate attitude toward corporate property*, with the expectation that if differences in attitudes are to be found anywhere in our culture, they are to be found here. [3]

Before investigating how Jones attempted to get at the attitudes that people held toward corporate property, let us look at the social setting in which Jones was operating, the place where the attitudes, opinions, and sentiments were developed.

"GUMTOWN," U.S.A.

Jones selected Akron, Ohio, for his study for three reasons: [4] "(1) it is a 'one-industry town' and thus presents a relatively simple picture; (2) it has a high proportion of native-born white

[2] *Ibid.*, pp. 19-20. Used by permission.
[3] Italics, except for the phrase *attitude toward corporate property*, not in original.
[4] *Ibid.*, p. 20.

workers of native parentage; and (3) it has been the scene of exceptionally intense industrial struggle." Each of these reasons is related to the study of attitude toward corporate property and each will be understood more thoroughly if we take a brief look at the growth and struggles of Akron.

The story of Akron is intricately tied up with the story of an amorphous substance extracted from certain tropical trees. Prior to the "coming of age" of the rubber industry, Akron existed for the nearby farmers, supplying their needs and buying some of their produce. By 1900, however, Goodrich, Goodyear, Firestone, and several smaller companies had been established there and the rubber business was off to a good start.

A new era began when the Model T Ford rolled off the assembly line on its Firestone tires. Production and sales increased rapidly. In 1900, Firestone employed twelve men; in 1912, 2900. By 1920 there were 202,000 persons in Akron, representing a 202 per cent increase within the decade, and about 75,000 were rubber workers. Akron and the rubber industry were "booming" in the loudest way. Two depressions later the picture of Akron was that of a city characterized by gloom and room. In 1938, when Jones came to the city, the percentage loss in Akron's population was the greatest of any city over 25,000 in Ohio and the greatest of all but one city over 100,000 in the United States. The Akron *Times Press* reported that *one third* of the population of Akron was on relief or supported by WPA.

The People of Akron

Many ethnic groups are represented in the one third of Akronites who were foreign born. In order of size, the largest of these groups includes Hungarians, Italians, Yugoslavs, Germans, English, Poles, Czechs, Russians, and Austrians. Internal migration accounted for the large remainder of the early population increase of Akron. In an increasing half-circle the rubber companies extended their recruiting arms to the counties surrounding Akron, to western Pennsylvania and Maryland, to West Virginia, south-eastern Ohio, and Kentucky. Finally, Tennessee and the deep South were tapped. The migration reached its peak just after World War I, and when the total was computed it was found that West Virginia had contributed more of her sons and daughters than had any other state. Akron was referred to as the "capital of West Virginia." West Virginians became known as "Snakes" or "Snake Eaters," an indication of what Akronites imagined the diet of West Virginia mountaineers to be. The "Snakes" tended to stand together for a while, but gradually the earlier arrivals have been assimilated. Even the word *Snake* is no longer the fighting word it once was.

Labor Unions and Industrial Conflict

The early attempts of the Akron rubber workers to organize were met with repeated failures. The few strikes attempted were, if possible, even less successful. Perhaps the desire to organize and engage in concerted action was not sufficiently strong in the large horde of single males who seemed to have no intention of settling in Akron.

Reduced wages, the speed-up, the threat of decentralization of the rubber industry, and many other factors gradually produced changes among the rubber workers. The workers themselves were ready for organization but "help from above" did not come until the summer of 1933, when it was read in an abbreviated version of section 7*a* of the N.I.R.A. that "The N.R.A. gives workers the right to organize." This was the message that was repeated fifty thousand times in the form of handbills distributed by the Central Labor Union. In a few weeks, locals of the A.F. of L. were organized in each of the major rubber companies.

The period was also noted for many spontaneous work stoppages at the various rubber companies. January, 1936, will be remembered as the date of the first full-fledged sit-down strike. Its success at Firestone touched off an epidemic of similar affairs at other rubber companies. A month later a thirty-three-day strike was held at Goodyear. The issues involved were hotly argued on the verbal level through the medium of full-page advertisements in Akron's newspapers. The argument was almost conducted on a physical level when the street cleaning force of Akron, escorted by the police, attempted to tear down the picket shanties which had been hastily constructed outside the Goodyear gates. Violence was avoided, but feelings ran high.

In the years that followed, a major (eight-week) strike was held at Firestone and many companies endured numerous sit-down and wildcat strikes. The rubber companies were showing their resentment toward unionization through speeches, formation of company unions, and through the creation of a "Law and Order League," whose members were editorially labeled "vigilantes" by the Akron *Beacon Journal*.

We are now up to the period when Jones arrived in Akron to investigate "attitudes toward corporate property." Perhaps the preceding story of Akron will let us agree with Jones that "if there are differences in attitudes between economic groups, we may expect to find them around this issue and in this particular place...." [5]

DETERMINING ATTITUDES TOWARD CORPORATE PROPERTY

The purpose of Jones's study, we will recall, was to study the relationship between attitudes toward corporate property and the economic position of the people involved. It is easily recognized that he probably could not have obtained meaningful results by asking a few hundred people, "What is your attitude toward corporate property?" Jones, in fact, decided that it was best not to use the "opinion poll" type of questioning at all. Instead, he selected a number of respondents, how we will see later, and related to each one several brief stories that involved the rights of corporate property ("big business," "the banks," and the like) on the one hand, and the desires, needs, or "rights" of

[5] *Ibid.*, p. 22.

individuals, on the other. At the end of each story, the respondent was asked to tell what he thought about the action described.

This methodology is particularly fascinating when we realize that Jones's sample consisted of 1705 persons. Every person was told each of the seven stories and their responses were all recorded.

A few words should be said about the scoring of the responses. Jones used a five-point scale to evaluate the answers of his respondents. One of the stories, for example, dealt with unemployed coal miners who stole coal from the shut-down mines. Some of the coal they burned in their own furnaces, some they sold. After respondents were asked what they thought about the action on the part of the miners, their answers were scored as follows: [6]

Response	Numerical Weight
Unqualified approval	0
Qualified approval	1
Neutral	2
Qualified disapproval	3
Unqualified disapproval	4

In a similar manner the respondents' answers to the other six stories received a score. In this way a total numercial score could be obtained which combined an individual's score on each of the seven stories. Individual could be compared with individual and group could be contrasted with group with regard to their attitude toward corporate property.

It should be made clear that most of Jones's respondents did not respond in terms of the above categories, that is, they were not asked to "check" if they "approved," "approved with qualifications," and so on, of the action described. The people simply told the interviewers what they thought about the story in their own words. A numerical score was attached to their responses in order to make possible some kind of statistical compilation of the data.

[6] *Ibid.*, p. 158. Used by permission.

The Sample

A total of 1705 Akronites was selected. Jones defines fourteen separate subgroups within the sample. The number of interviews obtained from persons in each of the subgroups was as follows: [7]

1. Control Group (303). A random sample from the alphabetical list in the city directory.
2. Business Leaders (18). Selected leaders of various enterprises, including rubber companies.
3. Chemists (24). A random sample from two lists, the membership list of the American Chemical Society and the list of employees of a large rubber company.
4. Farmers (22). This sample was obtained through a house-to-house canvass along roads radiating from two villages near Akron.
5. Employee Association Rubber Workers (37). The "Red Apples," usually met at their headquarters.
6. Female Office Workers (97). A random selection obtained chiefly from a list of recent graduates of a secretarial school, but also from a list of "business girls" registered with the local Y.W.C.A.
7. Teachers (40). Thirty-three teachers were randomly selected from the Akron School Directory, seven picked up in the general random sampling.
8. Non-C.I.O. Rubber Workers (69). A random selection of production employees of two large rubber companies. C.I.O. members, but not members of Employee Association, were first removed.
9. Small Merchants (52). A random selection of thirty independent grocers and twenty-two proprietors of service stations.
10. Clergymen (26). A random selection of religious leaders, but Catholic priests (both Roman and Greek Orthodox) weighted more heavily because of their larger congregations.
11. W.P.A. White Collar Workers (72). These were obtained from a list compiled by the local Works Progress Administration from its files.

[7] *Ibid.*, pp. 372-375. Used by permission. The total number of persons in the fourteen subgroups is 1122. The remainder of the 1705 interviews were obtained from two general sources: (1) special categories such as four Negro insurance men, female factory workers, and adults attending classes conducted by WPA, and (2) groups consisting of foreigners including Serbs, Germans, Syrians, Italians, Rumanians, and Hungarians.

12. A.F. of L. Members (59). A random sample of members of building trade unions.
13. W.P.A. Manual Workers (110). A list obtained from W.P.A. files by a method similar to that of W.P.A. White Collar Workers.
14. C.I.O. Rubber Workers (193). A random sample from membership lists of two of the largest locals of United Rubber Workers of America plus names taken from the city directory.

Two significant facts should be abstracted from this summary of the make-up of the sample. First, there exists a large control group that was selected at random. This group should be representative of all Akronites. Second, slightly over half of the *individuals* chosen, when the control group is excluded, are, somewhat loosely, manual workers. Jones has this to say about the representatives of the sample: [8] "We cannot claim that the 1705 represented a uniform, proportional coverage of the city. For example, no special effort was made to include in the sample certain sections of the population, such as physicians, lawyers, the employees of manufacturing enterprises other than the rubber companies, municipal employees, etc. Small numbers of them appeared in the control group, but in the sample as a whole they are not given proportional representation."

THE STORIES AND THE ATTITUDES ELICITED

We cannot, in this summary, give a detailed description of how each of the fourteen subgroups within the sample reacted to each of the seven stories told to them. All of the stories will be reprinted and a selected number of responses to them will be described. In addition, we will present a description of some of the groups, while conclusions will be drawn from the data on the entire sample.

I. Bootleg Coal: [9] Anthracite coal mining in Eastern Pennsylvania was a "sick industry" even before the depression. In the 1930's still

[8] *Ibid.,* pp. 375-376. Used by permission.
[9] *Ibid.,* pp. 144-145. Used by permission.

more mines shut down, the companies deciding to keep their coal in the ground until prices for it should go up. There was great unemployment and distress among the miners. In these years the unemployed miners began going into the idle mines and taking out the coal. They did this without the permission of the companies that own the mines, and without interference of the local police, so that no violence or bloodshed resulted. They have both burned the coal themselves and sold it.

The question is, now, what do you think of this sort of action on the part of the unemployed miners?

The farmers divided fairly evenly on this issue. A distinction was made, by those who disapproved, between burning the coal and selling it, the latter eliciting greater disapproval. Responses of the farmers included expressions such as, " 'Times are different now than in the past,' 'These are unusual times,' 'If I wasn't properly fed myself, I believe I would do that,' and 'A man wouldn't have a right to go in my granary and take my wheat.' " [10] When these and the remaining responses were scored it was found that farmers averaged 1.9 on this question (zero represents the most unfavorable attitude toward corporate property; four stands for a high regard for it.)

Only one of the business executives indicated even qualified approval of the miners' behavior. The vast majority indicated quite definitely that they disapproved, but intermingled with their disapproval Jones detected a certain amount of sympathy for their colder and hungrier fellow citizens. He found it expressed in two ways: [11]

The first was in a certain fierceness. "I think the same as I would if you should go out to the warehouse and help yourself to tires for your car and your friends'. It's plain stealing." Perhaps the speaker really felt it was not the same thing, but he wished to leave no crack in the door. "If such actions spread to other industries, we would be in a bad condition." The fierceness comes out in other remarks, as well. We say it is a form of sympathy, but perhaps it would be more correct to say

[10] *Ibid.*, p. 163.
[11] *Ibid.*, p. 172. Used by permission.

that it is a substitute for the sympathy which was more directly expressed by some of the others; "There should be some way to take care of this situation." "It was up to the State of Pennsylvania to take care of the miners." The president of one of the rubber companies reduced his total score from 32 to 30 by refusing to commit himself on this issue. All he would say was that "preservation is the first law." Another said: "They had to live," but the action did not fail to be "confiscation of property," and "They have no right to help themselves to these resources."

The C.I.O. rubber workers, averaging 0.8, scored the lowest of any group on this question. They were quite definite in their approval of the miners' action and frequently identified with the miners. "I hold right with the miners. They were forced to do it." "They were hungry. I'd do the same." "They had to keep warm. I would have done the same thing." [12]

It turned out that the office girls scored about the same as the 1.5 averaged by the random sample of Akronites: [13]

From the majority, we heard comments such as this: "I didn't always feel this way, but lately I've been thinking that when some people have *so* much, other people have the right to at least the essentials of life." "They needed the coal. They were justified in taking and using it because it was for their self-preservation." "They *really* needed the coal.". . ."Of course the miners had no real right to the coal, but they tried to help themselves which is a good thing, and if they had a right to burn it, they also had a right to sell it and buy food and clothing. I suppose they were in real need." This was scored as a qualified answer, as were these two: "Since they needed the money and the heat, it would be all right, but it wasn't exactly honest toward the company." "They went against the law, but just the same, self-preservation is necessary."

II. The Utility Stay-In Strike: [14] In early 1938 negotiations took place between the Utilities Workers' Organizing Committee and the Consumers Power Co. of Michigan. The Union wanted a renewal of its contract with the company, which was about to expire, and a year's

[12] *Ibid.*, p. 260.
[13] *Ibid.*, pp. 198-199. Used by permission.
[14] *Ibid.*, p. 145. Used by permission.

guarantee against wage cuts. The company refused this and negotiations broke down at the same time as the contract expired. A strike followed, in which the workers took possession of the company's power plants, in the Saginaw Valley area, and expelled the company's superintendents and foremen. During the several days that this stay-in-work strike lasted, the property of the company was not damaged in any way. Nor was it a sitdown strike, since the workers continued to operate the power plant, so that the interests of the consumers did not suffer. Although the company officials were strongly opposed to this strike action, they settled with the union after a time and it is safe to say that the union won better terms by this action than they would have won in any other way.

What do you think of what the workers did in this case?

Every one of the business leaders except one, who refused to answer the question, disapproved wholeheartedly of the action of the power plant workers. Jones tells us "the workers were condemned with a bitterness that sometimes resulted in long and irrelevant speeches." [15] If the following is typical of their speeches, the label is apparently fitting: [16]

That was damn foolishness just like the TVA, Guffey Coal Bill, Labor Relations Act, and all this Union racket. Roosevelt has gone fishing today. The sooner he gets drowned the better it will be for the whole country. He is just like Hitler and the only reason he does not act like Hitler is because it would not be politically expedient.

The trouble with the present times is that America does not need labor unions of European background. To meet our problems they will have to be American—derived from American tradition. The C.I.O. had its origin in coal—a natural resource—not a man-made industry like rubber. Because the rubber industry is man-made it is movable—not fixed as natural resources are.

The "Red Apples" (rubber workers who were members of Employee Associations), who were similar to the control group in their responses to the Bootleg Coal story, answered more nearly like the business leaders with regard to this story. Although some registered qualified approval, in that they thought the stay-

[15] *Ibid.*, p. 173.
[16] *Ibid.*, p. 173. Used by permission.

in strike was better than the sit-down type, the majority thought
the workers "went too far."

Interestingly enough, the clergy approved of the workers'
behavior more than any other one group. (C.I.O. rubber workers
scored *almost* as low as the clergy.) Jones believes that the priests
and ministers were primarily influenced by three factors: (1) the
"strike" worked out well for the workers; (2) the interests of the
public were protected; and (3) no violence took place. Of the
three, the lack of violence seemed the most important.

III. Goodrich Decentralization Threat: [17] The B. F. Goodrich Company in early 1938 asked the workers in its plant in Akron, Ohio, to
accept a wage cut and a longer working week. The company maintained that if the workers refused, some departments would have to
be moved away from Akron, involving the removal of some four or
five thousand jobs. They held that only in this way could they compete with the other rubber companies which already had a smaller
proportion of their operations in Akron, where a strong union exists
and maintains high wages. Assume that the Goodrich Company can
stay in business and continue to pay the old wages. They will not make
much money, if any, but they will at least not be driven into bank-
ruptcy. Assume also that if they move out of Akron they will be able
to hire workers cheaper, make more money and pay more dividends,
at least at first.

The workers, at a meeting held by the union, refused to accept the
wage cut. The company now has the next move.

What would you think of its action if the company should move
these jobs away from Akron?

All Akron, with the exception of the business leaders, seemed
to disapprove of the contemplated move of the Goodrich Company. The farmers and chemists, with scores of 2.2 and 2.5 respectively were the only other groups whose scores fell toward
the "big-business" end of the scale. (A score of 2 is neutral.)

The small businessmen of Akron had an interesting reaction to
this story. As a group, they averaged about a "qualified disapproval" (1.2) on this question, but there appeared to be two

[17] *Ibid.*, pp. 146-147. Used by permission.

forces tugging at them. Their own immediate welfare could be at stake but yet some could not forget they too were business-men and would like to reserve for themselves the right to move if they so pleased. Inasmuch as more of the small business owners scored zero on this question than they did on any other one, and in the light of their over-all low scores, it seems the conflict was finally resolved in favor of the workers.

IV. Farm Mortgage Foreclosure:[18] During good times a farmer in the Middle West borrowed a considerable sum of money from a big Chicago bank, and gave a mortgage on his farm as security. When the depression came he could no longer meet the payments on his loan, and the bank, after waiting a reasonable time, foreclosed. They started legal proceedings and the local sheriff advertised a foreclosure sale. But on the day of the advertised sale, the neighboring farmers gathered on the property to be sold at auction and acted in such a threatening way that no genuine bid could be made. The farmer himself bid one dollar, and since this was the highest bid, he bought his farm back for this amount, which was all the bank got in place of the mortgage. The mortgage was lifted and the farmer remained in possession instead of being driven off the land.

What do you think of the action of the neighbors?

Only the business leaders, with their score of 3.9 out of a possible 4, could fully see the bank's point of view in this story. The control group of a random sample of Akronites split fairly evenly on this issue. One hundred and thirty-six completely approved of the action that effectually prohibited the sale of the "old home-stead," whereas 126 felt very strongly that "the bank should not be expected to make good the farmer's loss." [19]

Small businessmen were quite unlike their big brothers when it came to the fate of the near-dispossessed farmer. Two thirds of the merchants registered opinions indicating approval of the action of the neighbors: [20]

"I think the bank should have compromised with the farmer and given him a chance." "The farmer had no chance—not his fault."

[18] *Ibid.,* pp. 147-148. Used by permission.
[19] *Ibid.,* p. 177.
[20] *Ibid.,* p. 232. Used by permission.

"That's pretty hard to say, buddy,—it would be against the law, but I approve." "The neighbors were a help. It was hard to lose what he had saved." "The bank should have been more lenient. The mortgage was reasonable security for the debt." "The bank should give more time, or make other arrangements." "They should compromise." "The farmer should fulfill his obligation to the bank afterwards." But, "The neighbors were wrong; that man, when he borrowed the money, he borrowed it in good faith, and he should pay it back. If such things would be allowed then we may as well stop doing business." (Note the *we*.) "I don't like the neighbors to interfere." "The farmers were all wet. Of course there are banks that only foreclose on mortgages that are nearly paid so that they can make money on the properties; but in most cases the money loaned belongs to investors or depositors and it is hard on them to lose their money." "I don't think it was a legal sale. I don't agree to it." "I don't approve of the act of the neighbors but the bank should have given a moratorium." "They should have followed the golden rule. They were both wrong."

The farmers themselves were better able to see the bank's side of the story than the several groups of rubber workers and even the teachers, merchants, and white-collar WPA workers. Perhaps their own optimism prevented them from imagining themselves in the position of their less fortunate fellow farmer; perhaps they did not want it to appear that they were favoring their own kind. *Why* people respond (and presumably think) as they do is more difficult to discover than *how* they respond!

V. Expulsion by Tear-Gas: [21] In 1937 there was a sitdown strike against the Fansteel Metallurgical Corporation, in North Chicago. After warning the workers who had occupied the plant, and ordering them to leave, police and deputies threw tear-gas bombs into the building. This succeeded in dislodging the strikers. Tear-gas, as you know, is unpleasant, but not fatal in its effects.

What do you think of the action of the local authorities, such as the chief of police, in ordering that tear-gas be used?

Here again we notice something of a true split in the control group. Fifty-seven per cent disapproved of the use of tear gas,

[21] *Ibid.*, p. 148. Used by permission.

while 41 per cent registered approval. In both cases, only a handful qualified their answers.

Many people from all walks of life are willing to line up on the anti-corporation side when the case involves evicting a man from his home or moving a major industry from the city. Many of these same people, however, stated that they did not approve of strikes and particularly sit-down strikes and therefore could condone the use of tear gas on the striking workers.

The chemists, for example, tended to score a little higher than average on the whole interview, but scored much higher on this story. Only three of the twenty-four chemists disapproved of the use of tear gas. Typical of the remarks of chemists who registered approval of the use of tear gas were the following: [22]

I realize that this is contrary to my other answers, but the men should have left the plant and negotiated outside." "I see nothing wrong in the use of tear-gas by the police—better than a club or a gun." "I'd say to use it. The sitdown strike is destructive." "Some method had to be used." "That is the kind of police we need." "I do not approve of sitdown strikes *at all*."

The fact that the gas proved to be a relatively nonviolent means of removing the workers (more severe methods *could* be used) was brought up quite often. Akron clergy, for instance, scored higher (2.7) on this story than they did on any other and it appeared that they considered the use of tear gas less regrettable than the potential violence that sit-down strikes might elicit.

VI. Run-away Dress Shop: [23] In 1936, in New York, a strong union called the International Ladies Garment Workers Union and the various companies manufacturing women's dresses worked out and signed a standard agreement. One clause of the agreement provided that the company must not move its factory beyond the New York City five cent fare zone.

Later in the year the workers of the Blue Dale Dress Company came to work one morning as usual, and found the shop closed, the com-

[22] *Ibid.*, p. 194. Used by permission.
[23] *Ibid.*, pp. 149-150. Used by permission.

pany's property in the form of sewing machines moved out and themselves out of jobs. The company was later found in Archibald, Pa.,
far beyond any question of five cent fare, so the union took the case
to court. Toward the end of 1936, Judge McCook handed down a
decision fully upholding the union, upholding the contract, and ordering the company to return to New York.

As you know, any contract which is obtained by the use of force is
not considered to be legally binding. Many persons, among them authorities in these matters, would say that in this case the union was
strong enough to force the company to sign away its old traditional
right to move its property wherever it pleases.

Now here is a contract which prevents the company from moving
its property freely. Do you approve or disapprove of such a contract?

The highest average score on this question, for any group, was
2.24. Seven (out of eighteen) business leaders stated this contract
was fair and their average score was only slightly higher than
neutral. The remaining eleven labeled the contract "absurd" and
seemed to feel the union must have used some kind of force to
get such a contract in the first place.

Clearly this story involved a right of corporate property—the
right to move their property if they are losing money, deriving
what they consider too meager profit, or if for some other reason
they want to relocate. Some of those opposed to the contract that
would restrain them from moving pointed out somewhat un-
imaginatively simply that this is a "free country." Others emphasized the fact that a person (including the fictional person,
the corporation) should be able to do what he wants to with his
own property.

Those who thought the contract was fair insisted that corporations should not be able to do with their property as they will
and that it is fair to sign a contract that so restricts them. Such
individuals felt that corporations owe a certain stability to the
workers and to the town in general. The companies come to
town, hire local workers, entice others to migrate from neighboring states and then leave when a place is found to hire lower-paid
workers. C.I.O. rubber workers, and other, seem to think that

the cheaper production costs would not be passed on to the consumer but would merely result in fatter profits.

VII. Rent Eviction: [24] During the depression a bank in a big city obtained title to a tenement house for poor people, in which the average rent per apartment was $15 per month. When the agents of the bank who managed the building went over the records, they found that one of the tenants, who was unemployed, was several months behind in his rent. Eviction proceedings were started, but when the officers and the movers arrived to move the furniture of the man, his wife and three children out into the street, they found the halls and stairways of the building crowded with neighbors, who prevented the moving of the man's belongings.

What do you think of the action of the neighbors?

We must remember that about the time this study was made it was reported that *one third* of all Akronites were either unemployed or working for the WPA. Those who were working at the time may have recently been out of work or may have had reason to worry about the permanency of their jobs. In addition, rent evictions were not infrequent during the 1930's. Those who have witnessed meager household possessions being piled in the street next to their homeless and often hopeless owners can well imagine the pictures that were recalled when Jones told this story to his respondents.

It is not surprising, then, that Akronites in general (two thirds of the control group) found nothing wrong in the action of the neighbors who averted at least one re-enactment of an unpleasant but not unfamiliar scene. Their comments contained several themes: (1) no man should be put out of his dwelling and left without a roof over his head; (2) it is not the fault of the renter (in general) if he cannot pay rent, for jobs are scarce; and (3) the government should somehow take care of the matter. Thus, the majority concluded that the man's neighbors did no wrong *in view of the times.* It is interesting how frequently, in response

[24] *Ibid.,* p. 150. Used by permission.

to all the stories, a reference was made to changed morality by comments that certain behavior *would* have been wrong in the past, or that certain behavior is acceptable *today*.

These, then, are the seven stories which Jones told the 1705 Akronites. We have seen that people responded to them in different ways and indicated varying degrees of a favorable or an unfavorable attitude toward corporate property. Next, we will compare some of the groups with one another and with the control group.

Business Leaders

Eight of the eighteen business leaders interviewed by Jones were top executives of rubber companies. They differed little, however, from the remaining ten leaders of large enterprises such as a bank president, or a head of a publishing house. All eighteen are near the top of Akron's "social heap."

The average total score of the business leaders was 29.1 out of a possible 32 points, where 32 represents the highest regard for corporate property.[25] Usually the business leaders were quite definite in their disapproval of action that was against the interests of corporate property. Nothing should come before profits. In the case of the contemplated move of the Goodrich Company (Story III), one business leader commented: [26] "This is not a moral question, but a matter of sheer business. The company owes nothing to the workers or to the town. Its only obligation is to make money for the stockholders. If the management con-

[25] In addition to the seven stories told respondents, Jones had an eighth item, the scores for which also ranged from zero through 4. This makes a total possible score of 32. The eighth item, not strictly a story but a ranking procedure, has been omitted from this review, since it may require somewhat detailed explanations. Briefly, respondents were asked to imagine that they could dispose of the net profits of a given company and were given a list from which they were to choose which category (stockholders, workers, consumers, and the like) should benefit first from the profits of the company. The scores assigned to their rankings represented complete respect for the stockholders' rights, at one extreme, to complete disregard for them at the other.

[26] *Ibid.*, p. 176. Used by permission.

siders morals in this case, the stockholders ought to vote for a change in management."

No other group even approached the 29.1 score of the business leaders. The union rubber workers, by contrast, scored 6.2, whereas the average of the random sample of Akronites was 12.3.

Chemists

The Akron rubber chemists make up the most highly trained group of technical people in the rubber industry. Twenty-four of them were interviewed by Jones and he found that they were the most educated group in his sample. All were college graduates and ten had advanced degrees.

This group (with the average of 19.5) scored closest to the business leaders. The range of scores is the unique factor about the chemists. They scored all the way from zero to 32, and there was no tendency to cluster about any certain point.[27]

Jones was unable to discover anything in the objective backgrounds of the chemists to account for the split within their ranks and the great range in their attitudes toward corporate property. The group, of course, was small and Jones suspected that there may have been personality traits involved that accounted for their opposing reactions.

The Red Apples

This is the group of rubber workers who have chosen not to join the United Rubber Workers of America, but instead, have organized in what are called Employee Associations, or sometimes, Independent Unions or Company Unions. Their nickname was first used by the union workers who suspected them of trying to curry the favor of management by joining the associations which the unions believe are sponsored by management. The company officials and the leaders of employee associations, how-

[27] Farmers, for example, also averaged 19.5 but there was a greater tendency for their scores to cluster about the average. For the chemists the standard deviation from the mean was 7.70; for the farmers, 4.78.

ever, state positively that there is no connection between them. It is known that the Red Apples consider themselves to be a little different from other groups. It is known, too, that this group is disliked by the unions. Jones discovered that their attitude toward corporate property was like that of what might be termed the "middle groups." The scores of the Red Apples ranged from zero to 32, but there was a tendency for them to cluster about 18. Their average score of 17.6 fell about halfway between the score of business leaders and that of the union rubber workers.

The members of employee associations resembled the rubber workers as far as the type of work they performed and, thus, the wages they received. Why the Red Apples were so unlike their fellow rubber workers with regard to their attitude toward corporate property is largely left unexplained.

The "Little Business" Men

"The statements issued by the representatives of "little business" indicate that their economic demands are much the same as those of "big business." Both are against high taxation, against interference with wages and hours, against the Wagner Labor Relations Act, and against "extravagance" in government administration. Little business differs, as is to be expected, in wanting rigid enforcement of the antitrust laws, restriction by taxation of chain store operations, and measures directed against manufacturer-controlled consumer outlets. In such matters little business naturally seeks its own ends. In other matters of government policy it has seemed to consider that its interests lie with those of big business and against many of the measures taken by the Roosevelt administration, and backed by labor." [28]

Thus there were two forces tugging at the little businessmen. Their attitude toward corporate property turned out to be average, that is, very much like that found in the control group. Statistically, at least, their attitudes were more similar to the population of Akron as a whole than any other group studied by

[28] *Ibid.*, p. 225. Used by permission.

Jones. But it should be noted that the average for the small merchant (12.1) is considerably closer to that of the C.I.O. rubber workers (6.3) than it is to the 29.1 scored by the business leaders.

The Clergy

Eight Roman Catholic priests scored, respectively, 22, 17, 15, 11, 8, 8, 8, and 1, their average score being 11.2. Their remarks showed that there is no monolithic body of social doctrine in the Catholic church, at least as far as we can judge from our small sample of the Akron clergy. In diversity and quality, the free comment of the priests was just what we might have expected to hear from any group of Akronites that scored slightly below the general average. In taking one side or the other, the eight showed in various mixtures, compassion, harshness, gentleness, anger, and regard for the law. On the whole they showed a greater regard for personal rights than for considerations of property.[29]

The protestant ministers averaged four points higher than the Catholic priests' 11.2. The highest scoring minister, an Episcopalian, scored 29. His comments usually centered on property rights: [30]

"A general disregard of property rights will result in chaos," he said, and struck consistently to this point throughout the interview. "The miners were within their rights in burning the coal, but not in selling it." "The strikers in Michigan were lawless. Again, it was a matter of property rights." He listened to the Goodrich story, looked down at his desk, and picked up a paperweight. "This is mine. I have a right to move it where I choose as long as I don't move it onto some other person's property." Following the next story, he said, "The farmer's neighbors were kindly. However, they acted merely on their emotions. They might have acted differently had they owned stock in the bank." On the rent eviction case—"The property owners were within their rights. The action of the neighbors showed a commendable sympathy, but it was ill advised."

Ideas more typical of the majority of ministers appear in the following comments of another protestant minister: [31]

[29] *Ibid.*, p. 213. Used by permission.
[30] *Ibid.*, p. 220. Used by permission.
[31] *Ibid.*, p. 221. Used by permission.

When we told him the story of the Michigan stay-in strike, he remarked: "We are living in a time when new codes are being set up. It is awfully hard to approve of this action, but I suppose I do—with qualifications. It's a new angle. At least the public is not injured." To the farm mortgage foreclosure story, he said: "I would give unqualified approval to what the man's neighbors did. It is up to us to revamp our thinking." Along with seven out of the eleven ministers, the same man sided with the other tenants who prevented the rent eviction. "Fifteen or twenty years ago we would have condemned this action. I would now be one of the group who would commend the solidarity of the neighbors."

The average score of the clergy as a whole was 12.0, just slightly under the average for the control group. All in all, the clergy of Akron seem to be more on the side of the worker than the owners of corporate property.

C.I.O. Rubber Workers

The union rubber workers had the lowest score (6.2) of any group studied by Jones. Nineteen per cent of them scored zero. Not quite 10 per cent of the scores fell on the half of the scale that indicated a neutral or favorable attitude toward corporate property. No business leaders, on the other hand, were even neutral, and the scores of 90 per cent indicated the highest regard for corporate property. Thus, there would seem to be a wide gulf separating the opinion of the business leaders from the C.I.O. rubber workers.

There is a significant difference, but of course not as great a one, between the responses of the union workers and their cohorts who belong to employee unions. The difference was most noticeable, as we would suspect, in those stories that related the militant action of labor unions, Story II, The Utility Stay-in Strike, and Story V, Expulsion by Tear Gas (of sit-down strikers). In the case of the tear gas, for example, the vast majority of Red Apples sounded like the farmers, the chemists, and the business leaders in their approval of the action, whereas the union rubber workers disapproved by comments which showed "plain, hot workers' indignation." [32]

"The police forgot that they are supposed to protect the workers as well as the factory. When a man has a gun and some gas shells he feels like he owns the town. I'd say put the sons of bitches in the penitentiary and throw the key away." "I think the chief of police ought to get a good dose of it himself." "The workers had a right to stay there until the dispute was settled. I disapprove of tear-gas. Fumes came into houses up here in the Goodyear district when they had that riot and made children sick." "Gas is a disgrace to a community." "I think the chief of police should be kicked off his job. No one ought to interfere. The workers ought to be left to fight their own fight in their own way." "It was a dirty shame. The working class is doing nothing but fighting for its living the whole time." "I think the police go wild many times, specially the new cops. They had no business throwing tear-gas." "I think it's a dirty shame. It doesn't matter a damn if it's fatal or not. Things like that wouldn't help settle things sensibly. People are convinced that the law is against them and for the company. The police should show the workers that they are just as much for them as for big business. We know something about them in Akron." "It's okay to use tear-gas on criminals, but I don't consider these workers criminals." "If the workers would be left alone they would settle everything." "Workers don't sit down unless they're forced to by the big man. The cops and the government are always on the company's side anyhow. The workers never make enough." "These cases require arbitration, not violence." "I had some of this gas at the Goodyear riot, and I don't like it."

Perhaps even more enlightening is the difference in attitudes shown by the Red Apples and union workers toward the foreclosure attempt of the farm mortgage (Story IV). This story had really nothing to do with unions but did involve a conflict between individual rights and the rights of corporate property owners. The C.I.O. workers were willing to grant the farmer more "rights" than was any other Akron group. The workers who belonged to Employee Associations, on the other hand, once again responded more in favor of the owners of corporate prop-

[32] *Ibid.*, pp. 254-255. Used by permission.

erty. The average score of the Red Apples was the same as the chemists and was higher than that of the teachers, farmers, office workers, and small merchants but not as high as business leaders.

The General Reaction of Akronites

So far we have seen how various special groups of Akronites feel about corporate property. What we need now is a composite picture of these several groups, a picture of how Akronites in general reacted to the attitude-provoking stories. We need, too, to tie this study in with what we have already learned about social stratification in an effort to see more clearly how a person's position in the production system is related to certain of his attitudes and beliefs.

The generalizations that are made about the population of Akron as a whole are based on the data concerning the control group of 303 Akronites. These people were selected at random from the city directory and, since their number is sizable, there is reason to believe that the group should approximate the proportions of the total Akron population. Generalizations concerning certain groups of Akronites, however, are based on the specific studies of these groups. In this way, larger numbers of the desired segments of the population are used as a basis for generalization.

Figure 7 shows the attitude scores of the four groups, C.I.O. rubber workers, business leaders, composite manual workers,[33] and composite middle groups.[34] The most noticeable fact about the graphs is the tendency of the scores of the C.I.O. rubber workers to pile up at the opposite end of the scale from the scores of the business leaders. We notice, too, that the composite middle groups of Akronites exhibit a wide range of attitudes toward corporate property; the spread for this group is, of course, greater than the two with the extreme scores.

[33] The manual workers include C.I.O. rubber workers, non-C.I.O. rubber workers, A.F. of L. members, and WPA manual workers.

[34] The middle groups include chemists, female office workers, teachers, ministers, and small merchants.

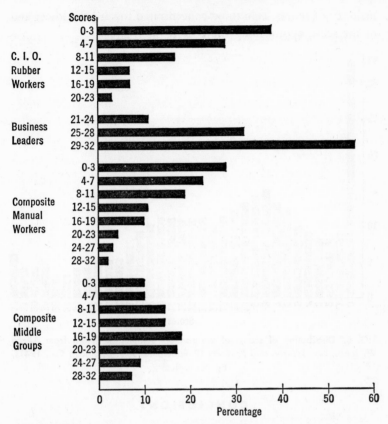

FIG. 7. Distribution of scores in percentages. (Redrawn from Alfred W. Jones,
Life, Liberty, and Property [Philadelphia, J. B. Lippincott Co., 1941], by
permission)

When we plot the scores of the control group, as in Figure 8,
we see that the extreme scores still stand out; the very low scores
are more predominant than the very high simply because there
are more people (union rubber men) who tended to achieve low
scores than there are those who achieved extremely high scores
(business leaders).

In addition to the cleavage or split in attitudes we note that the majority of scores seem to be concentrated toward the lower end of the scale, approaching the center.

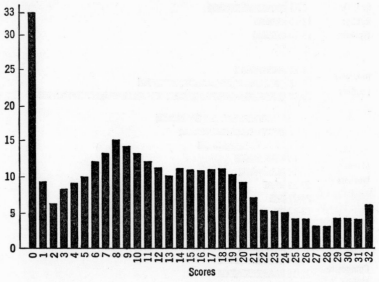

FIG. 8. Distribution of scores of the random sample. (Redrawn from Alfred W. Jones, *Life, Liberty, and Property* [Philadelphia, J. B. Lippincott Co., 1941], by permission)

CONCLUSIONS

We are ready for two conclusions: (1) some of the population of Akron showed a tendency to *extreme* attitudes toward corporate property; (2) the bulk of the population showed an even greater tendency toward an *intermediate* attitude toward corporate property, which was, however, more toward the lower end of the scale. Let us investigate these trends somewhat further.

1. Tendency Toward Polarization of Attitudes

Jones suggests that everything about the background and present make-up (1941) of Akron would tend to produce a great polarization of attitudes if such be found in any American city.

Chief among the unique features of Akron is the fact that the history of labor-management disagreements was not a peaceful one. Akron has the distinction of being the first city in the world where sit-down strikes were first employed on a large-scale basis. Sit-down strikes and other types of militant action between management and labor could be considered conducive to making Akronites "choose sides" between the major participants.

Jones points to still other characteristics that would tend to promote a true split in attitudes toward corporate property.[35]

Akron is a one-industry town, and the theory can be advanced and defended that extreme points of view and attitudes build up more readily and quickly the more homogeneous the population. Not only is social interaction in Akron heightened because all have in common an interest in the rubber industry, but there is also, owing to the preponderance of "American" stock, an unusual absence of ethnic heterogeneity. Furthermore, if extreme attitudes develop out of suffering, we might expect to find them in the city that had been earlier keyed to such high expectations and had then been so hard hit by the depression.

In view of these considerations it is not surprising that a tendency toward cleavage to the two extremes was discovered when the attitude-scores were plotted. Had this tendency been more pronounced, that is, had more of the cases been included at the extremes, we would be able to say that the population was split with respect to the attitudes of its members into two quite different groups; a case *could* have been made for the "class consciousness" of Akronites.

2. Tendency Toward Conformity with the Compromising Position

Even greater than the tendency toward polarization of attitudes, however, was that toward conformity to an intermediate or compromising attitude. Slightly over three fourths of the scores of the control group fell between 3 and 27. Jones calls this range the area of "central tendency," inasmuch as people so scor-

---

[35] *Ibid.*, p. 331. Used by permission.

ing do not clearly "side" with either corporate property or personal rights. Fully half of the control group, furthermore, scored within a narrower range, between 6 and 18 points.

If more cases had been distributed throughout the middle range and particularly if the curve indicated a definite reduction of cases as the extreme positions were approached, we would be able to speak of an absence of cleavage in attitudes. Since the actual situation approaches this hypothetical one, Jones interprets the findings as indicative of a certain thread of morality that runs through the attitudes of all, or most, of the population. This middle-of-the-road attitude he terms the "central morality" of Akronites.

The "Central Morality"

From his analysis of the attitudes of workers, owners, and "middle groups," Jones gathered a rather definite impression of the "central morality" that permeates the attitudes of the various groups.[36]

The central morality is humanitarian and approves of acts in the interest of human welfare and alleviation of suffering even if they entail the infringement of corporate property. It approves of trade unions, and would like to see a well-led, unified, strong labor movement, but one that refrained from violence. The central morality is not pacifist, however, and would even approve of violence if there were wrongdoers that it thinks could be met in no other way.

The central morality would also seem to include concession to corporate property, as evidenced by the fact that over half (55 per cent) of the people whose score fell between 6 and 18 sided with the bank on the farm mortgage issue.

Among the 155 of the control group (303 people) whose scores fell between 6 and 18, minorities varying between 25 and 42 per cent favored the rights of corporate property on stories other than the farm mortgage one.

[36] *Ibid.*, p. 339. Used by permission.

IS AMERICA MIDDLE CLASS?

Let us now combine the major findings. On the one hand, people of different social status tend to exhibit different attitudes and opinions. On the other hand, Jones has shown us that a certain "central morality" characterizes the collective opinion of a large mass of the people.

Can these findings be interpreted to mean that, by and large, Americans are middle-class people with fewer numbers in an "upper" and "lower" class? The answers to this question depend, as usual, upon our definition of "class." In a strictly objective sense, Jones's study has indicated that Akronites can be differentiated according to their economic and social statuses. The differences between the extremes of the hierarchy appear to be rather great. In this sense, then, we are certainly not a "classless" society.

The Akron study has also shown a close association between social status and attitudes. The data is the kind that is utilized by those who think of social classes in a subjective sense, usually defining them as groups of similar status people who think alike on basic issues.[37] But Jones's findings did not indicate any clear dividing line in the status-attitude breakdown that would permit the inference of any particular number of classes. The greatest attitude differences occurred between the extreme categories while intermediate groups formed a gradient series.

It seems best to conclude merely that Jones's study showed a distinct relationship between occupational status and attitudes toward corporate property. Because of the design of the study, we learn little that is directly related to the presence of social classes in Akron; nothing in his data, however, indicates that sharp cleavages exist whereby the population could be separated

[37] Representative of the subjective definition of social class is Centers' description of them as "political and economic interest groups tending to be structured primarily along the lines of socio-economic stratification...." Richard Centers, *The Psychology of Social Classes* (Princeton, Princeton University Press, 1949), p. 210.

into several clear-cut groups on the basis of either objective status differences or ideological differences.

EVALUATION

We will now attempt what might be called a "creative criticism" of *Life, Liberty, and Property*. By that we mean a criticism that is both positive and negative but which always takes as its starting place the point of view and the intent of the author of the study.

Methodology

We have repeatedly pointed out that methodological considerations are important, not because they offer ready footholds from which we can pick away at the entire structure, but because the findings of a study—the real reason for which the study was conducted—are inextricably tied up with the method by which the study was promulgated.

The way in which Jones chose to measure attitudes toward corporate property is a unique departure from the "opinion-poll" study that begins with, "Good morning, madam, I'm making a survey..." and receives, we sometimes suspect, equally stereotyped responses. We somehow sense that the responses of the 1705 Akronites were spontaneous and that they are most likely to represent how people "really" feel about certain issues.

Sometimes, however, the reader may find himself wondering just what sentiments were elicited by the stories told by Jones. The story of the rent eviction will illustrate what we have in mind. It is certain that the story gets at the attitudes people hold toward the financial well-being of the incorporated bank. Perhaps the story also draws a generalized reaction to "the times" or touches off a certain sympathetic feeling for one's fellow man that might have been elicited whether the story concerned man against nature, man against a single individual, or man against a "corporation."

Thus, the unstructured approach used by Jones has a distinct advantage in that it depicts scenes from everyday life to which people can react quite realistically. Its disadvantage could lie in the fact that the stories may have been interpreted differently by different groups of individuals.

Weighting the stories. Perhaps the really pertinent question concerns not *did* the stories get at the attitudes people held toward corporate property but *how much* they did so. Jones weighted each story equally, that is, a score of 3 on one story contributed the same amount to each total score as did a score of 3 on another story. It would seem, however, that a score of 3 or above on the rent eviction case where only one group scored over 2.2 is more meaningful than a score of 3 on the tear-gas story where four of the thirteen special groups scored over 3 and two more scored close to 3.

The problem of weighting is, of course, a technical point and is not one that is easily solved. It seems unlikely that even the most refined techniques of weighting would have altered the findings substantially, particularly those of a more generalizing nature (for example, the tendency toward cleavage in attitudes and the "central morality"). In planning a future study following similar methods, however, the matter of weighting would receive thoughtful consideration.

The Findings

In the first chapter Jones states, "Whatever the defects of method, the subject matter of this opinion study is of first importance." [38] With this we concur.

The over-all findings of Jones's study are quite significant in that they tend both to support and to qualify those of other investigations. He has indicated that there is a clear-cut difference in attitudes between individuals at opposite ends of the economic scale but that the entire range represents more of a gradation of attitudes. A difference in attitudes is exhibited by groups we

[38] Jones, *op. cit.*, p. 22.

would consider occupationally similar (Red Apples and union rubber workers) and a similarity of attitudes is shown by groups we would tend to think of as being different (non-C.I.O. rubber workers and small merchants). Basically, there is a core of opinion that is common to the various economic groups. This Jones calls the "central morality" of Akronites. All of this substantiates what Kornhauser [39] and others have discovered, but seems to temper the findings of those who think in terms of categorical class-differences in attitudes.

It is to be regretted that the scope of Jones's study did not include a direct measure of the relationship, rank by rank, between social status, and attitudes toward corporate property. Since various groups of workers were omitted from his study, the control group alone can be used to get an over-all picture of the relationship in question. If the control group had been ranked on a social status, occupational status, or economic status scale so that individuals at *many* different ranks could be compared with respect to their attitudes, the study could more meaningfully be compared to others of a similar nature. Perhaps Jones could have created several socio-economic status levels or divided the population into various income categories and then computed the average attitude score for each level. The differences in attitudes exhibited by persons at the various levels could then be compared with the attitudinal differences indicated by other studies when the population was classified according to three, four, or five broad categories.

In sum, it is to be regretted that the significant data gathered by Jones in an admittedly unique manner are not in a form that lend themselves to more direct comparison with those gathered by others who have studied the relationship between attitudes and social status.

[39] Arthur W. Kornhauser, "Analysis of 'Class' Structure of Contemporary American Society—Psychological Bases of Class Division," in George W. Hartman and Theodore Newcomb (eds.), *Industrial Conflict: A Psychological Interpretation* (New York, The Cordon Co., 1939), pp. 258-261.

SELECTED READINGS

CENTERS, Richard, *The Psychology of Social Classes* (Princeton, Princeton University Press, 1949).

KORNHAUSER, Arthur, "Public Opinion and Social Class," *American Journal of Sociology*, 55 (January, 1950), pp. 333-345.

McCORMICK, T. C., and SCHMID, R. C., "A System of Attitude Experiments," *Social Forces*, 19 (March, 1941), pp. 351-356.

MILLS, C. Wright, "The Middle Classes in Middle Sized Cities," *American Sociological Review*, 11 (October, 1946), pp. 520-529.

———, *White Collar* (New York, Oxford University Press, 1951), Part Four.

SAENGER, Gerhart H., "Social Status and Political Behavior," *American Journal of Sociology*, 51 (September, 1945), pp. 103-113.

10

"The Psychology of Social Classes"[1]

THE STUDIES of social stratification that we have summarized so far have measured the social status of individuals or have "stratified" communities into classes variously.[2] None of these studies, however, has paid serious attention to *where people would place themselves in the social hierarchy*, at least not to the extent of using self-identification as an integral part of their method.[3] Self-identification or "class consciousness," however, is one of the salient features of social classes, according to Centers in *The Psychology of Social Classes*.

It is not our task here to evaluate the importance of a person's own feelings about his place in a community as opposed to other criteria of social status. Rather we want to inspect this phenom-

[1] Richard Centers, *The Psychology of Social Classes* (Princeton, Princeton University Press, 1949).

[2] West, for example, drew upon community members of different social standing to determine the status structure of Plainville (see Chapter 4). Lenski (Chapter 5) and Hollingshead (Chapter 8) had "judges" rank community members on the basis of their social status while Kenkel (Chapter 7) inferred the nature of the social-stratification system of Columbus, Ohio, from the arrangement of the scores members of the community obtained on socio-economic status scales. Warner (see Chapter 6) utilized two different methods for obtaining the class placement of community members, but neither took serious account of where a person himself felt he "belonged."

[3] Other studies, not summarized in this book, have taken into account how individuals think they stand in the social hierarchy. See especially: Fortune Surveys, "The People of the United States—a Self Portrait," *Fortune* (February, 1940), p. 14. For a more particularistic study see Verner M. Sims, "The Social Class Affiliation of a Group of Public School Teachers," *School Review*, 59 (September, 1951), pp. 331-338.

enon of "class consciousness" more thoroughly and to investigate other aspects of Centers' theory.

The Interest-Group Theory of Social Classes

Without labeling a "definition" of social classes, Centers tells us what he considers them to be.[4]

Social classes in their essential nature can be characterized as psychologically or subjectively based groupings defined by the allegiance of their members. Integral to their structuring are tendencies toward common conceptions by their members of the qualifications for membership in them, tendencies toward common conceptions by their members of the occupational characteristics of their membership, tendencies toward common attitudes, beliefs, and behavior in political matters, and perhaps tendencies toward common attitudes, beliefs and behavior in many other ways as yet undiscovered and undefined. These constituent tendencies in the formation of social classes are the response of individuals to the whole complex situation of their lives, but are determined to a very large extent by their statuses and roles in their activities of getting a living.

The testing of this theory consititutes the bulk of Centers' research. His project can be broken down into several phases. The following outline will serve to identify the interdependent steps involved in testing the "interest group theory" of social classes.

1. Measuring the socio-economic status of individuals.
2. Determining the relationship between socio-economic status and certain attitudes and beliefs.
3. Determining the existence of social classes in the sense of consciousness of belonging to a social class.
4. Determining the relationship between class identification and occupational status.
5. Describing the social classes with which respondents identified with respect to other criteria.
6. Describing the relationship between attitude differences and social-class identifications.

[4] Centers, *op. cit.*, pp. 210-11.

Each of these phases will be described, but first some attention should be directed to Centers' general methodology and to the sample he selected for testing the theory.

Methodology

Centers obtained his sample, consisting of 1100 white males distributed throughout the United States, by what is called the "quota-control technique." This involves both control established by the researcher and a certain amount of selection by the interviewers. The researcher determines the number of people he needs in various categories (age, sex, geographical location) in order for his sample to conform with the make-up of a given population universe. An interviewer living near a rural area that was selected for sampling, for example, may receive an assignment to interview a specified number of people in different economic status groups, a specified number of people "over forty" and "under forty," and a specified number of farmers, since not all people living in rural areas are farmers. He is often instructed to include in his sample equal numbers of men and women. The interviewer then goes from door to door and sends in those completed interviews that meet his quotas for the various categories.

In this particular study, the interviewers were instructed to select respondents from different economic levels (average, above average, and below average) and to split the above average and below average into two groups "on the basis of their apparent wealth." [5]

How representative was the sample? Centers points out that there were several known sources of bias that prevented his cross section of American males from being a completely representative sample. He encountered the familiar "interviewer bias" which results in the selection of too few lower-status people. [6]

---

[5] *Ibid.*, p. 35.
[6] For a discussion of the "quota-control" technique and the "upward bias" often found in samples selected by this means see Hadley Cantril, *Gauging Public Opinion* (Princeton, Princeton University Press, 1947), pp. 143-149.

In addition, when his results were tallied, he discovered that the East and West coastal areas were under-represented. Centers also noted a bias in the occupational make-up of his sample inasmuch as proprietarial, managerial and professional persons were all overrepresented while various categories of wage earners, particularly "unskilled workers" and "farm laborers," were underrepresented. Centers concludes that his sample is "fairly representative" in terms of economic status of the general population and "reasonably accurate in terms of occupational stratification." There is no reason to dispute these modest claims. It should be added, however, that Centers' results, with respect to his sampling, appear to be as good as or better than those usually obtained when quota-control sampling is employed. Nevertheless, the biases indicated by Centers should be kept in mind when interpreting his results.

DETERMINING SOCIO-ECONOMIC STATUS

As indicated earlier, one of the first analyses that Centers made was the determination of the socio-economic status of his respondents. Three related indices were used to measure this variable: (1) respondent's rating by the interviewer (wealthy, average plus, average, poor plus, or poor); (2) respondent's occupation; and (3) the number of employees or subordinates (if any) supervised by a respondent. Farmers were classified according to whether they owned or managed the farm, rented the land, or were farm laborers. Urban occupations were classified according to seven categories: Large Business, Professional, Small Business, White Collar, Skilled Manual Workers, Semiskilled Manual Workers, and Unskilled Manual Workers. "The categories," we are told, "form a hierarchy in terms of skill, responsibility, and complexity of the occupational function or role in the total economy of production and exchange of goods and services." [7]

[7] Centers, *op. cit.*, p. 48.

Five categories were designed to rank the respondents in what Centers calls a "dominance-subordination hierarchy." These five were employers, managers, independents (self-employed workers and proprietors without employees), farm tenants, and employees (workers having no subordinates).

ATTITUDES, BELIEFS, AND OCCUPATIONAL STATUS

As we learned from Jones's study, individuals in different occupations vary in their attitudes toward corporate property.[8] In accordance with Centers' interest-group hypothesis, there should be a relationship between a person's occupation and various attitudes, particularly those of a political and economic nature. In this section, then, we will present Centers' findings pertinent to his question, "Do persons of differing status and role in the economic order (e.g., occupational strata) characteristically distinguish themselves from one another by the possession of differing points of view with respect to important political and economic issues?"[9]

Conservatism-Radicalism

On Centers' interview schedule there appeared the following six questions which were designed to obtain part of the answer to the above question concerning the politico-economic orientation of his cross section of United States males.[10]

1. Do you agree or disagree that America is truly a land of opportunity and that people get pretty much what's coming to them in this country?

2. Would you agree that everybody would be happier, more se-

---

[8] See Chapter 9.

[9] Centers, *op. cit.*, p. 55.

[10] *Ibid.*, pp. 39-40. It should be noted that although the order in which these questions appeared on the interview schedule has not been changed, in a few instances other questions, not used by Centers in his Conservatism-Radicalism battery, appeared on the schedule between the questions here presented.

cure and more prosperous if the working people were given more power and influence in government, or would you say that we would all be better off if the working people had no more power than they have now?

3. As you know, during this war many private businesses and industries have been taken over by the government. Do you think wages and salaries would be fairer, jobs more steady, and that we would have fewer people out of work if the government took over and ran our mines, factories and industries in the future, or do you think things would be better under private ownership?

4. Which one of these statements do you most agree with? (1) The most important job for the government is to make it certain that there are good opportunities for each person to get ahead on his own. (2) The most important job for the government is to guarantee every person a decent and steady job and standard of living.

5. In strikes and disputes between working people and employers do you usually side with the workers or with the employers?

6. Do you think working people are usually fairly and squarely treated by their employers, or that employers sometimes take advantage of them?

Centers established three categories for the answers to each of these questions, one indicating a "conservative" attitude, another a "radical" attitude.[11] A third category was set up for those cases in which the position of the respondent could not be determined. The sample was then divided into conservative and radical groups on the basis of the consistency of their responses in either direction, when all six questions were considered.[12]

[11] The reader may or may not consider the terms *conservative* and *radical* appropriate. It should be recognized that these are apparently just convenient labels for admittedly opposite positions with regard to the issue in question. In general, those answers that indicate approval of change are considered "radical" as are those that side with the worker in management-worker issues.

[12] The labels *ultra-conservative, conservative,* etc., were defined as follows: ultra-conservative, five or more (out of six) conservative responses; conservative, three or more conservative responses and at least two more conservative responses than radical ones; radical, three or more radical responses and at least two more radical responses than conservative ones; ultra-radical, five or more radical responses; indeterminate, all other combinations of responses including "don't knows," no response. (Centers, *op. cit.,* pp. 40-42.)

When the results were analyzed it was discovered that there is a difference between the "conservativeness" of people in the various occupational categories. As evidenced in Table 4, the differences are most noticeable with respect to extreme categories, either of occupation or of attitude. The over-all tendency is for persons in higher occupational groups to be more conservative than those in lower ones.

TABLE 4. Conservatism-Radicalism and Occupational Classification *

Occupation	N	% Ultra Conservative	% Conservative	% Indeterminate	% Radical	% Ultra Radical
Large Business	54	55.5	31.5	11.1	0.0	1.9
Professional	73	30.2	39.7	19.2	4.1	6.8
Small Business	131	45.8	28.2	17.6	6.9	1.5
White Collar	172	24.4	31.4	28.5	10.5	5.2
Skilled Manual	163	12.2	26.4	34.4	17.2	9.8
Semiskilled Manual ...	174	5.2	16.1	29.3	28.7	20.7
Unskilled Manual	77	2.5	20.8	39.0	20.8	16.9
Farm Owners and Managers	153	32.8	35.9	24.8	3.9	2.6
Farm Tenants and Laborers	69	11.7	31.9	30.4	18.8	7.2

* Based on Table 8, Richard Centers, *The Psychology of Social Classes* (Princeton, Princeton University Press, 1949), p. 57. Used by permission.

The exceptions to this, however, should also be noted. Fully 23 per cent of unskilled manual workers (the lowest occupational group) are either conservative or ultra-conservative, while over 10 per cent of professional, small business, and white-collar people are radical or ultra-radical.

Political Behavior

Centers also attempted to measure whether or not the politico-economic beliefs of the people are reflected in their voting behavior. His respondents were asked, "Whom did you vote for in the last presidential election?" (1944 election).[13]

[13] *Ibid.*, p. 67.

While about half (51.4 per cent) of the entire sample answered "Roosevelt," more people favoring the Democratic candidate were found in the ranks of the manual workers than among the large business owners and professional men.[14] White-collar workers stated they voted for Roosevelt just slightly less frequently (49.7 per cent) than did the sample as a whole.

These results are consistent, in a general sense, with those obtained regarding the attitudes elicited by questions cited earlier, for it has been the Republican party that could better be labeled the "conservative" party while in recent years, at least, the Democratic party has stood for more social change to the "left."

Respondents were also questioned about the usual voting of their parents. The relationship between occupation and voting behavior was similar, but it was not nearly as marked with regard to the parents' voting behavior. Centers has this to say about the meaning of this difference: [15]

The parents' voting habits do not show as great a difference along stratification lines as those of the younger generation. The cleavage has grown. *The suggestion is that in the future more and more manual workers will align themselves with a liberal party—as the Democratic party has sometimes been—and more and more of non-manual persons will cling to the conservative views of such a party as the Republican.*

Since the above was written (1949), we have witnessed an event that seems to temper Centers' predictions. Great industrial centers—Pittsburgh, Cleveland, Detroit—did not vote as expected in the presidential election of 1952. Although most of the big cities still went Democratic, the plurality of Democratic votes was smaller than in the preceding elections. The results are on hand for all to inspect; the question remains, "What do the results mean?"

[14] The popular vote in the 1944 election was: Democratic, approximately 53 per cent; Republican, approximately 46 per cent. Source: John Kieran (ed.), *Information Please Almanac 1953* (New York, The Macmillan Co., 1952), p. 209.

[15] Centers, *op. cit.*, p. 66. Italics not in original.

An obvious interpretation is that the results of the recent presidential election indicate that the trend noted by Centers is being reversed or, in short, that labor is "going conservative." But is there another explanation? Do these results truly indicate that the American working people are breaking their alliance with Democratic liberalism, an alliance that was initiated some twenty years ago when labor was offered a "New Deal" and an alliance that has apparently satisfied the workers' quest for employment security? *Not necessarily.* There is the alternative explanation that the American blue-collar workers felt that the benefits already achieved with regard to high hourly wage, weekly pay, and standard of living, and greater over-all security would not be in jeopardy regardless of the political party in power, due in part to their greater bargaining ability in the form of strong unionism. These same workers may have felt that there was something to be said for the oft-repeated slogan, "It's time for a change." In short, perhaps labor has not changed its attitude toward liberalism but has temporarily failed to support the Democratic party in full strength because of factors other than the liberal nature of the party's policies.

Behavior at the polls over the next twenty years should indicate which trend is the more permanent. The fact remains that at the time Centers made his study, his findings with respect to conservative attitudes of his respondents largely agree with those that measured conservative voting behavior.

Attitude Toward Unionism

Forty-five per cent of all the males interviewed by Centers reported that they belonged to some sort of a union while, of course, only 14 per cent of business, professional, and white-collar workers indicated a union affiliation.[16] These same people

[16] The complete union membership-occupational group breakdown is as follows: large business, 4 per cent union; professional, 7 per cent; small business, 8 per cent; white collar, 24 per cent; skilled manual, 49 per cent; semiskilled, 50 per cent; unskilled, 23 per cent. Centers suggests two explanations for the high degree of union affiliation among white-collar workers

were also asked, "Do you think belonging to a union usually hurts people's chances for advancement in their jobs, makes no difference, or helps their chance of advancement?" [17] Centers comments as follows about the response to this question: [18]

Belief in the advantages of unionism as far as personal advancement is concerned is, however, nearly everywhere stronger than actual memberships would suggest. Even the employing and managerial groups, who stand to lose rather than to gain by the combination of workers into unions, assert, more often than they do the contrary, that belonging to a union is beneficial to those who do belong to one. This, at least, is true when the business, professional and white collar groups are considered as a totality, and it holds for the farm owners and managers, though when the finer urban groupings are examined, the most distinctively employing and managing group, large businessmen, shows fewer who concede that unionism is advantageous to the worker than those who say it is disadvantageous to him. In general the tendency is for those in the lowest occupational ranks to manifest the largest approval of unionism, with the high point of such approval occurring in the semi-skilled grade.

Summary—Attitudes and Occupations

When we sum up all the evidence presented thus far we get a somewhat qualified affirmative answer to Centers' original question, "Do persons of differing status and roles in the economic order (e.g., occupational strata) characteristically distinguish themselves from one another by the possession of differing points of view with respect to important political and economic issues?" [19] The answer is affirmative because, by and large, the attitude responses cited have shown that the higher a person's

---

but particularly for the relatively high number of union members in the ranks of the business and professional people. The phenomenon may have been caused by occupationally mobile individuals retaining their union memberships or it may be the result of a confusion in terminology in that business people particularly may have considered trade associations or manufacturer's associations as "unions" in answering this question. (*Ibid.*, pp. 66-70.)

[17] *Ibid.*, p. 71.
[18] *Ibid.*, pp. 70-72.
[19] *Ibid.*, p. 55.

occupational status, the more likely he was to respond in a conservative manner.

CLASS CONSCIOUSNESS

The relationship between occupational status and attitudes that has been disclosed does not in itself indicate the presence of social classes. Rather, it is merely the kind of evidence that *may* be indicative of their presence. Thus Centers' next task was to discover whether his population accurately could be described as belonging to separate social classes.

We will recall that, according to Centers, one of the basic requirements for stating that an individual is a member of a certain class is simply whether the person himself feels that he belongs to that social class. After this has been determined, the question of definition of the classes can be pursued.

Class Identification

Centers recognized that if we are to speak of people possessing a consciousness of belonging to a group, these people must have a common name by which their group is called. In order to discover what names were in use for identifying social classes, Centers turned to the results of a then recent *Fortune* survey in which a cross section of Americans were asked, "What word would you use to name the class in America you belong to?" [20] The answers to this question are summarized in Table 5.

Over one fourth of *Fortune*'s sample replied they couldn't answer the question, and over half did not use the common expressions, "upper class," "middle class," and "lower class." Centers, however, accents the *positive* findings of this survey in telling how he chose the class titles that appeared on his ballot.[21] "Since *Fortune* had found that the terms *middle class* and *working* (or

[20] *Fortune, loc. cit.*
[21] Centers, *op. cit.*, p. 76.

laboring) *class* were the most frequently used of all, it was clear that these, along with the terms *upper class* and *lower class* which (together with apparently equivalent terms) constituted the next most frequent responses, should constitute the alternatives used in the present study." Members of Centers' cross section, therefore, were asked: [22] "If you were asked to use one of these four names for your social class, which would you say you belonged in: the middle class, lower class, working class or upper class?"

TABLE 5. The U.S. Is Middle Class *

What word would you use to name the class in America you belong to?

Upper	1.6%	2.9%
Other upper **	1.3	
Upper middle	1.7	
Other upper middle **	0.8	
Middle	38.6	47.0
Other middle **	5.5	
Lower middle	0.4	
Lower	1.2	
Other lower **	2.8	14.9
Working, laboring	10.6	
Unemployed, idle, unfortunate	0.3	
Business, executive, professional, white collar	2.0	
Other miscellaneous answers	5.7	
Don't Know	27.5	

* *Fortune* (February, 1940), p. 14. Used by permission.
** *Words without asterisks are the ones actually given.* Other upper *includes such words as* "best," "highest," *etc.; other upper middle* such words as *"above average," "better," etc.; other middle* such words as *"in between," "moderate," "normal," etc.; other lower* such words as *"poor," "poorest," "pauper," "third rate," "under class." The miscellaneous answers are legion, including* "American class," "free thinker class," "good citizen class," "foreign class," *and* "Negro class."

In Table 6 the answers given by the cross section of males in the main survey, as well as those in a later survey are presented. It is clear that when people are asked to identify with one of four classes, most will claim membership in "*a* class." Almost all (94 per cent) apparently prefer two of the four choices, working class or middle class. These results are noticeably different from

[22] *Ibid.*, p. 76.

those of studies of a similar design. If given only three choices, upper, middle, or lower class, about 80 to 90 per cent of the people have been found to pick "middle class" as the name of their class.[23] When given the additional choice of "working class," this category draws the heaviest response and the "middle class" responses drop to 43 per cent.

TABLE 6. Class Identifications of 1100 Americans *

Per Cent Saying:	Main Survey	Follow-up
Upper Class	3	4
Middle Class	43	36
Working Class	51	52
Lower Class	1	5
Don't Know	1	3
"Don't believe in classes"	1	—

* Adapted from Richard Centers, *The Psychology of Social Classes* (Princeton, Princeton University Press, 1949), p. 77. Used by permission.

Centers considers that his findings "convincingly dispel any doubt that Americans are class conscious" [24] and turns his efforts to discovering which people (occupationally) state they belong to the several classes and how they define the social classes with which they apparently identify. It should be recognized that the *descriptions and definitions of the classes also contribute to the problem of "class consciousness,"* for a number of people could not be said to "identify" with a given class if they defined it quite differently.

[23] The *Fortune* survey discovered that 79.2 per cent of their sample chose "middle class" in preference to "upper" or "lower" class, whereas Gallup found that 88 per cent stated they belonged to the middle class. These results were obtained when respondents were given the three choices, "upper class," "middle class," and "lower class." (See *Fortune, loc. cit.;* and George Gallup and Saul Forbes Rae, *The Pulse of Democracy* [New York, Simon and Schuster, 1949], p. 169.)

[24] Centers, *op. cit.*, p. 76.

CLASS IDENTIFICATION OF OCCUPATIONAL STRATA

First we will answer the question, "What is the relationship between a person's occupational status and his response concerning the class to which he belongs?"

The answers are tabulated in Table 7. It is clear from this table that a distinction can be made between those who claim membership in the middle class and those who choose the working class. *Almost two thirds (65 per cent) of large business, professional, small business and white-collar workers chose the middle class while somewhat more than three-fourths (77 per cent) of all manual workers chose the working class.*

TABLE 7. Occupation and Class Identification *

Occupation	N	% Upper Class	% Middle Class	% Working Class	% Lower Class	% Don't Know	% Don't Believe in Classes
Large Business .	54	13	78	7	—	2.0	—
Professional ...	73	4	81	10	—	1.0	4.0
Small Business .	131	3	70	24	—	1.5	1.5
White Collar .	172	2	61	34	0.6	0.6	1.8
Skilled Manual	163	2	26	71	1.0	—	—
Semi-skilled ..	174	1	14	83	1.0	1.0	—
Unskilled	77	—	18	75	7.0	—	—
Farm owners & managers ...	153	3	42	51	1.0	3.0	—
Farm tenants & laborers	69	2	16	73	2.0	7.0	—

* Based on Table 20, Richard Centers, *The Psychology of Social Classes* (Princeton, Princeton University Press, 1949), p. 86. Used by permission.

The differences in membership of the other two classes, upper and lower, can best be analyzed by considering the extremes. Thirteen per cent of large businessmen, for example, claim membership in the upper class as opposed to no unskilled laborers.

Professional men and small businessmen are only slightly more attracted to the upper class than are white-collar workers, skilled and even semiskilled manual workers. Since less than a dozen people from the entire urban sample claimed membership in the lower class, we can merely point out that five of these were unskilled manual workers and none of them were business or professional men.

The occupational composition of the two large classes could scarcely be called homogeneous. Slightly over half of the middle class, for example, are white-collar and small businessmen, about a fourth are large business and professional men, and the rest are various types of manual workers. It is natural to wonder whether these admittedly different types of workers had the same thing in mind when they answered "middle class" in response to the interviewer's query. At any rate, the problem of the definition of the classes should be investigated.

DEFINITIONS OF THE CLASSES

One way in which Centers got at the problem of definitions of the classes was by determining how people who claimed membership in a class described the class occupationally. In addition, he asked the entire sample which criteria other than occupation they would use to assign persons to the several classes. Although more information would be desirable, that furnished by these two inquiries should tell us something about what people think is the composition of the four classes. Some of our remarks, as those of Centers, will have to be restricted to the working and middle classes, due to the fewness of people who claim membership in the other classes.

Occupational Composition of the Middle Class

Each person who said he belonged in the middle class was given a card listing various occupational categories and was asked which he would say belonged in the middle class. The categories were:

Big business owners and executives
Small business owners and operators
Factory workers
Office workers
Doctors and lawyers
Servants

Farmers
Laborers such as miners, truck drivers, and shop-workers
Store and factory managers
Waiters and bartenders
Salesmen

Here is the self-portrait of the middle class. They generally agree (81 per cent so stated) that they should number among their ranks the owners and operators of small businesses. They are about equally as certain that their class does *not* include big business owners, servants, waiters and bartenders, laborers and factory workers. However, there seems to be considerable disagreement concerning whether or not doctors and lawyers, salesmen, office workers, and farmers belong to the middle class; about half of the middle-class people would include them in their class, the remainder think that they belong to some other class.[25] It is difficult to say, then, how clear a picture of themselves middle-class people actually have.

Occupational Composition of the Working Class

Those who said they belonged to the working class were shown the same list of occupational categories as were the middle-class people and were asked which they would include in their own (the working) class. Most working-class people (80 to 82 per cent) think of their class as being made up of factory workers and laborers, while a fairly sizable proportion (65 per cent) would include farmers. They are equally (or more) certain that "working class" does *not* mean business and professional men, store and factory managers, or salesmen. The working-class members split fairly evenly when it came to the inclusion of office workers, waiters and bartenders, and servants in their class.

[25] The actual percentages of people in the middle class who would include the several occupational categories in their class were as follows: 54 per cent included salesmen; 63 per cent included office workers, 45 per cent included farmers, and 40 per cent included doctors and lawyers.

Occupational Composition of the Upper Class

Ninety-three per cent of the people who claim membership in the upper class state that big business owners and executives belong to this class. About two thirds would include doctors and lawyers. All would exclude from their ranks servants, waiters and bartenders, laborers, and factory workers and most would exclude office workers. Upper-class people are fairly evenly divided over whether or not small business owners and operators belong to their class, and are prone to exclude store and factory managers, salesmen, and farmers.

Occupational Composition of the Lower Class

At least one lower-class person specified that each occupational category, other than big businessmen, belonged to the lower class. Generally there is good agreement that people within the highest six occupational categories do not belong to the lower class but there is little agreement concerning who *does* belong to this class. We must remember that the fewness of people identifying with the lower class limits the interpretation of these results.

Interclass Comparison of the Occupational Categories

We have seen how persons who identify with the several classes describe the occupational composition of their class. Let us look at the matter in a somewhat different way and attempt to draw conclusions concerning the "proper place" for people in the various occupational categories as judged by those who claimed them.

1. Big business owners—claimed largely only by upper-class people.
2. Doctors and lawyers—claimed by two-thirds of upper class and 40 per cent of middle-class people.
3. Small business owners—claimed by about 80 per cent of middle-class, over half of upper-class, and 20 per cent of working-class people.
4. Store and factory managers—most frequently claimed by middle-

class (63 per cent) but a sizable number of upper and working-class people specified this group as belonging to their class.

5. Salesmen—specified by no more than about half the people of *any* class but claimed most frequently by the middle class.
6. Office workers—claimed almost equally by middle and working classes but also by smaller numbers of upper-class and lower-class persons.
7. Farmers—claimed by every class but chiefly the working and middle classes.
8. Factory workers—largely specified by working-class people.
9. Laborers—claimed about equally by the lower class and the working class.
10. Waiters and bartenders—claimed by slightly under half of the lower class and slightly over half of the working class.
11. Servants—claimed about equally by the lower class and the working class.

Other Criteria for Class Membership

In view of the somewhat vague manner in which the sample used occupation as a way of describing their class, it should be clear that they considered "other things" as well. To determine just what were the other criteria for membership in the several classes, Centers asked his sample, "What would you say puts a person in the (upper, middle, working, lower) class?" [26] Their answers can be summarized by categorizing the free responses concerning each of the four classes.

Criteria for the upper class. People who call themselves upper class think of themselves differently than they are thought of by others. To an upper-class person, family origin, wealth, and education are all about equally important as criteria of status.[27] To others, wealth is the all important mark of an upper-class person. The upper class also tend to attach greater importance to attitudes and beliefs, character, and even personality, dress, and appearance, than do those who affiliated with the other classes.

[26] *Ibid.*, pp. 94 ff.
[27] In this section we are assuming that the "importance" which respondents attach to the various criteria is reflected in the frequency with which the characteristics were named as criteria for class membership.

Criteria for the middle class. Money again looms large in the middle-class picture, with something over a third of the people, regardless of class identification, naming money or income as the attribute that "puts" a person in the middle class. Another 20 per cent of middle-class persons tempered this somewhat by describing their class as the one of the financially average man (not rich, not poor, live comfortably, etc.). Members of the other three classes did not think of the middle class in these terms nearly so frequently.

Education was mentioned next most frequently as a criterion for middle-class membership but chiefly by the upper-class and middle-class persons. The working class is unique in its high regard for ownership of small business, profession, or trade as the mark of a middle-class man. To them, being an independent proprietor of some kind is second only to income as a middle-class characteristic.

Criteria for the working class. Despite the fact that the criteria sought for were those other than "occupation," factors seemingly quite related to occupation were stressed as indicative of membership in the working class. Most frequently mentioned by all respondents, but particularly by members of the working class, was the category, "working for a living." [28] To some, at least, there would seem to be an area of overlap between this reason for putting a man in the working class and three others labeled, "Manual, common, mill and factory work or labor," "being an employee or wage earner," and "kind of job, type of work." [29] When the number of times these three criteria and "working for a

[28] Centers acknowledges that this is a loose and general term but does not attempt to clarify its meaning. Apparently he feels its meaning is sufficiently understood. Although Centers and his interviewers are in the best position to describe what the expression meant to his sample, we can merely add that "working for a living" seems more often applied to wage and lower salaried persons than to those who receive large salaries, work on substantial commissions, or are proprietors. Doctors, lawyers, ministers, and school teachers, for example, are not generally thought of as "working for a living" in the sense that this expression is used here.

[29] *Ibid.*, p. 100.

living" are totaled it is found that about 67 per cent of the respondents named the four as criteria for working-class membership.

The upper-class and middle-class people stress the lack of education as a characteristic of working-class people, which is, of

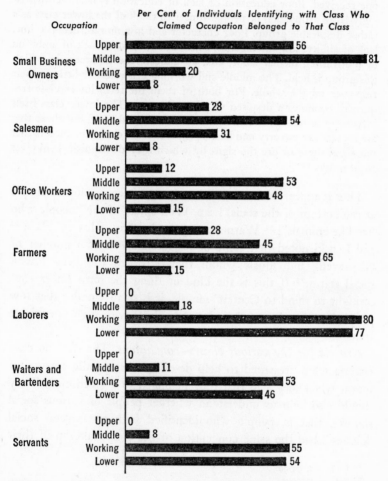

FIG. 9. In which class do these occupations "belong"? (Derived from Figs. 5, 6, 7, and 8, Centers, op. cit., pp. 80-83)

course, consistent with their emphasis of education as a characteristic of people of their own classes.

Criteria for the lower class.

What puts a person in the lower class? ... The most obvious answer is "being poor," and it is by a considerable margin the most frequent one received. Poor education or lack of education is next. A surprisingly large proportion of people appear to think of the lower class as a rather despicable group. Poor character and low morals, drink, crime, lack of ability, low intelligence, shiftlessness, laziness, lack of ambition or motivation, menial labor, etc., all indicate the disesteem in which this group is held. The middle and working classes differ little in their responses on the whole. For both of them the term lower class frequently connotes a despised or *déclassé* group. The lower class itself is scarcely present in sufficient numbers to defend itself, but those that are present say poverty and lack of education are either the factors that put them there or are the signs by which they distinguish themselves from others.[30]

Thus it appears that once again we encounter a group of people at the bottom of the social heap. West spoke of the "people who live like animals"; [31] Warner recognized a "lower-lower" class; [32] and Lenski noted that some of his raters spoke of a number of "depraved" individuals whom they afforded the very lowest social status.[33] If this is the kind of thing the term *lower class* brought to mind to Centers' sample, it is small wonder that few people cared to be numbered among those with such unenviable traits.

Criteria for the various classes—conclusions. The data on class criteria were presented to help describe what people apparently meant when they said that they belonged to a given class. They should also help us understand whether people of various social statuses, that is, people who identified with the several social "classes," had the same conception of the class make-up of their

[30] *Ibid.*, pp. 95-96.
[31] See Chapter 4.
[32] See Chapter 6.
[33] See Chapter 5.

society. On both of these points we can draw some tentative conclusions.

1. Individuals who identified with a given class showed a certain amount of agreement regarding the importance of various status criteria for membership in their class.

2. The extent to which class members agreed on the importance of various criteria varied. *In most cases no more than 30 to 40 per cent of the persons in a given class responded that a certain characteristic was responsible for "putting" someone in their class.*

3. There is some evidence that individuals who identify with different classes place somewhat different emphasis on the criteria for classes other than their own. Put differently, those who claim membership in a given social class think of the class in somewhat different terms than do "outsiders."

ATTITUDE DIFFERENCES AND SOCIAL-CLASS IDENTIFICATIONS

In an earlier section we discovered that a person's "politico-economic" orientation is related to his occupational status.[34] In Centers' terminology, the higher one's occupational status the more likely he is to answer questions of a political and economic nature in a conservative manner. Later we noted that there is also a relationship between a person's occupational status and the response he gives when asked to which social class he belongs. *Most* business, professional, and white-collar workers claim the middle class whereas *most* manual workers choose the working class.

In view of the fact that the social classes, as measured by respondent-identification, are not occupationally homogeneous, it remains to be seen whether people in the various classes differ significantly from one another with respect to their attitudes and beliefs. Due to the fewness of people identifying with the upper and lower classes our remarks, as were most of Centers', will be

[34] See also Chapter 9.

restricted to attitude differences between the working class and the middle class.

Politico-economic Attitudes

"Would you agree that everybody would be happier, more secure and more prosperous if the working people were given more power and influence in government . . . ? [35] Those identifying with the working class, as perhaps would be expected, were more prone to grant more power and influence to working people than were middle-class respondents.

The same type of relationship was discovered when the responses to other politico-economic attitude questions were analyzed. These can be summarized as follows:

1. Government versus private ownership of industry. Working-class people were more prone to agree that conditions would be better if the government owned and controlled various large industries and natural industries.

2. Individualism. Working-class people were less individualistic in that over half of them (as compared to about a quarter of the middle class) agreed that "The most important job for the government is to *guarantee* every person a decent and steady job and standard of living." [36]

3. Treatment of working people. Almost two thirds of the people considering themselves to be part of the working classes agreed that employers sometimes take advantage of working people. The urban middle class split about evenly on this issue.

Other Attitude Differences

Centers also investigated whether differences would be found between the classes with respect to other types of attitudes and beliefs. Again, the findings are reported only for the two large

[35] Centers, *op. cit.*, Appendix IV. The question continued, "or would you say we would all be better off if the working people had no more power than they have now?"

[36] *Ibid.*, p. 232. Italics not in original.

categories, those who claimed membership in the middle and working classes.

1. *Anti-Negro prejudice.* The working class was found to be significantly more prejudiced against Negroes than was the middle class. Centers has this to say about the findings:

This prejudice may or may not be economically determined; it is a fact, however, that people *in* the working class *are* more often prejudiced. It might be their greater poverty and more direct economic competition with Negroes that predisposes them to unfavorable views with respect to them, but it should be noted that, as a class, they are more poorly educated, and that, too, may play a role in prejudice.[37]

2. *Attitude toward religion.* People were asked, "Would you say that on the whole people take religion too seriously, or that they don't take it seriously enough?" [38] The answers to this question, plus a measure of church membership, were used to get at any differences in attitude toward religion between the classes. The first question did not differentiate between the classes inasmuch as most people (over three fourths) agreed that religion is not taken seriously enough. Those who identified with the middle class, however, stated somewhat more frequently that they were members of a church. Centers suggests that is perhaps a further indication of the more conservative attitudes of the middle class.

3. *Attitude toward working women.* In this case, however, it is the working class that shows itself the more conservative in that a higher percentage of this group stated that woman's place was "in the home."

4. *Attitude toward success and opportunity.* In order to find out if there were differences between people in their belief in the American ideal that hard work and ability will bring success, and that opportunities for success are free to all, Centers asked two questions: [39] (1) "Do you think most people who are successful are successful because of ability, luck, pull, or the better oppor-

[37] *Ibid.*, p. 144.
[38] *Ibid.*, p. 232.
[39] *Ibid.*, p. 233.

tunities they have had?" and (2) "Would you say that your children had just as good a chance, a poorer, or a better chance to rise in the world as anybody else's?" Once again differences were found between the two classes. In response to the first question, the middle class was more prone to answer "ability" than the working class and less prone to stress "pull" and "luck." Again, it was the middle-class respondent who was more likely to believe that his children had as good a chance to "rise in the world" as anybody else's.

5. *Indications of frustration.*

Most Americans seem, generally speaking, to be satisfied with the conditions of their lives and work. But significantly in keeping with all that has been said before is this finding: *the working class as a group tends to be distinctly more frustrated than the middle class.* More people who affiliate with the working class are dissatisfied with their jobs, their pay, their opportunities to get ahead, and their chances to enjoy life.... This is true for both urban and rural parts of the respective classes. The largest differences of all occur with respect to the issue of pay between the middle and working class sectors of the rural population, but differences of the order of ten to fifteen per cent are common on practically all comparisons on these questions.[40]

Are Centers' Findings Unique?

Centers discovered other differences in attitudes between people who claimed membership in different classes. It is not necessary to report them all; the questions that press for an answer are these: (1) Are Centers' findings consistent with those of other studies? and (2) What does Centers conclude from his findings about the reality of true social classes?

We will recall that Jones, in his study of attitudes toward corporate property among Akronites, discovered that different occupational groups showed varying degrees of favorable, and unfavorable, attitude toward corporate property.[41] In general, those whose occupation would be considered "high" or "better"

[40] *Ibid.*, pp. 148-150.
[41] See Chapter 9.

showed a greater willingness to grant corporate property its "rights" than were various manual workers. The methods of Jones and Centers are not comparable, nor is it claimed that the attitudes measured by each are the same. Rather, both studies can be said to have gotten at the same *kind* of attitudes with apparently consistent results.

Kenkel, in his study of social stratification in Columbus, asked his sample several attitude-evoking questions that seem to be the same type as those used by Centers. One such question was, "On the whole, which do you think would be likely to give the best value to taxpayers in making airplanes for the Army and Navy, a privately owned or operated plant or one that was owned and operated by the government?" [42]

We will recall that in the Columbus study, the people were not put into social classes but, rather, were simply ranked according to various objective measures of status. The various status continua (occupational status, etc.) were "cut" into two equal parts, then three parts, then four, and finally five. In most cases, but especially when fewer categories are used, *people in each status-category differed significantly from those in other categories with respect to attitude toward government ownership of airplane factories.*

Other attitudes were also measured, including attitudes toward labor unions, the Taft-Hartley law, strikes, government care for the needy, and price controls. In most cases, regardless of whether the sample was arbitrarily divided into two, three, four, or five equal-interval status categories, a direct relationship was found between social status and the attitude measured. Since this was the case, Kenkel found no objective reason for categorizing his sample into two, three, four, or five social classes on the basis of their differences in stated attitudes and differences in occupation. No one number of social classes was found to be more "logical" or more objectively warranted than any other. What was found,

[42] This question was originally cited in *Public Opinion Quarterly*, 11 (Spring, 1947), p. 146.

instead, was a continual gradation in attitudes as one progressed up (or down) the status scale. In this sense, then, the findings were consistent with Centers', for it was again demonstrated that *certain attitudes and social status are directly related.*

Kornhauser's findings further substantiate those already cited inasmuch as he, too, discovered a direct relationship between the attitudes on social-political issues elicited by various income and occupational groups.[43] His study was unique, in a sense, since he not only sampled on a large scale in Chicago but also utilized the findings of many public-opinion polls. The two polls most frequently cited were the "Gallup Poll" and those by *Fortune* magazine. Different types of classification were employed in the various polls, including a fourfold and a fivefold breakdown by income, several different occupational breakdowns, and a fourfold breakdown by general socio-economic level (prosperous, upper-middle, lower-middle, poor).

Despite the different number of breakdowns that were employed, Kornhauser was able to conclude that "Large and consistent differences do exist between income and occupational groups on a variety of broad social-political issues." [44] The evidence, according to Kornhauser, did not support the view that separate and distinct social classes could be distinguished on the basis of attitudinal differences.[45]

SUMMARY OF CENTERS' MAJOR FINDINGS AND CONCLUSIONS

In an earlier section of this chapter we indicated that Centers discovered that occupational groups differed in their politico-economic attitudes. In this respect his study is largely consistent

---

[43] Arthur W. Kornhauser, "Analysis of 'Class' Structure of Contemporary American Society," in George W. Hartman and Theodore Newcomb (eds.), *Industrial Conflict: A Psychological Interpretation* (New York, The Cordon Co., 1939), Chapter 11.

[44] *Ibid.*, p. 260.

[45] *Ibid.*, p. 250.

with many others. Other data collected by Centers led him to conclude that he had also discovered the existence of social classes in the sense of groups of people who are conscious of belonging to a social class which they define similarly, and who think alike on basic issues. The steps involved in reaching this conclusion, and the findings with regard to each step, can be summarized as follows:

1. Class consciousness was determined by asking the sample to which of four classes (upper, middle, working, or lower) they belonged. When the respondents were asked to identify with one of four classes, 3 per cent chose the upper class, 43 per cent the middle class, 51 per cent the working class, and 1 per cent chose the lower class. Two per cent would not respond in these terms.

2. The homogeneity of the classes was determined by discovering the occupation of each person identifying with a given class. "*Nearly three quarters of all business, professional, and white-collar workers identify themselves with the middle or upper classes. An even larger proportion of all manual workers, 79 per cent, identify, on the other hand, with the working and lower classes.*" [46]

3. Commonality of interests and attitudes among class members was measured by comparing the responses given by people who identified with one class to those of people who identified with other classes. Significant differences were found between the way the "working class" and the "middle class" felt on political and economic issues.

4. The agreement concerning what characterizes the various classes was determined by (1) asking each person identifying with a given class which occupations characterized his class, and (2) asking the entire sample what characteristics, other than occupation, would "put" someone in the several classes. People within a given class agreed that some occupations "belonged" in their class and that others did not. Concerning various occupations, however, Centers found considerable disagreement in that

[46] Centers, *op. cit.*, p. 85.

the occupation was claimed about equally by two classes or was claimed and disclaimed equally by members of the same class. Individuals who identified with a given class agreed to a certain extent regarding the importance of various criteria, other than occupation, for membership in their class. Centers also discovered that those who claim membership in a class think of the class in somewhat different terms than do "outsiders."

EVALUATION

Our evaluation of Centers' work will begin with comments on the over-all design of his research and his sampling technique. Further methodological considerations will be met, however, when we analyze what we consider the major findings of this study. Finally, to end on a positive note, we will present what we believe are some of Centers' more important contributions to the field of social stratification.

Research Design

"The method decided upon for the present study was that of a public attitude survey of a *representative* cross section of the adult white male population. Such a method is peculiarly designed to give macroscropic, over-all results rather than the kind that might be obtained by studies of specific populations in limited areas. . . ." [47]

Centers' attempts to help fill the need for an over-all picture of social stratification cannot go unrecognized. Such a task, depending upon its scope, could require more elaborate planning and could be more difficult to execute than a study of a more delimited universe.

The question that must be raised, however, concerns the applicability of Centers' sampling methodology for testing the hypotheses phrased by him. More specifically we might ask, "Why did Centers limit himself to a representative sample?" One

[47] *Ibid.*, p. 34. Italics not in original.

reason, of course, would be that such a sample would permit the making of broad generalizations. This type of sampling, however, does not yield enough cases from all levels of the status hierarchy. In Centers' terminology, the upper class and lower class are represented by so few cases that little can be said about their make-up. It *is* significant to know that only 1 per cent of people from a representative sample choose the lower class as the one to which they belong. It is also important to know something about this lower class. Who *does* identify with the lower class? How do *they* describe their class? What do lower-class people think about the remaining classes? These and many more questions press for answers, *particularly* since so few admit to belonging to this class.

This criticism, we believe, is particularly relevant in view of the fact that Centers could have predicted that few people would choose the upper and lower classes. He had access to, and, in fact, referred to, several public-opinion polls which discovered that Americans, if given some other choices, apparently do not like to claim membership in the upper or lower classes.[48]

Thus, it is suggested that if Centers had sampled more heavily among the people that could be expected to choose the upper or lower classes his results would have lent themselves to broader interpretation.[49]

It is not necessary to comment on *how representative* Centers' representative sample turned out to be. Centers recognizes that it reflects the biases often connected with this type of study. Apparently, all biases worked in the same direction with the result that various categories of individuals (occupationally higher, economically higher, etc.) tended to be overrepresented while the lowest ones were under-represented.[50]

[48] Particular reference is being made to the *Fortune* poll cited by Centers.
[49] See also J. J. Eysenck, "Social Attitudes and Social Class," *British Journal of Sociology*, 1 (March, 1950), pp. 56-66. Eysenck shows similar concern over Centers' sampling technique.
[50] This bias is in the expected direction for a study in which the sample was obtained by the "quota-control" technique. Katz, for example, discovered that even trained interviewers obtained about a 10 per cent over-representation of high school graduates in their sample. Even more impor-

Forced-Choice Questions

Centers used that type of question most often employed by opinion surveys. Such questions are generally called "forced-choice" since in the question are contained several choices, one of which the respondent *must* choose. Another approach would be to use the "open-ended" type of question, in which the respondent phrases his own answer. The advantage of the forced-choice type of questioning lies in the greater ease of statistical manipulation of answers. Serious questions can be raised, however, concerning the meaningfulness of answers obtained by this technique.[51] The use of questions with predetermined responses assumes, among other things, that the responses have the same meaning for all respondents, that the alternatives suggested are exhaustive, and that the choices represent genuine opinions rather than accepted stereotypes. At least one study has shown that when opinions tend to be vague and unstructured quite different results are obtained with the use of "free-response" and "forced-choice" question types.[52]

It should not be concluded from the foregoing that this type of questioning will *never* yield meaningful results. It is simply suggested that in this particular study, admittedly exploratory in nature, the answers to forced-choice questions should not be unequivocably accepted as indications of the respondents' true attitudes. Of particular concern, in this respect, is the question through which class consciousness was purported to be measured. Let us turn to this, then, as the first of Centers' findings to be evaluated.

---

tant than the type of respondents selected by interviewers is the kind of opinions such respondents report to "middle-class" interviewers. This same study discovered that opinions reported to a group of specially trained working-class interviewers were generally more radical than those recorded by the usual staff of trained interviewers. See Daniel Katz, "Do Interviewers Bias Poll Results?" *Public Opinion Quarterly*, 6 (Summer, 1942), pp. 248-268.

[51] Eysenck also seems to think that this type of questioning is inappropriate for the type of opinions Centers was attempting to measure. See Eysenck, *op. cit.*, pp. 64 ff.

[52] Cantril, *op. cit.*, pp. 39-40.

Class Consciousness

An integral part of Centers' theory of social classes is that people are conscious of belonging to *a* social class. Class consciousness was determined, we will recall, by asking the subjects, "If you were asked to use one of these four names for your social class, which would you say you belonged in: the middle class, lower class, working class, or upper class?" [53] The answers to this question (containing four choices) were used to demonstrate that there are four social classes.[54] It is no mere speculation to suggest that people would also respond to a question containing more or fewer than four choices.[55] If Centers had tried several types of questions and had then discovered that people responded more readily to one type (i.e., containing one number of classes) than they did to the others, we would have greater reason to believe that class consciousness was, in fact, determined.[56]

It should also be indicated that Centers' respondents were not given the opportunity to respond in anything but this one, class-oriented manner. One study has shown, however, that people are able to indicate their social position in a community without the use of the traditional class concept.[57] Individuals simply indicated their place, relative to others in their community, on a social-status continuum. This should serve to indicate how much care

[53] Centers, *op. cit.*, p. 233.

[54] The responses, "don't know" and "don't believe in classes," were recorded but were not contained in the question. Essentially, then, there were only four choices.

[55] As we have indicated earlier, in several places, various studies have used the choices, "upper," "middle" and "lower," and the subjects responded in terms of these choices.

[56] Lenski, for example, did not structure his status-ranking procedure but merely instructed his raters to rank 173 families according to their relative "standing" in the community. Not more than one third of the raters agreed on the number of social strata into which the 173 families should be placed; three, four, five, six, and seven levels were utilized by the raters. On the basis of this study, therefore, it is impossible to conclude that any one number of status groups is more "natural" than any other. For a summary of Lenski's study see Chapter 5.

[57] Stanley Hetzler, "An Investigation of the Distinctiveness of Social Classes," *American Sociological Review*, 18 (October, 1953), pp. 493-497.

should be taken in choosing the methods by which phenomena are to be measured. When the question wording implies the existence of three classes, respondents respond in terms of three classes; the same holds true when four classes are used in the question. If a status-continuum concept is employed, individuals appear equally as able to respond in these terms.

Composition of the Four Classes

Centers discovered that almost three fourths of all large business, professional, and small business workers chose the middle class when asked to state to which class they belonged. In addition, 61 per cent of white-collar workers, and 19 per cent of all skilled, semiskilled, and unskilled workers answered "middle class."

Thus there is a decided trend for people classified in the higher occupational categories to choose the middle class. About 80 per cent of both large business and professional people stated they belonged to the middle class, whereas only 18 per cent of unskilled manual workers "identify" with the class.

The occupational categories used by Centers are admittedly broad; all urban occupations are placed into seven categories. Some categories are particularly difficult to describe; for example, the classification "large business owner or executive" could include the president of General Motors, the owner of an urban department store, and, perhaps, the manager of a small chain of super-markets.

Particularly, then, since the occupational categories are broad, it seems safe to conclude that there is a great variability in the kind of people, occupationally speaking, who claim membership in the middle class.

The choice "working class" also drew the response of seemingly dissimilar individuals. *Every occupational category was represented in the "working class,"* although the choice was most frequent among manual workers. Interestingly enough, almost *one fourth* of all people who chose the working class as their own were business, professional, or white-collar workers. This, of course, is a sizable minority.

Since only twelve of the 1097 people in Centers' sample said they belonged to the lower class and only thirty-two claimed the upper class, a breakdown by occupational status is precluded for these two classes.

Similarity of Class Definitions

As we have indicated previously, individuals who identify with a given class tended to agree that a few occupations "belonged" in their class and that others did not. There were always other occupations, however, about which considerable disagreement was found. In some cases, those claiming membership in the same class split almost evenly concerning whether or not their class included people of a given occupation. In other cases, a given occupation was "claimed" about equally by individuals identifying with different classes.

There is a problem, too, connected with the definition and delineation of the occupational categories used by Centers on the list from which respondents picked the ones "belonging" in their class. Not only were the eleven categories broad (for example, "store and factory managers") but we do not know whether the subjects responded in terms of national standards or in terms of their own "home town." [58]

We will recall that when people were asked which characteristics, other than occupation, "put" a person in each of the classes, those claiming membership in a given class showed a certain amount of consistency in the responses. *In most cases, however, no more than 30 to 40 per cent of persons in any one class responded that a given trait was responsible for "putting" someone in their class.*

In summary, then, the evidence presented by Centers does not

---

[58] A similar point is made by Robert S. Lynd in his review of Centers' study. See Robert S. Lynd, "Tiptoeing Around Class," *New Republic,* 121 (July 25, 1949), pp. 17-18.

seem to warrant the conclusion that even those people who claimed membership in a given class defined that class similarly. In other words, the choices "working class" and "middle class" seemed to have different meanings for the people who picked them as representing the name of their class. It is hard to conclude, then, that all those who chose a given class are conscious of belonging to the same social class.

Commonality of Interests and Attitudes

Significant differences were found between the way in which people identifying with the working and middle class answered questions eliciting various attitudes, particularly those of a political and economic nature. We should recall that most business, professional, and white-collar workers picked the middle class and most manual workers picked the working class as their own. Since there is a relationship between occupational status and certain attitudes and beliefs, almost any classification of people that is made along occupational lines will indicate that people in one category "think" differently from those in another category. This was indicated in both Kornhauser's study and that part of Kenkel's study that was concerned with this phenomenon.[59] Centers' evidence *alone* does not seem to substantiate the "interest-group" theory of classes. It does indicate that when people are classified somewhat along occupational and economic lines, differences in their attitudes will be noted. It is, we believe, difficult to accept the proposition that the people were accurately classified in terms of "true" social classes, and that, therefore, the attitude differences displayed are indicative of clearly delineated "interest groups."

Status Differences and Attitudes

Regardless of whether or not we accept the "interest-group" theory of social classes, it is unmistakably clear that Centers' study has demonstrated a direct relationship between socio-eco-

[59] See pp. 251-252.

nomic status and political and economic attitudes. Other studies, as we have seen, confirm this phenomenon.

Although most of Centers' analyses are in terms of occupational status, his findings with respect to a single criterion based upon occupation, power (in the work situation), and economic status (as judged by interviewers), indicate that there is a definite trend for individuals with a high socio-economic score to respond more conservatively toward a series of politico-economic issues.

The retesting of this relationship in a single study that used for a sample a cross section of people of the United States represents a valuable contribution to the field of social stratification.

SELECTED READINGS

CANTRIL, Hadley, *Gauging Public Opinion* (Princeton, Princeton University Press, 1947), Parts I, II, and III especially.

———, "Identification with Social and Economic Class," *Journal of Abnormal and Social Psychology*, 38 (January, 1943), pp. 74-80.

GALLUP, George, and RAE, Saul Forbes, *The Pulse of Democracy* (New York, Simon and Schuster, 1940), Part I especially.

JONES, A. W., *Life, Liberty, and Property* (Philadelphia, J. B. Lippincott Co., 1941).

KATZ, Daniel, "Do Interviewers Bias Poll Results?" *Public Opinion Quarterly*, 6 (Summer, 1942), pp. 248-268.

KORNHAUSER, Arthur W., "Analysis of 'Class' Structure of Contemporary American Society—Psychological Bases of Class Divisions," in George W. Hartman and Theodore Newcomb (eds.), *Industrial Conflict* (New York, The Cordon Co., 1939), pp. 199-264.

———, "Public Opinion and Social Class." (See bibliographic note, p. 225.)

McCORMICK, T. C., and SCHMID, R. C., "A System of Attitude Experiments." (See bibliographic note, p. 225.)

SAENGER, Gerhart H., "Social Status and Political Behavior." (See bibliographic note, p. 225.)

11

"Who Shall Be Educated?"[1]

The American public schools are, in the opinion of the people of the United States, basic and necessary parts of our democracy. We are convinced that they must, and we hope that they do, provide equal opportunity for every child. This means that those at the bottom can compete through education for life's prizes with those at the top.[2]

So RUNS the introduction of a book provocatively titled, "*Who Shall Be Educated?* It questions how fully "those at the bottom" of our social-status hierarchy *can* compete, in our public schools, with those of higher status. *Who Shall Be Educated?* draws upon the results of various studies that describe how social status relates to who and what is taught in our schools and who does the teaching. Chiefly, however, it is concerned with the school systems in three towns: "Old City," a southern town of 13,000; "Hometown," a 6000 inhabitant town in the Midwest; and "Yankee City," a New England town with a population of about 17,000.

The stratification systems of these towns were analyzed in much the same manner in which Warner studied Jonesville.[3] Thus, the social status of individuals frequently will be reported in terms of the familiar six "classes" utilized by Warner. At other times, special studies are cited and status is in terms of such characteristics as income and occupation.

---

[1] W. Lloyd Warner, Robert J. Havighurst, and Martin B. Loeb, *Who Shall Be Educated?* (New York, Harper and Bros., 1944).
[2] *Ibid.*, p. xi. By permission.
[3] See Chapter 6.

EQUALITY OF EDUCATIONAL OPPORTUNITY

If all children were able to continue their formal education as long as they were able to profit from it, and wished to pursue it, then we could say that educational opportunities are available to all. There is considerable evidence, however, that this ideal is seldom attained; a person's opportunity to remain in school seems to be closely linked simply with the socio-economic status of his parents.

Warner reports on a study of 910 Pennsylvania grade school children, all with I.Q.'s of 110 or above, and thus all "college material." The group was separated into those of "above average" and "below average" economic levels. It was evident that children of similar intellectual ability were not receiving a similar amount of education. Slightly over one fourth of the "superior" children of below-average socio-economic status did not even finish high school; approximately 60 per cent more finished high school but did not attend college. Not quite 13 per cent of these intellectually potential college students eventually attended college. About 57 per cent of the superior children of above-average socio-economic status, by contrast, attended college. Only a handful did not at least graduate from high school.

A study was made of a similar group of students in Milwaukee. From the standpoint of ability, the students were much the same; all had I.Q.'s of 117 or above. The yearly income of their parents, however, ranged from under $500 to over $8000. Table 8 clearly indicates that the higher the yearly income of the parents, the more likely it was that the child attended college.

Other studies have also discovered this direct relationship between economic status and school attendance. If, however, the children of lower economic origins do not *want* to remain in school to the same extent as do their wealthier intellectual peers, the statistics do not necessarily indicate a status-bias in our school system. Warner presents three types of evidence which would seem to indicate that economic factors bear heavily on the decision to remain in school. (1) One study discovered that many students give "lack of money" as their reason for leaving school.[4] (2) There was a large response to the National Youth Administration school program which offered financial aid to school students. It is difficult to estimate how many of the students would have dropped out of school were it not for this financial assistance. To be eligible for this aid, however, a child had to demonstrate he "needed" the funds to remain in school. (3)

TABLE 8. Relation of Parental Income to Full-time College Attendance of Superior Milwaukee High School Graduates *

Parental Income	Per Cent In College Full-time
$8000–	100.0
5000–7999	92.0
3000–4999	72.9
2000–2999	44.4
1500–1999	28.9
1000–1499	25.5
500– 999	26.8
Under 500	20.4

* Adapted from W. Lloyd Warner, Robert J. Havighurst, and Martin B. Loeb, *Who Shall Be Educated?* (New York, Harper and Bros., 1944), p. 53. Used by permission.

There is the fact that it *does* cost money to go school, even to the so-called "free" schools in the United States. One study, for example, discovered that even ten years ago, the "incidental" expenses connected with attending a public high school amounted to $125 a year.[5]

This type of evidence, though certainly significant, does not give us the full story. Many a lower-status child will probably say that he dropped out of grade or high school or failed to go to college because this is what he "wanted" to do. But let us

[4] Howard M. Bell, *Youth Tell Their Story* (Washington, D.C., American Council on Education, 1938), pp. 64 ff.

[5] A Committee of North Central Association of Colleges and Secondary Schools, *General Education in the American High School* (Chicago, Scott, Foresman and Co., 1942), pp. 17-20.

investigate how the school system "works" in selecting students for higher education. Perhaps then we will better realize why it is that many lower-status children "want" to leave school.

SEPARATE SCHOOL CURRICULA AND DIFFERENTIAL SOCIAL STATUS

Elementary Schools

It may seem that social status would not affect the course of training in our elementary schools, since all students in the public schools usually receive the same formal training. We must remember, however, that the "best" families sometimes do not send their children to the public elementary schools. They register their sons, instead, at an "exclusive" military school and send their daughters to a "nice" girls' school where "music is emphasized" and where the "young ladies" can learn to ride and swim and cultivate the "right" friendships. Thus, children in our public elementary schools do not often even get to know their age-mates from socially prominent families. During Christmas vacation, perhaps, they may hear exciting tales of life in the different "cottages" or of strict but easily outwitted "headmasters," but all in all they learn little about how the highest 1 per cent live. In this manner, then, social status enters into elementary school education; at a very early age children are somewhat segregated according to the possessions and prestige of their parents.

But social status operates at this time of life in still other ways. A child in the higher grades in elementary school is well aware that in high school he can "elect" some courses or can choose from several different curricula. His parents, perhaps, have already instructed him concerning which courses he should choose and his teachers may have talked to him to assure that he will make a "wise" decision. Most children of lower status are not encouraged to talk about college-preparatory courses but are told of the "fine vocational courses" that they can take. Even while still in grade school, children of higher status begin to realize that high school, for them, is but a means of preparing themselves for college. Let us see, then, what happens when children of various statuses get to high school.

High Schools

In Yankee City, a typical small New England town, the high school has four curricula. Two, the science and the Latin courses, prepare the students for college; the general and the commercial curricula are usually considered terminal.

The college-preparation curricula are said to be "better" than the terminal ones for these reasons:

1. Scholastic standards are higher in the Latin and scientific courses. A "D" is not considered a passing grade in these courses, whereas it is in the general and commercial ones.

2. The college-preparatory courses are taught better. The principal of Yankee City High School stated that the standard of teaching lowers as one goes from the college-preparatory curricula to the general and commercial ones. "It is like having two schools within one building." [6]

3. The college-preparatory courses are more difficult and comprehensive. The principal cited, as one example, the difference between the General Science Course III and the Chemistry course in the scientific curriculum. "The latter," he stated, "is more difficult and includes more material...." [7]

4. The goals of the college-preparatory curricula are "higher." They prepare students for the occupations which directly or indirectly can place them in a higher social position.

In view of these differences, one might suppose that the more able and ambitious students would choose the Latin and scientific courses. Social status, however, seems to affect the students' choice of curricula in the Yankee City and Hometown high

[6] Warner, op. cit., p. 62.
[7] Ibid.

schools. In general, the higher an adolescent's social status, the more likely he is to choose the Latin and scientific courses.

Thus, the status system is, in part, perpetuated. Children from families of higher status generally prepare themselves for higher statuses; many children of lower-status origin prepare themselves for a social position similar to that of their parents.

Table 9 indicates, however, that a sizable minority of lower-class children do enroll in the college-preparatory curricula. Some of these children will eventually graduate from college and will accomplish a substantial rise in status. But why do not more lower-status children prepare themselves for college? Several "reasons" are offered to explain this phenomenon.

TABLE 9. College Expectations and Social Position *
Proportion of High-School Students Expecting to Go to College

Class	Hometown Per Cent	Yankee City Per Cent
Upper upper		
Lower upper	100	100
Upper middle	80	88
Lower middle	22	45
Upper lower	9	28
Lower lower	0	26

* W. Lloyd Warner, Robert J. Havighurst, and Martin B. Loeb, *Who Shall Be Educated?* (New York, Harper and Bros., 1944), p. 66.

1. *Lower-status children lack ability.* No objective studies support this theory. Intelligence differences between children of different status are not sufficient to account for their differential preparation for college.[8]

2. *Lower-status children lack "ambition."* It is sometimes suggested that lower-status children lack the "will to get ahead" and that anyone with ability who "really wanted to" could manage a college education. Many high school students, however, have

[8] For conclusions regarding the relationship between ability and status and appropriate references see Stephen Abrahamson, "Our Status System and Scholastic Rewards," *Journal of Educational Sociology*, 25 (April, 1952), pp. 441-450.

stated that they would like to go to college, but simply cannot afford it. Among those who state that they do not want a college education there are many, undoubtedly, who have accepted what they believe is the inevitable. Their knowledge of the cost of a college education and the experiences of their friends support this belief.

3. *Lower-status children lack encouragement.* It cannot be denied that some lower-status families encourage their children to pursue a course of study that will enable them to "get a job" after completion of high school. In many cases this is probably a quite "realistic" approach to the situation, because of the inability of the parents to pay for a college education. It is probably not as well known that teachers, too, dissuade students from preparing for college. Sometimes they "have a talk" with the student; other times they give failing grades to those who they think should not pursue the college-preparatory curricula. Warner implies that in Yankee City, status factors, and not necessarily achievement, enter into teachers' judgments of who "belongs" in the college-preparatory courses.

We have some evidence, then, that students' choice of curricula is in part dependent upon their social status rather than upon their ability to learn. There are some who do not like to admit that factors other than ability seem to determine who goes to college and especially that these "other factors" are closely tied up with our stratification system. Such people emphasize the fact that *some* lower-status children do, in fact, go to college. They point out, furthermore, that each year college scholarships are offered to able students and that a certain proportion of the scholarships always go unused. Later we will investigate factors in our schools, other than curricula differences, that are related to social status. Perhaps this will help answer these objections. Let us turn first to those schools that have but one curriculum for all students.

SCHOOLS WITHOUT DIFFERENT CURRICULA

In some public high schools there is no differentiation of curricula; the same courses are available to all students. In general, there are three types of undifferentiated high schools: (1) the school whose enrollment is too small to permit different curricula; (2) the school whose population is similar in its status make-up; and (3) the school that is large enough to permit differentiation but chooses instead not to have hard divisions based on collegiate intentions.

The small high school. In Hometown, as in most small cities, the high school enrollment is too small to have a separate curriculum for the college-bound students. There are, of course, a certain number of "elective" courses, but students of all statuses are in the same "required" courses. It should be added, however, that in many such schools the curriculum is built around college-entrance requirements.

The high school that serves a relatively homogeneous population.[9] In homogeneous suburbs such as Lake Forest (Ill.), Grosse Pointe (Mich.) and Shaker Heights (Ohio) it is usually unnecessary to have different curricula. Most of the students are college-bound and the remainder seem to accept the curriculum that is built around the needs of the majority.

The large, undifferentiated high school. In some large cities the high schools contain no separate curricula despite the fact that their enrollments are large enough to make differentiation possible.[10] The distinguishing characteristic of the undifferentiated high school is the lack of the split between the college-preparatory group and the "others" and the differential prestige that is attached to the two groups. In such a situation children should have a greater chance to compete with one another and to demonstrate their ability.

[9] Warner, *op. cit.,* p. 70.
[10] *Ibid.,* pp. 69-70.

Perhaps if we examine how social status affects still other aspects of the school situation we will understand why even in the undifferentiated high schools students who go to college do not come from the various status levels proportionately.

STATUS AND THE "SECTION SYSTEM"

Some elementary schools have a section system by which the students in the same grade are separated into two, three, or more groups. In Old City, for example, each grade has three sections: A, B, and C. The sections meet in different classrooms and are taught by different teachers. In Old City the children are said to be divided into the sections on the basis of their ability. The junior-high-school principal explains that the "ability" of the students is estimated simply by teachers' judgments.[11, 12]

Accordingly, if ability is distributed more or less evenly among children of various statuses, we should expect to find the same proportion of children from each social level in each of the three sections. But this is not the case. The higher-status levels are represented in Section A up to twice as frequently as they are in the total sample, whereas there are over three times as many lower-status students in the sample as there are in the highest section. These facts lend themselves to two interpretations: (1) higher-status students in general have more ability than do those of lower status; or (2) students are placed in the section on the basis of factors other than ability alone. Perhaps the statement of two school officials will help us decide which is the more likely

[11] *Ibid.*, p. 73.

[12] A recent study discovered that teachers in small schools can estimate a student's I.Q. with a fairly high degree of accuracy. Errors in estimates were made, to be sure, but the coefficient of correlation between teachers' rating of their students and their subsequent scores on an I.Q. test was discovered to be +0.72. (Robert E. Hubbard and William R. Flesher, "Intelligent Teachers and Intelligence Tests—Do They Agree?" *Educational Research Bulletin*, 32 (May 13, 1953), pp. 113-122.) If we can generalize on the basis of this study, it would seem that teachers *can* estimate the ability of their students. The question in relation to this study concerns whether they estimate ability *alone* when assigning students to various sections.

interpretation. When the junior-high-school principal was asked whether there were any status distinctions between the sections he responded: [13]

There is to some extent. You generally find that children from the best families do the best work. That is not always true but usually it is so. The children from the lower class seem to be not as capable as the others. I think it is to some extent inheritance. The others come from people who are capable and educated, and also the environment probably has a great effect. They come to school with a lot of knowledge already that the others lack.

The principal's theory seems to support the first interpretation. A teacher in the junior high school had a somewhat different story when asked if there was "much class feeling in the school." She replied: [14]

Oh, yes, there is a lot of that. We try not to have it as much as we can but of course we can't help it. Now, for instance, even in the sections we have, it is evident. Sections are supposed to be made up just on the basis of records in school but it isn't and everybody knows it isn't. I know right in my own A section I have children who ought to be in B section, but they are little socialites and so they stay in A. I don't say there are children in B who should be in A but in the A section there are some who shouldn't be there. We have discussed it in faculty meetings but nothing is ever done....

Of course, we do some shifting around. There are some borderliners who were shifted up to make the sections more nearly even. But the socialites who aren't keeping up their standard in the A section were never taken into B or C section and they never will. They don't belong there socially. Of course, there are some girls in A section who don't belong there socially, but almost everyone of the socialites is in A.

Studies dealing with the relationship between ability and social status would support this teacher's viewpoint that it is not always ability that places a student in the highest section.[15] Whatever

[13] Warner, *op. cit.*, p. 74.
[14] *Ibid.*
[15] For the relationship between academic achievement and social status see Stephen Abrahamson, *op. cit.*, p. 443. See also pp. 172-173.

the interpretation, however, the fact remains that higher-status students are overrepresented in the A section. By and large, students from a given status level are placed with one another, and thus learn to exclude those of quite different status.

YANKEE CITY SCHOOLS

There are two kinds of groupings in the Yankee City elementary school system: (1) there are different schools for children from different sections of the city; and (2) the schools employ the section system for grouping the students in each grade.

Dorland School is situated in the south end of Yankee City. Over 80 per cent of the children in this school are either upper-lower or lower-lower class. Most higher-status children go to Ashton School, situated in one of the "better" neighborhoods. "In the case of those who live near the borderline of the school districts the assignment of the students by the school authorities is based more on class status than ability." [16]

Social status is reflected in the physical facilities of the Yankee City schools as well as the make-up of the school populations. The Dorland School has the dubious distinction of being the only school in town without lighting in all of its classrooms. Its heating system has been called inadequate and even hazardous. In general, the school is dirty and run-down. The school authorities spend less money for this and other schools in the poorer areas than for other schools. With respect to this situation Warner concludes, "There can be no doubt that the powerful middle-class, by their influence on the schools, tend to contribute to the subordination of the lower classes by refusing equipment to schools which are predominately lower class." [17]

The Dorland School operates with a section system similar to that previously described. The children purportedly are placed in the sections according to their ability but the superintendent

[16] Warner, op. cit., p. 75.
[17] Ibid., p. 76.

of schools commented that, "A section is for Hill Streeters, B for the middle group, and C for the Riverbrookers." [18] The school principal does not seem to like the implications of this remark and emphasizes that students are allowed more individual attention because of the section system.

But status differences among students in the three sections *are* evident. All of the upper-middle class (the highest class in the school) students are in A section, while 91 per cent of the students in C section are lower-lower class. Regardless of how we account for this, it is manifest that children tend to be segregated along lines of social status in some of our grade and high schools.

COLLEGES AND THE STATUS SYSTEM

Most students are probably well aware that there are status differences among the many colleges and universities in this country. The "Ivy League" institutions and a few others largely attract the higher-status students. State universities and liberal-arts colleges draw mainly from the middle-status levels. College students of lower status are found disproportionately in our teachers' colleges and municipal junior colleges.

Equally as significant as the status differences among institutions of higher learning is the relationship between the curricula choices of college students and the economic status of their families. In a study cited by Warner, an interesting pattern is discovered when the college courses are ranked according to the median income of the families of students pursuing each. (The study was first published in 1940, so it is to be expected that the average incomes are lower than those that would be found today.) It seems safe to generalize from Table 10 that status differences are often related to curriculum choices at the collegiate level.

Concerning social status and the school system Warner concludes: "The evidence from the Yankee City schools demonstrates that the school reinforces the class standards in the general

18 *Ibid.*

community, from an early period in the child's life through high
school and into college." [19]

TABLE 10. Parental Income and College Courses *

Curriculum	Median Parental Income
Law	$2118
Medicine and Dentistry	2112
Liberal Arts	2068
Journalism	1907
Engineering	1884
Teaching	1570
Commercial	1543
Nursing	1368
Industrial Trades	1104

* W. Lloyd Warner, Robert J. Havighurst, and Martin B. Loeb, *Who Shall Be Educated?*
(New York, Harper and Bros., 1944), p. 72. Used by permission.

SOCIAL MOBILITY THROUGH EDUCATION

So far we have shown only one side of the picture, how the
school system operates to fit students into social positions similar
to their parents'. But there are always a number of "exceptional"
cases. Some boys and girls of lower status are placed in the higher
sections of elementary school, choose the college-preparatory
course in high school, and eventually graduate from college.[20]

Education as a means of social mobility operates differently for
different children, however. It depends, in part, on how far the
mobile person rises and from where he starts. Warner cites some
case histories of successful social mobility which illustrate how
education fits into the picture. One is the story of Martha, a
lower-status girl from one of the poorest residential areas of
Hometown. "When Martha first appeared at school," we are told,
"she was a shy, thin blonde child, looking like a fresh version of
her pale, prematurely old mother." [21] She soon attracted the

[19] *Ibid.*, p. 80.
[20] *Ibid.*, pp. 81-82.
[21] *Ibid.*, pp. 88-89.

attention of her teachers, however, by her seriousness, her willingness and ability to learn, and her persistence in doing simple tasks for them during recess. Her teachers generally reciprocated with extra help in school work, and sometimes they gave her a book or two. As a result of her presumably pleasant experiences in grammar school, Martha had no misgivings about enrolling in high school.

Apparently Martha readily adjusted to high school and was very happy there. Despite the fact that her mother died and she was forced to keep the family going, she managed to remain in high school with the help of a scholarship arranged for by her teachers. Her school history was in marked contrast to her half-brothers and half-sisters who disliked school, were "kept back" at one time or another, and generally "grew to be unrecognizable among the other Boxtown children." [22] Finally, Martha graduated from high school and took a job as a domestic in a "respectable" home.

From the Browns, Martha learned "refined ways" and "some of the niceties of living room conduct." For quite a time she was happy with them, then she announced one day that she was going to visit her mother's people in Indiana. The real story was this. She had become enamoured of a magazine salesman who professed both his love for her and his intentions of marriage. Martha's letter informing him she was going to bear his child had been returned with the conclusive stamp, "not known at this address." She bore the child in a maternity home in a nearby city and six months later returned to Hometown where she obtained a job through the assistance of her former employer, Mrs. Brown.

Another chapter in Martha's life began the night she met Dick Johnson, a run-of-the-mill lawyer, at a dance sponsored by a women's organization.[23] A few months later they were married.

And so the shy little girl from the tarpaper shack in Boxtown settled down in a neat white house in a "nice" neighborhood.

[22] *Ibid.*, p. 90.
[23] *Ibid.*, pp. 94-95.

Throughout her story many factors stand out as having contributed to her successful mobility. Martha had ambition; she was determined and calculating as well. She knew what she wanted and soon learned how to satisfy her wants. But we are concerned here with how education fits into the story of our socially mobile heroine.

From the time that Martha started school it was apparent that she was not like the rest of "those Boxtowners." Her clean clothes and person belied her lower status. Nor did she *act* like the typical "slum kids." She took an interest in school, helped her teachers, and so on. Her teachers, in turn, were willing to put forth some extra effort when they discovered that she was interested in "getting ahead." It was through their help that she managed to graduate from high school, a somewhat rare accomplishment for the "typical Boxtowner." Her first job was found by one of her teachers. Certainly education alone was not responsible for Martha's rise in status but it is almost equally as certain that it played an important part.

Most cases in which education contributes to a rise in status are not so spectacular as that cited. The more frequent cases are those of children who are able to raise their status only a little above that of their parents.

Teachers and the Social-Status System

School policies and other features of the school system were shown to be influenced by social status. Teachers, too, fit into this pattern in ways that are not always understood. We would want to know, for example, what the position of teachers is in the status hierarchy of American towns and cities. From what point in the hierarchy did they come? Finally, and what may be even more important, how do status factors influence their role as teachers of American youths?

The social status of teachers. Most Americans, apparently, think that a public-school teacher has a "good" occupation. When jobs are ranked according to their prestige, the position of "public-school teacher" receives an "above average" rank. The job of teacher carries *more* prestige than such jobs as radio announcer, undertaker, and insurance agent, but it carries *less* prestige than such positions as physician, lawyer, and civil engineer.[24] In Warner's terminology, most teachers are "middle class." Table 11 shows how the public-school teachers are distributed in the status hierarchy in the three towns studied by Warner.

TABLE 11. Social-Class Distribution of Teachers *

	Hometown Per Cent	Yankee City Per Cent	Old City Per Cent
Upper-upper	0	2	2.5
Lower-upper	0	1	2.5
Upper-middle	26	76	72.5
Lower-middle	72	21	20.0
Upper-lower	2	0	2.5
Lower-lower	0	0	0.0
	100	100	100.0

* W. Lloyd Warner, Robert J. Havighurst, and Martin B. Loeb, *Who Shall Be Educated?* (New York, Harper and Bros., 1944), p. 101. Used by Permission.

The parents of teachers. From Table 12 it is apparent that the parents of a generation of school teachers were largely farmers and businessmen. "It is safe to say," according to Warner, "that the businessmen are mostly owners of small businesses—grocers, druggists and the like."[25] It is significant that a sizable number of prospective teachers are recruited from the families of laborers. Apparently, the teaching profession attracts a large number of socially mobile individuals; in the study cited by Warner, probably over half of the students in the teachers' colleges will achieve a status higher than their parents.

Thus, teachers are either born of middle-class families or have

[24] The relative prestige of these occupations are based on Cecil C. North and Paul K. Hatt, *Occupations Ranked According to Prestige* (unpublished manuscript). A partial reproduction of this scale appears in Logan Wilson and William L. Kolb, *Sociological Analysis* (New York, Harcourt, Brace and Co., 1949), p. 464.
[25] Warner, *op. cit.*, p. 101.

achieved this status by virtue of their occupation. Considering their status origins and eventual social positions it is not surprising that, as a group, they tend to take on and to emphasize the values of the great "middle class." [26] This affects their role as educators of American youth.

TABLE 12. Occupations of Parents of 1080 Women Students in Fifteen Teachers Colleges *

Type of Occupation	Per Cent Engaged in Occupation
Professional	8.1
Manufacturing	3.1
Business (proprietary)	42.1
Farming	45.2
Public Service	4.5
Business (clerical)	5.0
Skilled Labor	14.8
Unskilled Labor	4.0

* W. Lloyd Warner, Robert J. Havighurst, and Martin B. Loeb, *Who Shall Be Educated?* (New York, Harper and Bros., 1944), p. 102. Used by Permission.

The Boards of Education

In every community there is a group of citizens, usually elected, whose function it is to represent the general public in matters of educational policy. Several studies have shown that these boards of education are made up largely of business and professional men.[27] In terms of social status, the members of the school boards of Old City, Hometown, and Yankee City were somewhat higher than the teachers. A few board members were upper class, while none came from below the middle. It would appear, then, that the "middle-class bias" of the teachers would find approval and reinforcement through the boards of education.

[26] A recent study, for example, found that the vast majority of teachers in one community "identify" with a status level above skilled workers and, to a lesser extent, above white-collar workers. The teachers, moreover, were found to be "very conservative" in their views. See V. M. Sims, "The Social Class Affiliation of a Group of Public School Teachers," *School Review*, 59 (September, 1951), pp. 331-338.

[27] Warner, *op. cit.*, p. 118.

Democratic Values and Educational Facts

In the foregoing sections we have attempted to describe how the American school system is related to the social-status system. The school system simultaneously operates to perpetuate our existing social-status system and to provide for a certain amount of social mobility.[28] It is clear that children from lower social levels, many of whom have average or even above-average ability, do not participate in our schools as frequently or for as long a time as do children of higher status. In view of the differential treatment that is afforded children of unequal status, this is not difficult to understand.

It should be made clear that Warner is not advocating a system of *identical* education for all children. Rather, he is stressing that it is in keeping with our democratic ideals that all children should have an opportunity to achieve as much education as they desire and from which they can profit. We have shown that this is not the case in America today. Warner also points out that America cannot afford the luxury of filling its top positions chiefly with the competent from among our higher-status citizens. "We must," he tells us, "use fully *all* our human resources if we are to have the necessary personnel to administer efficiently the work that society must have done." [29] With this in mind, Americans should be able to answer for themselves the provocative question, "Who Shall Be Educated?"

[28] The extent of social mobility is difficult to estimate and it is even less certain how much mobility can be traced even partially to education. As a result of a recent study Mulligan seems to conclude that the actual mobility through education is exceedingly less than the potential. See Raymond H. Mulligan, "Social Mobility and Higher Education," *Journal of Educational Sociology*, 25 (April, 1952), pp. 476-487.

[29] *Ibid.*, p. 142. Italics not in original.

EVALUATION

Methodology

Social status in this study is reported in terms of Warner's familiar six-class scheme. Thus, for most questions relating to the adequacy of this scheme and how it was derived, the reader can be referred to Chapter 6. It has probably been noted that in this study the definitions of both the six classes and the criteria for membership in them have remained unclarified. This, it is thought, limits the possibility for grasping the dynamics of the relationship between our social-stratification system and our public schools. Perhaps if we knew more precisely what is meant by, for example, the "lower class" we would be better able to understand why children from this level received differential treatment in schools and responded differently even when afforded similar opportunities.

Warner's use of many different studies and investigations can be considered part of the "methodology" of *Who Shall Be Educated?* This technique has enabled the student to realize that the problems and situations reported are not unique to one or two communities. The findings, therefore, should be more meaningful and, indeed, are more thought-provoking.

This same technique, however, has resulted in a certain amount of confusion. Individuals are variously classified according to their yearly income, occupation, and over-all social status. The reader frequently is forced to "shift gears" to relate these factors both to one another and to the variable under study.

Findings

This study attempted to demonstrate how the American school system both perpetuates the existing social structure and provides for a limited amount of social mobility. Considerable evidence was produced to indicate that children of various statuses are treated differentially in our schools. In fact, there is a certain amount of segregation along status lines, which means that at an early age children associate with equals and near-equals and learn to avoid those of quite dissimilar status. In these, and other ways, the schools perpetuate the present status system.

Less objective evidence is furnished on the successfully mobile children. A few case histories are presented in which it is evident that education played a part in the social mobility of the people concerned. What is lacking, however, is factual data of the type that could be compared with and possibly verified by studies of a similar nature. It is difficult to abstract "principles of social mobility" from the limited number of personal histories of successfully mobile individuals. It is the need for these "principles" which is most strongly felt.

It has been said that "much that the authors present is already well known." [30] Undoubtedly much of the data could be duplicated from the records of most of our schools. This study, however, illustrates the fruitful results that can be obtained when a common situation is dealt with in an uncommon way. Although the "facts" have been present for all to inspect, few, apparently, have realized the systematic way in which social status pervades the entire school system.

SELECTED READINGS

ABRAHAMSON, Stephen, "Our Status System and Scholastic Rewards," *Journal of Educational Sociology*, 25 (April, 1952), pp. 441-450.

HAVIGHURST, R. J., and BREESE, Fay H., "The Relation Between Ability and Social Status in a Midwestern Community. III," *Journal of Educational Psychology*, 38 (April, 1947), pp. 241-247.

JANKE, L. L., and HAVIGHURST, R. J., "Relations Between Ability and Social Status in a Midwestern Community. II" (See bibliographic note, p. 191.)

MULLIGAN, Raymond A., "Social Mobility and Higher Education," *Journal of Educational Sociology*, 25 (April, 1952), pp. 476-487.

[30] Malcolm M. Willey, review of *Who Shall Be Educated? American Journal of Sociology*, 50 (September, 1944), p. 148.

MULLIGAN, Raymond A., "Socioeconomic Background and College Enrollment," *American Sociological Review,* 16 (April, 1951), pp. 188-196.

NEUGARTEN, Bernice L., "Social Class and Friendship Among School Children." (See bibliographic note, p. 191.)

SIMS, Verner M., "The Social Class Affiliation of a Group of Public School Teachers," *School Review,* 59 (September, 1951), pp. 331-338.

———, "Some Correlates of Social Class Identification Among High-School and College Students." (See bibliographic note, p. 192.)

Part III
CONCLUSIONS

12

Position and Mobility in the American Pattern

INTRODUCTION

OUR MAIN SURVEY of the literature of social stratification, incomplete though it has been, has now largely been concluded. We shall, however, refer from time to time in the concluding sections to materials not already explained. Two important tasks still remain: (1) to *evaluate* the now familiar empirical data in somewhat larger compass than we have already done in the various chapters; and (2) to *integrate* our knowledge of widely scattered and differently conceived studies, so that they may be brought to focus upon a half dozen or so important theoretical, and sometimes also practical, questions pertaining to social stratification in the United States.

To accomplish these objectives we shall need first to *weigh evidence*—evidence which, it will be recalled from preceding chapters, is often incomplete and sometimes contradictory. But it is not enough to examine evidence; we need to go a step further. In a very real and literal sense, there is need to examine also the *evidence for the evidence*. This latter phrase is no mere play on words. Social-science research all too frequently presents a comixture of fact and factiousness, of spuriousness and of solid information. As has been pointed out repeatedly, this will take us into social-science methodology quite as much as into so-called "content." For content is not self-evident; rather it is *constructed* as content, through the pursuit of *certain* research methods, the selection of *certain* data to be studied, and the use of *certain* logical exercises in the derivation of the conclusions from data. There is a subtle but persistent illusion, common both to some scholars and to many laymen, that "the facts" are somehow independent of human judgment, that there are such things as "bare facts" and "inescapable facts" and facts with all sorts of adjectives intending to connote that some particular item of information is unaffected by the human equation. In the study of human behavior it is at least doubtful whether there are any facts in this sense, and certainly in the field of social stratification there are relatively few facts which can safely be accepted without careful scrutiny.

In this effort it is hoped that the reader, quite as much as the authors, will not hesitate to draw upon personal experience and observation and upon logical analysis as aids to the formation of conclusions. It is hoped further that neither of us will choose to fly in the face of impressive empirical evidence in order to buttress hopes or fears or judgments derived from "authority" or "intuition." This is a hard discipline, but it is a necessary one; for unless conclusions from objective data and intricate theory make some real sense, they will only give the learner a vague feeling that social-science methods are not quite to be trusted, or that there is something unreal and "merely academic" about conclusions derived by these methods. As specialists in the social sciences, the authors would be the first to acknowledge that some of the work done by sociologists on stratification and on other matters has been presented in a form and also sometimes a spirit which is hardly conducive to trust and respect. That this is a minority of our research and theoretical output is probably obvious, but as in so many aspects of human experience, it is frequently the conduct of comparative minorities that attracts the greatest attention.

We have said that we shall attempt to marshal whatever data we can in an attempt to answer, however tentatively, certain meaningful and important questions about social stratification in the United States during the 1950's. What are these questions? The following seem to us to constitute such a series of important and basic questions. We offer no evidence to prove that they are "basic" in importance, since we consider it self-evident from the frequency with which they are asked that they are considered important. It is also our judgment that they are scientifically basic. Obviously, there are other questions that could be asked, and these could be asked in other forms.

1. Is there a single American stratification system?

2. Does every person and/or family have *a* more or less clear position in the stratification system?

3. Can we reach a conclusion relative to the truth or falsity of the American Dream as an explanation of social mobility in the United States?

4. Do the facts of stratification in the United States warrant the use of the term *social class* in the sense that the persons in each "class" are *objectively* "set off from" the persons in other "classes"?

5. Is the American stratification system "functional" and, if so, in what sense?

6. What are some of the larger implications of the structure of power in American society? What attending issues have formed? How, and to what extent, are they being resolved?

7. What about class consciousness and class conflict in the United States? Do they exist? How are they manifest? What is their significance?

8. What negative judgments of the American stratification system can be made, using as a base for evaluation the *stated objectives* of American society?

9. What favorable factors in the system can be found, using the same criteria as in Question 8?

10. What imminent developments in the stratification system in the United States can we anticipate?

Questions 1 through 3 will be considered in this chapter, Questions 4 and 5 in Chapter 13, Questions 6 and 7 in Chapter 14, and the last three in Chapter 15.

IS THERE A SINGLE AMERICAN STRATIFICATION SYSTEM?

Our reply to this question is, in the light of evidence reproduced here, a qualified, "probably no." Four lines of evidence converge to support the negative conclusion.

1. First of all, *communities of comparable size and similar gross characteristics apparently differ from one another* in a number of important respects. It will be recalled that Lenski,[1] using the same method Warner [2] allegedly used, found in a highly similar city completely different public consciousness of class than that found by Warner. Replication studies of this sort are exceedingly rare and consequently it cannot be asserted dogmatically that communities do in fact differ fundamentally, but it *can* be safely asserted that the evidence to demonstrate that they do not differ is conspicuously lacking. This will be recognized as contrary to the position taken by Warner and his associates. Although we respect the Warner group's undoubted efforts at objectivity, we are unable to overlook the existence of other careful studies like those of Lenski and Kenkel,[3] which reach distinctly different conclusions.

Apparently there are idiosyncratic elements on the community level. For example, some communities are one-industry towns, others are diversified; some have altruistic—even if paternalistic—X families.[4] Others have X families essentially exploitative in their social influence, and some communities have no clear-cut X families at all. Ideologies of local ethnic groups, churches, and

[1] See Chapter 5.
[2] See Chapter 6.
[3] See Chapter 7.
[4] This reference is to "The X Family," Chapter III in Lynd and Lynd, *Middletown in Transition* (New York, Harcourt, Brace and Co., 1937).

especially educational institutions are by no means the same in every community, and these may be presumed to exert considerable influence upon judgments of "who belongs where" and of feelings about invidious status comparisons and attitudes toward mobility. Whether we are right or wrong in offering these explanations, the data *as presented by the researchers* themselves would seem to document the basic proposition.

2. Not only are communities of a similar size different from one another in their status structures, but *additional differences appear to be introduced by* the *differing sizes of the community aggregates.* The justification offered for this position is partly inferential, but more largely empirical. Inclusive stratification studies of large urban aggregates like New York City or Chicago or Detroit or Los Angeles have not been made. But practically everyone who has written on the subject of stratification from the viewpoint of community analysis has said, in effect, that he would expect these large population aggregates to be "different" from communities like Middletown or Jonesville or even Columbus, and we know of no sociologist who would be inclined to challenge this assumption.

Moving down the scale of size, the evidence becomes more empirical. Compare, for example, the findings on Plainville,[5] Elmtown,[6] and Columbus.[7] Surely these status systems are constituted differently, even though there are some similarities in the alleged *bases used* by the people to judge status. It appears probable to us that, as the size of the population aggregate increases and the opportunity for face-to-face or even second-hand personal knowledge of persons and families diminishes, the tendency to judge by external symbols of status increases, although we recognize the possibility of entertaining alternative hypotheses on this point.

3. Apparently there are also *regional differences among com-*

[5] Chapter 4.
[6] Chapter 8.
[7] Chapter 7.

munities, which differences appear to be related to ecological and historical factors. Despite a somewhat dubious methodology, Adams [8] appears to have discovered significant differences in the social-mobility patterns of lawyers in different regions of the United States. Moreover, it seems a reasonable inference that differences in the origins and make-up of the racial and immigrant stock would affect the status systems of some communities. Historical evidence from such regions as the American Southwest, notably Texas and Oklahoma, show the effect upon the stratification system of successive waves of prosperity, following the discovery and exploitation of oil in a country which had as its chief economic base cotton, cattle grazing, and other types of agriculture. It will be recalled, further, that nearly a fourth of the American states are less than 100 years removed from an economy based on Negro slavery, and even less removed in time from an interstitial form of stratification during the Reconstruction period. Summarizing our case tersely, we have already pointed out (*a*) the failure of any studies clearly to demonstrate the absence of regional difference, (*b*) a few studies which document the existence of differences, and (*c*) what appear to be reasonable inferences from differential history, that regional differences cannot be ignored.

4. Despite evidence, not presented here but well known, that *earlier extremes of rural-urban differences are rapidly diminishing, it would be a mistake to assume that they have been entirely obliterated.* Current estimates indicate that around 15 per cent of Americans live in rural areas. This figure, of course, represents a census category rather than a count of functional living and economic arrangements. In rural areas, whether the preponderant system of agriculture is a traditional farm family unit or a newer and growing absentee-owned corporation-type of agricultural endeavor, the community structure is basically different from

[8] Stuart Adams, "Regional Differences in Vertical Mobility in a High-Status Occupation," *American Sociological Review,* 15 (April, 1950), pp. 228-235.

that of cities. Numerous studies [9] document the fact that the stratification characteristics of rural communities have many different elements from the urban. To be sure, some similarities do exist, such as the ever-present importance of wealth and income and of lineage, but despite these similarities, the stratification differences between Plainville and Jonesville cannot be generalized without doing violence to both.

Having answered chiefly in the negative the question of whether there is a single over-all American stratification system does not mean that we do not find some evidence of basic similarities which run through the American society, regardless of region and difference in community size or ecology. Certain kinds of possessions everywhere appear to bestow upon the possessor and his family status advantages over the non-possessor. Everywhere we encounter, in some degree at least, widespread aspiration to achieve higher status and some willingness to defer gratification of immediate needs for the purpose of achieving upward social mobility. Virtually everywhere we find the same complex of institutions, through which successful individuals secure the necessary skills to enhance their mobility. Probably education, the church, and the military services are the clearest illustrations, although to some extent government service (both civil service and "politics") and the corporation constitute effective ladders whereby certain individuals with no previous claim to upward mobility do achieve mobility and sometimes to a marked degree. Moreover, it appears probable that with the constantly increasing exposure of persons in all regions and in virtually all strata to our many mass media, the idiosyncratic elements in region and community type will gradually tend to be diminished. Such seems a

[9] See Chapter 4. Also Harold F. Kaufman, *Defining Prestige in a Rural Community*, Sociometry Monograph, Number 10 (New York, Beacon House, 1946); John Useem, Pierre Tangent, and Ruth Useem, "Stratification in a Prairie Town," *American Sociological Review*, 7 (June, 1942), pp. 331-342; and Otis D. Duncan and Jay W. Ortis, "Social Stratification in a Pennsylvania Rural Community," *The Pennsylvania State College of Agriculture, Bulletin 543* (October, 1951).

reasonable inference, but this eventuality cannot be demonstrated factually at present.

POSITION

Does every person and/or family have a single more or less clearly defined position in the American stratification system? With rural areas and small towns *possibly* constituting an exception, the evidence would seem to indicate that a given person or family does *not* have a *single* status position in the community of his residence. Again we must recognize some contradictory evidence and logic, but on the whole it can be concluded that a person has *multiple statuses*, based not only upon *multiple dimensions* and *different reference groups*,[10] but even more upon the *lack of correlation among the different criteria* by which he is evaluated. Some writers have discussed "status position" as if income, lineage, possessions, occupation, and other status-giving attributes of a person were somehow "averaged up" by a community, the way a college registrar averages the course grades to determine who shall make the honor roll. Outside of rural communities, and possibly not even there, we find little evidence to support this neat formulation. Consistent with more of the evidence seems to be the view that persons and families have multiple stratified statuses based upon (*a*) *who* does the evaluating and (*b*) *what* criterion is being employed at the moment.

The Hatt-North scale of occupational prestige has been mentioned several times.[11] It will be recalled that the highest prestige occupations in this study were not the highest *paid* occupations, or necessarily the occupations requiring the highest *education*. (At least, occupations requiring comparable education rated wide

[10] Reference-group theory seems to us to be a very fruitful approach to understanding stratification, especially on a social psychological level. See, e.g., Herbert H. Hyman, "The Relation of the Reference Group to Judgments of Status," in Reinhard Bendix and Seymour Lipset, *Class Status and Power* (Glencoe, Ill., The Free Press, 1953), pp. 263-271.

[11] National Opinion Research Center, "Jobs and Occupations: A Popular Evaluation," *Opinion News*, 9 (September, 1947), pp. 3-13.

differences.) Yet occupation, income, and education are rather uniformly reported as being prominent among the bases used for the assignment of status to persons. It seems that something like the following represents a true and realistic picture of how a person or family is "stratified" in the community of residence.

The *A* family apparently has a good deal of money. They have two cars, a nice house. *But* they don't go to church, they don't help in the community chest drive, and they never go to the PTA. *But* they've all gone to college, subscribe to a lot of newspapers and magazines and buy a lot of books. *But* you would think that a man with his education would do something better than just be a contractor for building silos and grain storage bins. *But* not many are inclined to criticise openly because Mr. *A* has a lot of power in this town—can hire and fire a lot of people and he also has some kind of an "in" with the Bank—maybe owns some of its stock.

With the criteria for ascribing status showing as low intercorrelations as they do, such instances as the above are by no means unusual. It could not be otherwise under the conditions.

Not enough attention, West's *Plainville, U.S.A.* being one conspicuous exception, has been given to measuring differences in the status ranking of individuals and families in a given community from the point of view of *groups evaluating from different reference points.* Probably the reason for differing concepts of who belongs where and why is that the bases for assigning status are by no means as uniform as it is sometimes alleged that they are. For example, it is one thing to observe that, practically universally, money and possessions are a basis for awarding positive status and another thing to note the differences in the *amount of importance attached* to money and to certain kinds of possessions by the Prairie people of Plainville and by the Hill people. Quite conceivably, comparable differences might be expected between the importance attached to wealth by a Quaker family on an Iowa farm and by a Catholic merchant's family in Brooklyn. Similarly with education: families differ greatly in the kinds of traditions which they have or are trying to build with respect to education.

One major difference is the valuation of education per se as against valuation of education for ulterior reasons such as "you'll get an easier job," or "you'll make more money." It is at least questionable in the latter case whether it is education that is being valued at all. Moreover, there are substantial numbers of persons, and even organized groups, who either place no value on college education or actually disvalue it. These persons are a minority of the population, but they are *in* the population and their evaluation of themselves and others on the basis of these varying criteria of education are quite as socially real as are those of the lower-middle-class housewife who is doing her own washing so that Junior "can get through Normal School and be the first teacher on either side of the family."

Some statistical procedures tend to foster an illusion of uniformity. This is particularly true of the use of measures of central tendency (averages of various sorts,—means, modes, and medians). Probably because they are the simplest of all statistical concepts they are overused. To illustrate, let us take the case of the "Insurance Agent" on the Hatt-North scale of occupational prestige.[12] We say that he rated 68. What does this mean? It means that of the persons interviewed, each evaluating the occupation on a five-point scale, the *average* came out 68. Actually, some persons may have rated the occupation very superior, others superior, some average, some below average and some very inferior, but this *average* rating resulted. For purposes of comparison with other occupations, it is entirely legitimate, of course, to do this averaging. The error lies in the easy supposition that there is a *uniformity in the judgment* of Americans about the occupation, when all we know, from the published data, is that the people who thought well of it canceled out the people who thought poorly of it, leaving it in an approximate midway position. In other words, averages tend to blur differences.

One of the seemingly important aspects of personal placement in a stratification system, which no study seems to have under-

12 *Ibid.*

taken and few persons have chosen to discuss, is whether the informant, except when he is pushed by the investigator, *actually* thinks in terms of a single unitary placement when evaluating others or himself. In the absence of evidence, we are perhaps entitled to speculate on the matter, and our speculation runs somewhat as follows. Do not individuals tend mostly to think in some such terms as these: "I am not the wealthiest man in town, but I have as much education as any and I guess I am as well liked as average. Few people drive better cars and have better homes, even though I'm kind of a nobody because I didn't grow up in this town and nobody ever heard of my parents." If the man is ambitious, he might strive to make more money in order to improve his position, or change occupations to improve his standing, or brief himself on "how to win friends and influence people" if he wishes to improve his popularity. To be sure, a man might generalize, average out, his various ratings and conclude, "Well, all in all I guess I'm above average," or, "Maybe my education will compensate for defects in my lineage." But even if he does this, he would probably do it with the full knowledge that people do not react to him as a set of abstract averages, but rather in terms of concrete attributes—what he is, what he has, what he does, and these apparently always comparatively.

How are status striving and upward mobility related to the fragmentized stratification picture which has just been described? Although we know of no way to prove it statistically, our observation is that individuals seeking to improve their positions select some dimension which they consider to be important and seek to enhance it. Many times, in fact, one is forced in the practical situation to choose *between* status criteria, since it is not possible to have one's cake and eat it at the same time. For example, many men every year make the choice between going to college or professional school to train for a moderate paying position (such as teacher or clergyman) or accepting an immediate and relatively high paying position (such as a small business with a future). Whichever the choice, the individual is acting logically in terms of the inconsistent imperatives in the American status system. He says in effect, "I would rather have *A* than *B*," and, whichever he chooses, he finds a ready-made set of cultural rationalizations, like a ready-made suit, to justify his decision. And, whichever his choice, he will have no difficulty finding persons to confirm it.

In summary, the American society contains a collection of individuals and families with varying judgments about the stratification systems and their places in them. Apparently persons generally have some notion of where they belong on each of the various continua—at least those of which they are aware and which they value. Some persons are content with their current evaluations and give little thought or attention to improvement. Others, often called "strivers," are discontent with one or more of their status positions and seek, in varying degree and with varying success, to improve their positions. Rarely can they improve on all fronts at once, so an element of choice enters in as to which strife has the highest priority. Some persons go on from conquest to conquest, others strive for a while and then slow down, some never start.[13] This is the kaleidoscope of Americans in the American stratification systems.

THE "AMERICAN DREAM" AND UPWARD MOBILITY

Can we reach a conclusion relative to the truth or falsity of the American Dream as an explanation of social mobility in the United States? Frequently sociologists have written as if their data on stratification have dealt deadly body blows to the American Dream. And so indeed they may. Much depends, first, on what is meant by the "American Dream." Probably, as we have said earlier, the phrase stems from the "rags to riches" sagas of

[13] See, e.g., Seymour Lipset and Reinhard Bendix, "Social Mobility and Occupational Career Patterns II: Social Mobility," *American Journal of Sociology,* 57 (March, 1952), pp. 494-504.

selected persons from American history and from contemporary life. Individuals reared in poverty, if not squalor, have risen in American society to high positions in government, industry, the professions, and the church. What has apparently fired the imaginations of historians and journalists, who have largely nurtured this theme, is that in many other parts of the civilized world these instances would have been either impossible or markedly less frequent. To be sure, Ramsey MacDonald started life as a worker and Stalin was of comparatively low origin, but these are relatively modern cases; the origins of the American Dream lie earlier in history. It is altogether natural that the known instances of the rags-to-riches climb would be overgeneralized, since no one made a count of them. Not only is a recital of the theme ego-satisfying to some, it makes excellent inspirational copy for Fourth of July addresses, school commencements, and children's literature. Frequent repetition of a pleasing fantasy adds a certain credulity.

Many persons, however, who seem to give verbal assent to the American Dream also give other evidence, when observed closely in their actual lives, that they know full well that the statistical probability of attaining some aspiration is not high enough for them to count on it. Heeding the old advice to the soldier, "Pray to the Lord, but keep your powder dry," most American parents seem to have been willing to teach the American Dream to their children when seated on one knee, but also to instruct them about differential life-chances when they are seated on the other.

The American Dream has been a sitting pigeon for those who wish to fire loads of familiar facts about differential life-chances. Some writers have written as if, when they have demonstrated that appreciable numbers of lower-class children of college ability do not go to college, they have abolished a vile myth about American life and education. They often do not point out, or do not know, that the fact of differential aspiration enters in, that all of the people with college ability may not *wish* to go to college. And, despite the large number of lower-class World War II veterans who went to college because of the availability of the

G.I. Bill, we should also document the fact that at least a million eligibles did not elect to accept the gratuity!

There is, of course, little doubt that some of the excesses of the American Dream are sheer nonsense. The formulation that "Anyone can do anything, if he wants to badly enough and works hard enough" is, of course, ridiculous. It is doubtful if many mature adults really believe this, although some children and college students in the writers' experience have said that they did. It is easy to document, with the data on differential life-chances, that the proposition simply is not true. Low life-chances can in many cases weave so inexorable a web around and within one's personality that from birth to the grave he cannot extricate himself from their consequences. Just as it is easy to exaggerate the frequency and ease of upward social mobility, so, also, is it easy to exaggerate the determining influence of low life-chances.

Little progress can be made in analyzing the validity of the American Dream when attention is paid only to the extremes of "rags to riches" glory or frustration in the "perilous web of circumstance." Neither of these characterizations applies to more than a small minority of individuals, except, perhaps, during extreme periods like depressions or war booms. Instead, attention should be drawn to the larger numbers of less dramatic cases.

Here a serious theoretical question is at once encountered: *How much* social mobility is to be regarded as desirable, either on moral or on practical grounds. Returning to an earlier illustration, suppose that 50 per cent of the persons in the ranks of semiskilled labor have minds capable of earning a college degree. Is it morally wrong that only 4 or 5 per cent of these shall actually graduate from college? Or, what may be more pertinent, suppose that all of the barriers to college and attendance were removed— financial, moral, and academic. What would the society do with the millions of unemployed baccalaureates? With the number of higher-status jobs relatively limited—not necessarily to the present numbers—our problem would resolve itself into so organizing the competitive structure that all of the jobs could be filled by the most worthy applicants. This is more easily said than done. There now exist a number of competitive systems for mobility, but many persons think that the systems are not fair, and at many points it seems that they are not. This question will be discussed at length in Chapter 15.

One unfortunate aspect of the American Dream has been its glorification of the final personal triumph, as if all would be well with the person once he succeeded. Although the evidence to the contrary is fragmentary, there is some evidence, and it is not pretty. Psychiatrists such as Karen Horney,[14] for example, have reported that they have observed as patients a disproportionate number of mentally ill persons who had been particularly successful in their upward mobility. In general, the view seems consistent with that implied in a recent cartoon in which one man says to another, "Go ahead, Joe, *you* take the promotion; I'd rather not have an ulcer." This caricature is sustained in at least two studies, one published and one not, which have attempted to measure the personality byproducts of upward social mobility. The first study was of successful career women who had been upwardly mobile.[15] Their positions were currently 10 points or more higher than those of their fathers on the Hatt-North scale of occupational prestige. In comparing this group statistically with a control group of women holding comparable positions, but not much different from those of their fathers, Ellis discovered a significantly higher incidence of poor mental health and psychosomatic illness among the mobile group. The second study, also using a control group, and based on samples of patients diagnosed as "psychosomatic" and "non-psychosomatic" in several hospitals, reached a number of conclusions essentially in harmony with the study first cited.[16] In presenting these data, it

[14] Karen Horney, *The Neurotic Personality of Our Time* (New York, W. W. Norton and Co., 1937), pp. 80-82 and 178-179.
[15] Evelyn Ellis, "Upward Social Mobility Among Unmarried Career Women," *American Sociological Review*, 17 (October, 1952), pp. 558-563.
[16] Unpublished doctoral dissertation by J. D. Folkman, in the Ohio State University Library.

should be stressed that we do not regard the results as conclusive, although the studies are carefully done, are consistent with one another and also with the expectations based on the explanations of such psychiatrists as Horney.

An interesting, and possibly significant, unanswered question remains in the interpretation of the two studies. We refer to the question of cause and effect. Assuming that bad mental health is correlated with upward mobility, are the persons mentally ill because they are upwardly mobile, or are they upwardly mobile because they are mentally ill? The conventional explanation is, of course, the former. Everyone has heard anecdotes about so and so, who worked so hard getting ahead that he developed ulcers or a psychosis. It is quite as tenable, however, to postulate that the reasons for the person's high aspiration and intensity in deferring gratification, which resulted in the successful upward mobility, may have been the frustrations, the bad interpersonal relations in the family and friendship groups in which he originated. These could result in a high level of anxiety, which could in turn result in a high motivation to become a high achiever. The piper is really paid, however, when the person has achieved his goals, or more, only to find that the anxiety does not subside nor the insecurity abate. Instead of reaping the rewards for having undergone deprivation, he still suffers from the sibling rivalry or parental hostility or minority-group psychosis or whatever it was that made him so acutely dissatisfied with his earlier status. This explanation is not offered as necessarily preferential to the more conventional one. Rather it is offered as an *alternative hypothesis* applicable in some cases to explain the relationship found in these studies, with the implication that, all factors considered, it is at least as tenable as the more conventional one.

Thus we are left not knowing how much of high aspiration for social mobility is neurotic in origin and/or contraindicative of good mental and physical health. Moreover, we do not know how much of low aspiration should be considered as rational. A person may have low aspirations because he recognizes that he has low ability and judges that it is better, so to speak, "never to have loved" than to have "loved and lost." Or the low aspirant may have calculated the cost of upward mobility better than the romantic thinks. He may have weighed the necessity for deferring gratifications, the risks involved, the negative aspects of the achievement of success, and concluded, simply, that the prize is not worth the race. Finally, the low aspirer may be sufficiently well adjusted in the lower-status position, finding his values quite in keeping with those of persons to be found there and, withal, finding his life fulfillments, if not the pot of gold, in his own back yard. For these and probably other reasons, the low aspirer, so often looked upon with benign pity by his social superior, may be much wiser than we think, and altogether also a rational man.

It is considered by some not in good taste when writing scientifically to refer to the popular concept "luck" in any serious way. We find it impossible to write realistically about upward social mobility *without* using that term. For beyond the known or knowable statistical probabilities, many life outcomes for successful upwardly mobile persons must be so interpreted. In the interest of fairness, it would have to be admitted that at crucial points in their careers some unforseeable, uncontrollable factor altered their destiny. It is fashionable to point out that it was "not really luck," that the person had to have the wit to capitalize on the opportunity; but this is often only a shallow rationalization, since without the opportunity brought about by the luck, the assumed wit would have been wasted. The purpose of this paragraph is simply to point out that in addition to what we may *know* about differential life-chances in a statistical sense, there is another category of influence, which we have called "luck," which is *a* factor influencing individual instances of social mobility. To omit it would be to leave out an important piece of the puzzle.

In summary, then, our examination of the American Dream and certain known facts about social mobility in the United States would lead to the conclusion that the American Dream does not exist in a form which is readily testable. It is in some ways a useful concept around which to marshal certain kinds of data and logical analysis. Whether the reader believes that form in which he has held the American Dream, if he has, is still tenable in the light of this analysis, will probably depend not so much upon the analysis as upon his temperament, his philosophical orientation, and his own conception of his origins and present status.

SELECTED READINGS

The selected readings for the chapters in Part III will be found on pages 347-350.

13

The Continuum Theory and Functionalism

THE CONTINUUM THEORY

WHAT SHALL we conclude about the concept *social class?* Are the facts of stratification in the United States such as to warrant the use of the term in the sense that the category called a "class" includes a group of persons demonstrably set off from others? Are the various categories found in the several studies we have examined anything other than convenient class intervals in an array of data?

Warner,[1] Hollingshead,[2] and West[3] seem to be correct in their approach to "social class" as a group of people *assigned* a more or less similar status, or status range, within the community, using as criteria of this unity the agreements among the persons in the community (*a*) that these units exist, (*b*) that a certain definite number of people are "in" and "out" of each unit, and (*c*) that it makes a difference both subjectively and objectively in which segment of the community one is. Warner is perhaps most explicit and original in the methods which he and his group use for the discovery of the classes and the methods for determining who is in each. Hollingshead's findings are quite consistent

[1] See Chapter 6.
[2] See Chapter 8.
[3] See Chapter 4.

with Warner's. But, as we have seen in examining published reviews of the specific studies and their methodologies, most professional reviewers are unconvinced that these studies have actually *demonstrated* what they have *asserted*. These and similar studies represent one of the more sizable social-science expenditures of our time, but it seems to us, as also to the numerous other reviewers, that a negative evaluation on the basic issue must be made, despite other utilities of the studies. The data and methods cited simply do not sustain the conclusions claimed about the discreteness of the various "classes."

Two lines of criticism are offered in contradiction of Warner's and others' claims that the community divides itself into six or some other set number of distinct categories. The first line of criticism was developed at length in our evaluation of the Warner studies and applies equally to Hollingshead and to other studies which reach the conclusion being discussed here, namely, that the methods stated by the researchers in question fall short of statistical research methods which have now come to be generally accepted as essential if reliability and validity are to be claimed. A generous hypothesis might be held that Warner's methods were imperfectly reproduced in his works, and that actually they were better than they appear in print. We doubt that this can be taken seriously, however, because numerous reviewers of Warner's several studies over a period of several years have questioned his methodology, and yet, when the summary volume was published, no indication was given by Warner that he had any rebuttal to the widespread criticism of his method. We can only conclude that the methods stated were the methods used and that the researches must be evaluated on this basis.

In short, those ubiquitous proponents who claim that the society divides itself into clear-cut categories seem to us to fail in establishing the burden of proof. By the "burden of proof" is meant the obligation upon him who asserts that something is true to demonstrate conclusively and beyond reasonable doubt that it is true. It is not at all uncommon in the complex and often emotionally charged questions and issues with which social scientists frequently deal, to find that the burden-of-proof principle, known to be fundamental by the logician, is either ignored or mishandled. A common vulgarization on the part of those who "feel" or consider that it is "obvious" that there are or "must be" social classes is the defensive challenge, "Well, maybe we (or they) have not conclusively proven that discrete social classes exist, but you can't prove that they don't." This is tantamount, of course, to saying that I have a right to assert that there is a man in the moon, because you cannot prove that there is not! It would seem that the burden of proving that there is a man in the moon is the claimant's burden, and unless we can demonstrate it conclusively, the person who thinks otherwise need demonstrate nothing.

A second line of reasoning which adds considerable weight to our questioning of the discrete-classes hypothesis is that other research studies using methods comparable to, if not identical with, Warner's have resulted in radically different conclusions on this question. The studies of Lenski [4] and Kenkel [5] are notable in this regard. Lenski, it will be recalled, found in a neighboring city in the same region studied by Warner that a representative sample of community members held no such general conception of the number of classes, or who belonged in each, as was claimed by Warner not only for the communities actually studied but also for the whole United States. Kenkel, using a different method, found in a somewhat larger city that a random sample, chosen from the city directory, invariably gave responses yielding a continuum, not a set of discrete categories.

In addition to the Kenkel and Lenski studies, another study offers further substantiation of our thesis. Hetzler [6] also employed a random sampling technique, but instead of asking *questions*

[4] See Chapter 5.
[5] See Chapter 7.
[6] Stanley Hetzler, "An Investigation of the Distinctiveness of Social Classes," *American Sociological Review*, 18 (October, 1950), pp. 493-497.

regarding class affiliation, he gave each informant a 12-inch scale, indicating at the top "the person of highest status in your community" and at the bottom "the person of lowest status in your community," and requested the informant to mark the point on the scale where he thought he ranked. When these check points were superimposed upon one another, the result showed a continuous, approximately normal, curve of distribution, with no breaks which could possibly be construed as marking off one class or stratum from another. (For the statistically minded reader it might be added that the consulting professional statistician [7] on this research project judged that the statistical procedures to insure reliability and validity were satisfactory, as were also other aspects, such as sampling.)

If we are to reject the conventional hypothesis that social classes exist as more or less discrete social units, conscious of their own identity and of the existence of other units, *what sort of stratification theory may we accept as consistent with the evidence and useful for research and theoretical purposes?* It will be anticipated from what was written in the introductory chapters, that we consider the continuum theory to be tenable. At that point we set forth a somewhat *a priori* set of reasons for preferring a continuum theory over the categorical theory. Recapitulating in part but also integrating data from the various field studies discussed in Part II of the book, our final reasons for rejecting the categorical theory and adhering to the continuum theory are these:

1. All data, even from studies which claim to have found discrete classes, are consistent with the continuum theory. By this we mean that all data which have been reported by researches yield results along a continuum. This is true of income, wealth, education, possession of goods, attitudes, power, occupational prestige, and general reputational prestige. The data of no study failed to show this hierarchical arrangement, even though persons

[7] Profesor Raymond Sletto, The Ohio State University.

who claim to have "found" discrete categories emphasize, of course, the demarcation lines rather than the continuous character of their data.

2. Claims that the society "divides itself" into these oft-discussed class categories seem to be unsubstantiated by the methods which the researchers have said they used. We have discussed this in detail in the central portions of this book and have summarized it again in a few paragraphs above.

(It should perhaps also be explicitly stated that some students of social stratification have claimed the existence of some number of classes, but have not stated *operationally* how they derived this particular number, or precisely what evidence, how gathered and how processed, yielded the conclusions. Studies of this sort are, of course, impossible to evaluate or recheck, and must simply be cited as impressionistic treatments of the subject, yielding no definitive results which can be relied upon.)

3. A number of studies, notably Lenski's, Kenkel's, and Hetzler's, using careful, checkable statistical techniques, have presented impressive evidence favorable to the continuum theory. One used a city of nearly half a million in the Middle West, one a city in New England, and one a county seat village in the Middle West.

4. Most of the objective studies of stratification, which have largely sidestepped the issue of categorical versus continuum theory, have yielded materials which are in no way incompatible with the continuum theory. It would be impossible to do more than to refer summarily to these, although from time to time we have referred to specific social-mobility studies, life-chances studies, intermarriage studies, occupational prestige, wealth and income data, and attitude research.

The authors reject the pedantry which holds that for the sake of consistency we should now not use the term *social class* and should recommend that others do not. We see no objection to the use of the verbal convention *social class*, so long as the reader and the listener are aware of the proximate nature of the reference and of the essentially statistical character of the construct. Such expressions as *middle class, working class, lower class, business class, professional class* have undisputed utility in facilitating communication. It is obvious that they overlap and often will need qualifying adjectives, but this is not unique to our universe of discourse. It adheres in the problem of language, which we always have with us.

A final note should perhaps be appended that deals with research data based on the forced-choice technique. The forced-choice technique consists simply of allowing the informant a certain number of choices and requesting him to check whichever one applies to himself. Thus, the Purdue Opinion Panel,[8] probably taking their cue from Centers who did likewise, gave their informants a four-choice classification—upper class, middle class, working class, and lower class. They then presented tables showing the attitudes or other social characteristics of these four classes, or one of them compared to another. Although there is no inherent objection to this statistical procedure, it has the unfortunate concomitant of reinforcing the notion that these classes were *found* in the research instead of having been *superimposed* on the data at the outset. The researchers could just as well have used three classes or five classes or two classes; and whichever they used, the informants would be left with no option but to make a choice from among the alternatives offered. This kind of research procedure, while yielding useful information, is entirely outside the issue which we have had under discussion in this section.

The authors are unwilling to close the door, however, to the possibility that sometime someone using other research techniques, perhaps, than have been used so far, may demonstrate that the continuum theory is not good enough. The scientifically minded student should always leave the door open to new evi-

---

[8] Purdue Opinion Panel, "Teen-Age Personality in Our Culture," Report of Poll No. 32, May, 1952, Purdue University, Lafayette, Ind., mimeographed.

dence and new theory. But the open mind need not be a gullible mind, and it is not inconsistent to hold the proponent of a new idea responsible for a vigorous and objective demonstration of each proposition which he claims to be true, of the evidence upon which it rests, and of the procedures by which it was derived.

A RE-VIEW OF FUNCTIONALISM

Is the American stratification system "functional" and, if so, in what sense? What modification needs to be made in the tentative disposition of the issue which we made in Chapter 2 (p. 28-30)? It will be recalled that none of the researches which we have subsequently examined dealt explicitly with the functionalist issue. Consequently, our conclusions of necessity must be somewhat speculative, although some of the "facts and figures" with which we are now familiar may have relevance to this undertaking.

It will be recalled that in Chapter 2 we examined one of the most clear and articulate formulations of functionalist theory, the Davis and Moore thesis that the differential-reward system found in a society is functionally necessary and justifiable in order adequately to staff the important positions in the society with persons of skill, training, and responsibility. We raised the issue, at least with reference to American society, whether there were too many exceptions to the proposition to permit it to go unchallenged. That is, there seemed to be numerous occupations of high prestige and material reward whose functional relationship to societal survival or efficiency would be very, very hard to demonstrate. The fabulous material reward and prestige of persons ι the entertainment world is an excellent, but by no means exclusive, case in point. It is not obvious that entertainment is a fundamental prerequisite of societal survival or efficiency, nor is it possible to demonstrate, we think, even if professional entertainment is functional, that it warrants a reward pattern higher than that for workers in education, religion, and administrative government. Later, we granted that if psychic and prestigial factors were included with financial rewards, then the apparent contradictions could partly be explained away.

Perhaps care should be taken not to make too much of what may be only exceptions. It may be unfair to hold a theoretical proposition to a "no exceptions" level of perfection. Perhaps, even if what we have said about the entertainment occupations is accepted as completely true and without bias, these exceptions may not alter the validity of the basic proposition; that is, there may be no necessary contradiction between the functionalist theory as a statement of *broad proximate relationship* and some specific conflicting social values. The situation may be a little like the theory and practice of giving examinations and grades in a college class. Some sort of procedure presumably is necessary as a basis for arriving at qualitative differences. Obviously, the examination and grading system is not perfect; sometimes we reward the wrong kind of activity (as in successful "apple polishing") and it is possible for outstanding talent to go unnoticed while mediocre talent sometimes gets a big play. But, *on the whole*, the system is reasonably functional in that it does work as a motivating device for most people most of the time, and it does sort out and reward outstanding talent sufficiently frequently to maintain a good supply of able young men and women to take the place of their ever departing elders in the professions, business, and government.

Probably what troubles some critics of functionalist theory is their unwillingness to justify *ethically* some of the concomitants of the *current* system of rewards and punishments. For example, for a person deeply and sincerely committed to the democratic philosophy, it is distressing to see year after year many moderately talented high school boys from the lower classes go to work in factories and at other relatively low-status and low-power occupations with limited futures, while many less able sons of middle- or upper-class origins clutter the colleges with halfhearted application to study. Nor is it easy to justify the wide range of differential reward, both financially and prestigially, particularly when one thinks in concrete cases. But these may be but imperfections and false starts, the aberrations in a functioning social system which, like the squeaks and rattles in a machine, are admittedly undesirable but not crucial. For the time being these imperfections do not seriously prevent the machine from getting its work done with reasonable efficiency. This analogy to a machine is not to be taken literally, of course. Society is not a machine and the criteria for efficiency and inefficiency are not as clearly computable as in the case of the machine. But, within the limits necessarily imposed by analogical description, the logic seems to hold.

Stratification, moreover, may be functional and disfunctional at the same time. That is to say, some aspects of the reward and punishment and social-mobility pattern of a society may be functional in the sense claimed and some others may be contrary to it. For example, by a system of differential reward American society is able to recruit enough people most of the time to keep its essential services running and its survival moderately secure. But in some respects, and especially at some times, the differential-reward system breaks down. As this is being written, for instance, there is one reasonably high-status occupation for which there are not enough recruits, namely, elementary school teachers. This position pays *relatively* well and has higher than average prestige. To be sure, it has also some aspects of negative prestige. The supply of recruits can, and undoubtedly will, be increased by increasing the rewards—higher salary, better working conditions, and/or some kind of added non-pecuniary incentives. At various times, presumably, the reward system will break down, so that insufficient numbers of aspirants for given status positions will present themselves, and presumably, also, these conditions can again be rectified by altering the reward pattern.

Similarly, some of the *allegedly* inequitable elements, admittedly playing a large part in a differential-status system, may be coming under stricter rational control, or, at least, presumably *could* do so. Illustrations of this from the recent past are easy to cite, some of them of tremendous practical importance. During the last few decades, for example, there has occurred a leveling of income in the United States, largely through the device of progressive income taxation. Some persons believe, as apparently did the late President Franklin D. Roosevelt, who once recommended to Congress that it legislate a personal income ceiling of $25,000 a year after taxes, that the financial aspect of our reward system is not maximally functional in that it still allows "too-great" discrepancies. If the number of persons who believe this becomes sufficiently great, there is no reason, under constitutional government, that some such proposal as Roosevelt's could not become the law of the land. Concurrently with the leveling of income extremes, there has also occurred a growing concept of public welfare, which holds that there is an ethical and practical justification for such practices as social security for old age, unemployment insurance, minimum wages, and other kinds of public assistance to keep incomes from falling too disastrously low and to obviate the necessity of individuals falling to the status of public paupers or poor relations. In offering these illustrations we do not intend to endorse income limitations or the welfare concept; we only intend to illustrate the fact that the specific functional relationships found in a society are subject to periodic evaluation and possible change.

Practically every institution, moreover, which provides a structure for promotion or recruitment for progressively higher positions, such as education, the military, and the corporation, is more or less regularly giving conscious thought to ways and means of improving the efficiency of its recruitment and advancement system. There is a general recognition that too much talent gets lost and too much mediocrity gets ahead. The higher echelons of administration, for the sake of efficiency at least, often wish to see these conditions rectified. It is easy to be naive, however, and to expect too much too soon from these efforts. Sometimes they are not sincere—are used only for "window dressing" or for other public-relations reasons. In other instances, however, major policy changes in recruitment and promotion philosophy and procedure have resulted, and sometimes, at least, they would meet the approval of even the most idealistic democrat.

Functional elements in a society may be seen as intermittently in conflict not only with nonfunctional and disfunctional elements stemming from tradition, but also with the forces of crude individualism flying in the face of collective need. In fact, there is much in the legislative struggle between the public interest and special interest to suggest just such an interpretation.

Finally, functionalism for whom? By this we mean that there are varying kinds of, and motivations for, functionalist theory. There is the naive functionalist who sees all conventional social forces of reward and punishment as a beneficent providence from an omniscient "Society." He usually begs the question of *what kind* of a society: a democratic society, a fascist society, or a communist society? Not all of the same functions are required, at least not in the same relationship, by each of these, and the sophisticated functionalist knows that. He is likely to speak not in terms of categorical "efficient" or "inefficient," but rather in terms of "if . . . then." More concretely, the more enlightened functionalist might say "*if* currently we wish to have a democratic society in America with a maximum use of existing, potential talent, *then* changes must be made in the educational system so that unused talent does not get lost as it now does." *But*, he would go on to say, "*if* you want a more fascist-like society, one with high prestige positions largely the monopoly of self-perpetuating elites, *then* there is no need to worry about recruitment of talent from the lower classes; give them vocational training and be done with it. But give the best possible educational opportunities to the sons and daughters of the elite."

We would conclude, then, that in broadest outline the functionalist theory is *probably* tenable, but we would hold to two qualifications. (*a*) Any given concrete social system, notably the United States, should be recognized as also having many disfunctional and nonfunctional elements in its status-reward-power system, which may be corrected or accentuated from time to time. (*b*) When thinking *concretely* about a given social system and its functionality, the functional and disfunctional elements are not to be regarded as inherently so; they can be judged so only in the light of the kinds of societal goals which are being sought. For this reason it is to be expected that different men, of equivalent ability and good will but with different philosophical orientations, may be presumed to judge differently what is functional and disfunctional in the status-reward-power system. In a very real and basic sense this may be the difference between being a liberal and being a conservative.

SELECTED READINGS

The selected readings for the chapters in, Part III will be found on pages 347-350.

14

Power, Class Struggle, and Class Consciousness

POWER

THE HIERARCHICAL distribution of power, regarded by some analysts to be the most important differential among the various stratification dimensions, is probably the least often discussed aspect of stratification. It will be recalled that the studies which we examined have largely omitted any systematic treatment of this question. There are probably several reasons for this abdication of professional opinion on the subject of power. First, there is the matter of difficulty. Prestige, being essentially judgmental and comparative, is relatively easy to study. Such privilege categories as income, wealth, education, and the possession of status-giving goods are *prima facie* demonstrable. But power is difficult even to define, types of power are almost endless, and the relationships of the various types to one another involve comparisons which are not readily additive.[1] How is one to compare, for example, the "power" of Arthur Godfrey in selling merchandise and influencing public values in general to the power of a Supreme Court justice, the chairman of a Senate investigating committee, and a multimillionaire financier? On a descriptive verbal level, comparisons seem easy and sometimes obvious, but how are

[1] See our previous discussion of power, pp. 7-10. The serious student should read the excellent treatment of the subject by Robert Bierstedt, "An Analysis of Social Power," *American Sociological Review*, 15 (December, 1950), pp. 730-738.

we to *measure* whatever units may be involved in such rather obvious concepts as "prestige power," "the power of suggestion," "constitutional power" and "delegated power"? And how shall we compare the power of a man's millions with that of a saint?

But perhaps we should try. Lacking plentiful empirical data, we shall have to whip those data we have pretty hard. Moreover, we may have to be rather inexacting in what we regard as "data."

Our first step, of necessity, would seem to be some attempt at classifying types or forms of power. If we start with the already adopted concept of power as the degree to which an individual or group is able to control the behavior of other individuals and groups in accordance with the former's desires, we arrive at the obvious need for spelling out the operational forms which such control presumably takes. Classification of "types" of power is, of course, an almost endless pursuit. Since we are striving for an economy of terminology and concepts, we shall largely restrict our discussion to one distinction which is considered basic, namely, the distinction between legitimate and non-legitimate power. (It is to be noted that the formulation *non*-legitimate rather than *il*legitimate is used. This is because the latter carries the implication of being demonstrably *against* the rule, so to speak.) *Non*-legitimate power is that twilight zone between clear, legally, or customarily defined rights of control by one person over another and clear violation of these proscriptions. For example, a traffic policeman has the legal right to judge when a violation has occurred and to arrest the violator. This is his legitimate power. Clearly he does *not* have the right to try the offender on the spot and collect a fine. This would constitute *il*legitimate power. But in between the two, the officer has a large area of discretion. So great is this area that he may, and in instances often does, discriminate between persons of different classes or ages or sexes or races with respect to judging that a violation has occurred and that it warrants an arrest.[2] Even though discriminations of a relatively gross sort, as seen by the disinterested

[2] See, e.g., Walter Reckless, *The Crime Problem* (New York, Appleton-Century-Crofts, Inc., 1950), pp. 57-60.

observer, may take place, the officer may properly claim that he has not usurped power, but simply has used his judgment as provided for in the rules and regulations. Practically every person carrying out the duties of a job is in much the same situation as the policeman in the above illustration: the teacher, the foreman, the person who hires and fires in a personnel office, the dean of women, the insurance adjuster, the tax collector, and so on.

It is not intended to imply that non-legitimate power presents a problem solely because of the opportunities for discrimination offered to the power-wielding functionaries of a society. Important as these may be, there are other aspects of non-legitimate power which have attracted comment (and criticism) in American society. Considerable protest is found in the literature on stratification against such non-legitimate extensions of power as the following.[3] Industrial or commercial concerns may participate in propaganda tactics under the guise of advertising their products, having for the apparent purpose an essentially political objective, namely, to create public hostility toward some acts or decisions of government, so that the offending administration may be turned out and a more favorable one brought in. Legally there is probably nothing objectionable about the practice, but criticism has arisen because there is no channel by which opposing views can be given comparable publicity. The cards seem to some to be stacked politically in favor of the power giant.

Lobbying is perhaps another illustration. Theoretically, every person has access to his legislator, but in practice only those individuals and interest groups which can secure able, and usually expensive, persons skilled in the art of manipulating legislators actually exercise their constitutional rights of petition. The Speaker of the House of Representatives of a Midwestern state recently admonished the legislators "not to mistake the voice of the lobbyist for the voice of the people." So general, however, is the practice of lobbying and so ineffective are the attempts to

[3] One, probably not unbiased, well-known book dealing largely with this matter is Robert A. Brady, *Business as a System of Power* (New York, Columbia University Press, 1943).

control it that no one seriously expects that the voice of the people will usually be heard. A criticism commonly leveled against big business, and applying comparably to the attempts if not to the success of labor unions, farm organizations, and other groups, is to the effect that minority groups with large concentrations of votes and/or money exert power out of all proportion to their numbers and, moreover, often exert this power, whether so intended or not, deceptively. A similar charge is often brought against newspapers, and to a less extent against radio and TV, usually that these mass media, while purporting to serve "the people" in stated ways, really mean only to serve *some* people, such as the advertisers who pay the bills or the media owners.

Defenders of these practices usually contend that the critics either exaggerate, or are not themselves unbiased, or are simply naive about the way "the system works." There is nothing illegal, we are reminded, about a corporation's decision to spend a fraction of its profits for propaganda. Similarly, since advertising space in newspapers or on the air is bought and paid for, anyone who can pay the price can buy it. Moreover, everyone using mass media is limited in his use of these media by existing laws pertaining to truthful advertising and to libel. If educational institutions can make evaluations of business, why cannot business participate also in education? Moreover, many of the efforts of lobbyists and other pressure activities are at variance with one another, leaving the public presumably free to "make up its mind" between the claim and counterclaim of the various proponents.

The role of arbiter in this conflict is not an easy one, particularly if one accepts the obligation of evaluating *within* the value structure of American society. An exhaustive analysis of this problem is clearly beyond the scope of this book, but it ought to be pointed out in the interest of clarification of the issue, at least, that a major part of the insolubility of the issue arises from the fact that there coexist in the United States two value emphases, each with a widespread following, which are apparently inconsistent, at least in their application. On the one hand, we have the acquisitive capitalistic values which hold, simply, that an individual is entitled to use his property rights in any way he wishes, providing the uses are legal and it cannot be demonstrated that the property rights of others are injured thereby. Specifically, advertising of any kind and lobbying are simply the extensions of the property rights of those who pay the bills. One is not forced to read the advertisement nor is the legislator forced to do the lobbyist's bidding. But there is, on the other hand, a humanitarian or "general welfare" objective which may stand in direct contradiction to some forms of using wealth. This humanitarian view has resulted in the introduction of a number of legal limits upon the use of wealth, such as the obligation of a radio station to give equal time to proponent and opponent at the same cost, regardless of the station owners' personal preference, the obligation of advertisers to advertise truthfully, the illegality of bribing and blackmail and various other curbs on "abuse of power." Some humanitarians have frequently objected that these regulatory devices are too weak and are too half-heartedly enforced to be effective. Again, however, another aspect of power intrudes, this time "indirect" power taking the form of manipulation of public opinion so that there will not be effective curbs upon the existing manifestations of power.

Other stratification analysts have much more to say about power, especially of the non-legitimate forms. Sutherland [4] coined and popularized the phrase "white-collar crime," by which he meant that our theoretical concept of equality before the law is summarily and continuously violated by surrounding many kinds of criminal offenders with technical protections, immunities, and even by the absence of legal enforcement of many kinds of crime. He pointed out that the advantage of the "white-collar" classes are several. First, white-collar people typically commit crimes against property and not against persons directly—for example,

[4] Edwin H. Sutherland, *White Collar Crime* (New York, Dryden Press, 1949). For a sharply contrasting view see Paul Tappan, "Who Is a Criminal?" *American Sociological Review*, 12 (February, 1947), p. 100.

embezzlement, defrauding, false advertising—whereas persons of the lower classes typically commit such crimes as breaking and entering, assault and battery, or theft. The prevailing value standards of the society are such that the latter appear to be more heinous than the former, and hence wrongdoers are dealt with more summarily. The higher-income classes, moreover, are in a better position to know their legal rights and to hire attorneys to represent them, who sometimes succeed in proving innocence or lack of ill intent by some technical device or another which the layman rarely understands. Finally, Sutherland notes the high incidence of settlement out of court, dismissal of cases, nominal fines, and other types of slap-on-the-wrist penalty. He is careful not to say that this is any sort of conspiracy, but rather implies that in the present structure of power these outcomes seem natural if not inevitable to many people.

Another aspect of non-legitimate power which has attracted attention is the large part allegedly played by personal acquaintances and personal preference in the distribution of high-status positions, not only in government but in industry and the professions as well. "It isn't what you know, but whom you know" is the common complaint of the unsuccessful aspirant. In general, higher-status positions are filled at the discretion of other higher-status persons, who with predictable uniformity seem to conclude that it is other high-status persons who are most eminently qualified for the responsibilities of the positions. The problem here is more than mere personal favoritism; it is rather the superior advantage in the competitive struggle for the person who enters the struggle from a more advantaged position. As has been pointed out many times in analyzing education, the teacher usually chooses her "pets" from the upper-middle or higher range in the status continuum, apparently because children coming from these strata in society have less to learn and consequently appear brighter, are more co-operative, and altogether seem (and are) competent. From this advantaged position they then move on to further advantage—the appointments to responsible duties, schol-

arships to higher education, and so on. And, indeed, it appears
that the classroom microcosm is as the larger social macrocosm.

One unpublished study of stratification and power, conducted
several years ago, dealt with an analysis of the public-welfare
structure of a Midwest metropolitan city.[5] Specifically, the author
examined the make-up of the boards of the social-welfare agencies
of the city of Columbus, Ohio, and found that they consisted
almost exclusively of men and women from the professional and
business classes, with scarcely any representation from clerical,
industrial, or agricultural groups. Meanwhile, of course, the
reverse was found to be true of the recipients of the services of
these agencies, who were almost exclusively, as would be expected, from the lower-income and less-privileged groups. Very
probably the findings of this study can safely be generalized
beyond the city studied and beyond the field of public-welfare
agencies. The same thesis can be amply documented from studies
of boards of education [6] and very probably also from the administrative boards of churches. The rebuttal that this under-rep-
resentation of substantial segments of the community is "functional" in that only the professional and business classes have the
necessary skill and leisure to "run" community affairs has an
element of truth in it, but is an oversimplification of a more
complex process. Many of the activities of church, school, and
community boards are not so complex and do not call for so
great display of education or genius that some significant representation at least could not be granted to the groups making
up the majority of the community. Moreover, it is an unproven
assumption that there could not be found within the ranks of
labor the relatively few persons willing and able to serve in these
capacities. It is not known to what extent there is a conscious
aspiration on the part of lower-status persons to serve in commu-

[5] Susan McAllister, unpublished doctoral dissertation, The Ohio State
University Library. See also "The Social Control of Philanthropy," *American Journal of Sociology*, 58 (March, 1953), pp. 451-461.

[6] See, e.g., August Hollingshead, *Elmtown's Youth* (New York, John
Wiley and Sons, 1950), pp. 122 ff.

nity agencies on the policy-forming level, but some students of stratification have reported that there is rather clear consciousness among the rank and file that they are unrepresented and that community agencies—particularly the schools—are being conducted more consistently with the values of higher-status people than with the values and needs of persons of humbler standing.

Returning now to our original question, namely, what is the relationship between power and other stratifications, we may recapitulate somewhat as follows: Starting from the fact of an hierarchical arrangement of persons with differential privilege and status, it can be observed that one of the attending inequalities is the differing ability to have one's own way, to control the behavior of others. A functional analysis of the situation readily shows that a part—how much is debatable—of differential power is simply an aspect of the reward system, that is, one of the privileges resulting from the ability and willingness to defer gratification is the fact that, if successful in the enterprise, the person will then have more of some kind of power. Sometimes there is a frank recognition that the power sought is of the non-legitimate variety as, for example, when an individual seeks a political office for a time in order to get business contacts which will "pay off" later, or when an individual chooses a high-status college, not because he will learn more there, but because he will "make contacts" which will pay off in preferential treatment later on.

But this is an incomplete picture. Differential power is more than the prize for success. Differential power is also a *factor* in success, and sometimes a decisive one. Financial power alone, although by no means the sole advantage in the competitive struggle, is clearly demonstrable as a factor making competition among persons significantly unequal. Whether we consider the student working his way through school and the fully supported student competing, say, for Phi Beta Kappa, or the wealthy industrialist suing or being sued by one of his employees, it is obvious that the adversaries do not compete on equal terms. It is as if many persons are running a race over the same course, but are forced to carry unequal loads. The fact that sometimes one of the competitors carrying a relatively heavy load is outstanding enough to surpass another with a lighter load should not obscure the fact that the naive concept of competitive equality in a stratified society is a myth unworthy of a mature mind.

Thus far, then, we have concluded that power is one of the rewards for success, and that power is circulatory, that is, power, like money, tends to make more. The picture would not be complete if we did not point out also, however, that there are *forces in American society which work against the circulatory effect of power*. We should also examine these to get a more accurate conception of the matter. First, there are a large number of institutions which are essentially socialistic in character, which give an approximately equal service to all persons regardless of power or even discriminate in favor of low-power persons. At least such is the goal and to some extent it is realized. Heading the list is the public school system from the kindergarten through the professional schools and graduate school of the state university. Although the more advanced stages of education are not truly free, neither does the student pay completely for the cost of education on this level. Normally a tuition-paying student in a state university pays around 10 or 15 per cent of the actual cost of educating him, and if he has a scholarship, he may not even pay that fraction. Moreover, the university may lend him money, find him a part-time job, give him contacts with employers, and serve him in many ways so as more nearly to equalize the competition between low- and high-status persons.

As we have mentioned before, the income tax structure is based on the "progressive" principle, i.e., the *rate* of taxation rises with income. Not all aspects of the tax structure work in this way, however. Sales taxes, for example, bear more heavily upon low-income groups and so do many kinds of flat-rate taxes like auto licenses. But, on the whole, progressive taxation seems to be the preponderant pattern.

Moreover, the society supports a number of institutions aside from education which are dedicated more or less idealistically to the free competition principle in personal advancement, notably the church and the military services. Each of these institutions has within it a system of evaluation and promotion, with policies usually so prescribed as to resist at least some of the contaminating influence which might work against the merit system. Thus, many a young man finds out in the army that his father may be the village banker, but he still has to do K.P., and if he goes AWOL a trip by his mother to the commanding officer will not result in putting the penalty aside! In making this point it is not overlooked that these institutions are also subject to some of the pressures of the larger society and "undue influence" does creep in, but the point is that it is often identified as undue influence and there are rules and policies designed to hold it to a minimum. Despite the negative criticism which can be brought against our public institutions for what has been termed *class bias*, the fact remains that they present perhaps the best approximation of democracy in the competitive scramble for higher status.

The ethically sensitive and value-sophisticated student will readily note that in our discussion of power we may not have been bias-free. That would be impossible, even if desirable. We have tried, however, to discuss these fiercely controversial questions with candor and as much objectivity as our best efforts could muster. We grant the existence of alternate hypotheses and sometimes have even stated them expressly. Beyond that, there seems nothing that can be done, except to have avoided the question, which would have been remiss to say the least.

CLASS STRUGGLE

Ever since Marx and Engels [7] formulated the concept of "class struggle," the phrase has been bantered about with far more venom than scientific detachment. It has been, to borrow Weber's phrase, one of the words which we have used as "swords" with which to do battle rather than as "ploughshares to loosen the soil

[7] *The Communist Manifesto,* 1848.

of contemplative thought." [8] The patient analyst of social stratification must be understood to be the inheritor of a dubious
legacy.

Strictly logically, of course, if one denies the existence of
classes, then there can be no class struggle, because something that
does not exist cannot struggle with something else that does not
exist either. This facetious view may have more realism than
readily meets the eye. Restating the question, if, as we have
shown, the continuum theory of stratification is in the light of the
evidence more tenable, that there are no clear-cut classes or strata
to be in conflict with others, then we would be forced to conclude that class struggle is but a shibboleth. Viewed somewhat
less pedantically, however, there does seem merit in the phrase
as a theoretical proposition and there is empirical evidence with
which to document it.

Classes of persons, *in the statistical sense*, not only can but do
struggle against one another in many conspicuous ways; and
these struggles are and have been among the most dramatic and
significant characteristics of the American scene. It would be
impossible within the scope of any book or even series of books
to chronicle all of these conflicts as they have occurred during
the last two or three decades. It must suffice to point out in very
broad terms something of the nature of this conflict. At each
session of each of the state legislatures, not to mention county
legislative units and city councils, and even more patently in the
Congress of the United States, the activities consist almost exclusively of the struggles of one group against another to make laws,
abolish laws, or change laws. Commonly the term *interest groups*
is used, and sometimes *pressure groups*,[9] to indicate these collec-
tivities. Some of the most important of these struggles have been
between persons of dissimilar position on one status continuum
or another, and perhaps this fact has contributed to the impression

[8] Max Weber, "Science as a Vocation," in Logan Wilson and William
Kolb, *Sociological Analysis* (New York, Harcourt, Brace and Co., 1949),
p. 11.

[9] See, e.g., V. O. Key, *Politics, Parties and Pressure Groups* (New York,
The Thomas Y. Crowell Co., 1942).

that they are of necessity always in conflict. Thus, currently organized labor is pushing for the revision of the Taft-Hartley act in one direction and, more quietly, groups representing management are pushing for revision in the other. Some farmers' organizations are lobbying for higher parity support prices. Real-estate lobbies are striving to discourage government housing. Though many of these groups find it advantageous for public-relations reasons to talk about the "Great Principles of American Democracy," the fact remains that what they want is some law or laws which will improve their own position relative to others.

It is important to note, however, that many interest and pressure groups include persons from wide ranges along continuums measuring wealth or occupational prestige or income. There are pressure groups like the American Legion, the Catholic Church, or the Women's Christian Temperance Union. These groups sometimes have sponsored powerful and effective lobbies, and the goals which they have fostered could hardly be construed, except by the most paranoid Marxist, as being "class interests" in the Marxist sense of the concept.

It should also be noted that interest-group struggle differs significantly from class struggle (in the Marxist and neo-Marxist sense) in that the same individual may belong to a variety of interest groups and pressure groups which may, and often do, work at cross purposes. The same man may be a member of the American Legion and an industrial worker belonging to the C.I.O. and an absentee owner of an inherited farm. These separate interest groups take different positions on issues before the Congress and to a considerable extent nullify one another. Moreover, even a single occupational group may have several different interest groups with different, often opposing, goals. Present-day farmers, for example, have three major nation-wide interest groups, each with a legislative program, lobbying, propaganda, and all the rest—the Farm Bureau Federation, the Grange, and the Farmers Union. The legislative programs of these three organizations are rarely in complete unison and sometimes are in very sharp contrast. Similarly, classroom teachers have two interest groups of marked differences in goal—the National Education Association and the Teachers Union, affiliated with the A.F. of L. Labor has its American Federation of Labor, C.I.O., Railroad Brotherhoods, and a miscellany of smaller groups. Policies of these groups are by no means the same, nor are the tactics.

Before leaving the subject some comment seems in order about such studies as Centers' and Jones's in which, it will be recalled, it was claimed that statistically significant differences in attitude existed, at the time the studies were made, between certain defined groups. Centers, for example, found political radicalism very significantly different between the working class and the upper class, with the middle class highly variant within itself, but occupying, in general, a midway position. This was in the 1940's, during the New Deal-Fair Deal political era. Since then, the American political climate has materially changed with a decisive popular vote against the party which stood most near the position preferred by the "working class." Numerically, the working class predominates and it would be reasonable to presume that with some support from the middle class, it could have returned the Democratic party to power easily in 1952. This obviously did not happen, and one is forced to conclude either that Centers was incorrect or, as appears to us much more likely, many working-class people changed their minds. Even if we are wrong in the above inference, it can hardly be disputed that the political action of the working people—even since the fruition of the large and aggressive C.I.O.—has not exerted a preponderant influence in American politics,[10] even through the working people having the numerical strength to do so. As far as can be determined, working people seem to follow in their political attitudes and socio-economic moods much the same oscillation between radicalism and conservativism as characterizes the nation as a whole.

[10] For a lucid, brief discussion of this subject see, e.g., Rudolf Heberle, *Social Movements* (New York, Appleton-Century-Crofts, Inc., 1951), pp. 174-179. Heberle's position is essentially the same as ours.

It is not denied that there may be a "hard core" of labor-class voters who are more consistent and tenacious than the above sentence would imply, but they are insufficient in number and/or have an insufficiently dependable following to make possible concerted group action at the polls. Probably contributing to this fact are some of the characteristics of the American party system which work to prevent sharp issues from developing between the parties on fundamental matters, so that issues in which there is a clear labor-versus-someone-else line up tend not to develop.

In sum, we are obliged to say that *from the evidence* which can be marshaled, the only conclusions which can be drawn on alleged class struggle in the United States are in the form of interest-group issues, more or less familiar to any informed citizen. Consequently, we prefer that the mysticism of "the class-struggle" concept be dispensed with, and we talk instead in terms of demonstrable interest-group conflict which is everywhere and always apparent.

CLASS CONSCIOUSNESS

What can be concluded about the concept "class consciousness," so freely bandied about by journalists and some social scientists? As usual, we shall need first to clarify our meanings. Greatest justification, both logically and empirically, for such a language convention is found in the now familiar phenomenon of interest groups. Obviously, unless the persons in an interest group were in some degree conscious of their common interest, there would be no group. Thus, the very existence of an interest group is *prima facie* affirmation of a sort of class consciousness in this limited sense. The question becomes more complicated, however, as soon as we recall that a given individual may and often does belong to multiple interest groups, which may work at cross purposes, or at least exert influence in different directions.

The chief difficulty with this familiar concept, however, is that it carries a secondary meaning with a strong implication that there is some small number of classes, that all or practically all persons know what class they are "in," and that these persons exert whatever influence they can to form concerted impact on the decision-making processes of the society. Empirically, this conception of the matter is impossible to sustain with the evidence at hand, despite its constant reaffirmation, often supported by mystical semantic contortions of the Marxists and neo-Marxists. Studies such as Centers' and Jones's, despite imperfections which have been pointed out, seem to us to lend credence to the view that there probably are some typical attitudinal concomitants of certain status positions in American society. This is but another way of recognizing that, being somewhat rational beings, people recognize diversity of interests and they view objects and ideals variously, depending on the relationship of these to their own needs and objectives. Thus, for example, in so far as a low-income person is aware of the facts, he could be presumed to favor more sharply progressive income taxes, whereas a person at the other end of the continuum would presumably be of reverse inclination. Since, however, all data seem to indicate that our status system is based on *multiple* criteria—not merely on money—these two disagreeing individuals might conceivably also agree substantially on, say, the high status of a Supreme Court justice or the importance of being able to trace one's lineage to the Mayflower. As we have seen so many times, then, the absence of any single criterion of status and value not only makes classes and class struggle in the literal sense of these terms improbable, but also tends to make consciousness of class a variable phenomenon dependent upon the particular values of the particular persons involved. Since the values are not intercorrelated, consciousness is likewise fragmentized and no unitary consciousness of belonging is manifest.

SELECTED READINGS

The selected readings for the chapters in Part III will be found on pages 347-350.

HOW DO *YOU* INTERPRET THESE RESEARCH DATA?

1. *Sixty-three per cent of college students were represented in college by* neither *parent; only 13 per cent by* both *parents.*[1]

2. *Between 1910 and 1940, the percentage of "professionals" whose fathers were also professionals" increased from 21 per cent to 28 per cent.*[2]

3. *Between 1910 and 1940 the percentage of "semi-professionals" and "proprietors, managers and officials" whose fathers were of the same occupations, decreased by roughly 30 per cent and 25 per cent respectively.*[2]

4. *Physicians who had physician fathers decreased from 22 per cent of the total physicians for those born 1870-1879 to 9.4 per cent for those born 1910-1919.*[3]

5. *During 1952-53, 20 per cent of the graduate assistantships in engineering available in American colleges and universities and 37 per cent of the graduate assistantships in the "health fields" were* unused. *The figures for unused fellowships were essentially the same.*[4]

6. *"In the United States, since 1929, the employee-compensation share of the before-tax national income has risen one-ninth from 58.1 to around 65 per cent, while the property share ... has declined about one-sixth.*[5]

[1] Data from Patricia S. West, "Social Mobility Among College Students," in Reinhard Bendix and Seymour Lipset, *Class, Status and Power* (Glencoe, Ill., The Free Press, 1953), p. 699.

[2] Data taken from Tables I and II in Natalie Rogoff, "Recent Trends in Urban Occupational Mobility," in P. K. Hatt and A. Reiss (eds.), *Reader in Urban Sociology* (Glencoe, Ill., The Free Press, 1951).

[3] Stuart Adams, "Trends in the Occupational Origins of Physicians," *American Sociological Review*, 18 (August, 1953), Tables 3 and 4, p. 407.

[4] Data from "Financial Support Available for Graduate Students," National Science Foundation, Washington, D. C., Release of August 1, 1953, mimeographed.

[5] From J. J. Spengler, "Changes in Income Distribution and Social Stratification: A Note," *American Journal of Sociology*, 59 (November, 1953), pp. 249 and 250.

15

An Evaluation of the American Stratification System

To EVALUATE the American stratification system is an ambitious and hazard-fraught undertaking. So pervasive is the stratification system that it reaches into every nook and cranny of American society. It involves the economy with its complex web of functions and functionaries, the endless process of allocation of income and economic power, and such earth-shaking issues as the struggle between management and labor, agriculture and the consumer. It includes the family, with important implications for mate choice, style of life, child-rearing patterns. It embraces education, posing such dramatic enigmas as who shall be educated, what shall they be educated for, who shall do the educating, and, most important of all, whose answers to the preceding questions are the right answers. Our question also engulfs religion. What are the functions of religion? Can they be the same for the "haves" and the "have nots"? Must it be, as some critics of our age have said, that for the "haves" the function of religion is to appease their consciences, whereas for the "have nots" it is an opiate to dull their sensitivity to their social world, with promises of pie-in-the-sky—but tomorrow? Stratification is, thus, not a thing apart from the American social system. Rather it inheres in the warp and woof of the fabric. Consequently to "evaluate" the American social system is in a very real sense to evaluate America.

Not only is our order a big one; there are those who think it an inappropriate one. Although one does not hear the admonition quite as frequently as he did a decade ago, it is still all too commonly asserted that social scientists should not evaluate, that science is only "a study of what is," that philosophers, theologians, and other phyla of "mystics" [1] should attempt whatever valuation may be involved.

There are also those who would advise us to eschew evaluation, not because it is inappropriate, but because it is ineffective. We are told that society, despite the efforts of rationalists and planners and idealists, evolves much more like Topsy than like the neat, polite boy at Exeter. Why kick against the pricks? Few succeed in "bucking city hall." It is not the small voice of the reasoning academe that will influence the design for tomorrow, but rather the bellicose slogans of the public-relations firms.

Although we recognize that there may be much in fact to support the logic of these viewpoints, we choose to exercise the right to evaluate the social scene, cognizant that there are those among us who do not know the difference between dissent and disloyalty, between evaluation and espousal. In this evaluation we shall make a very real effort to maintain the social scientists' skills in objectivity without abdicating the American citizen's traditional rights to speak out in town meeting. We shall, accordingly, devote ourselves (a) to negative judgments of the American status system, and (b) to positive judgments in an effort toward "balancing the books." The time is past, we think, when the social scientist can cavalierly dismiss his responsibility for judging the meaning and value of that which he describes. [2]

[1] See, e.g., George Lundberg, *Foundations of Sociology* (New York, The Macmillan Co., 1939), pp. 29 ff., for a vigorous support of this view of the matter.

[2] For a vigorous and well-documented defense of our position see Robert Lynd, *Knowledge for What?* (Princeton, Princeton University Press, 1939).

SOME NEGATIVE JUDGMENTS

Negative judgments of the American stratification system abound. They are found in the literature of social protest—poetry, drama, and the novel. A study of these alone would constitute a major undertaking. Similarly, "liberal" journalism of the *Nation* and *New Republic* vintage can be depended upon to point out with predictable consistency that some Americans play for stakes with loaded dice and marked cards. What can the social scientist add to or detract from this well-known literature of social protest? Probably little. Except, perhaps, to examine the charges in the light of what evidence exists, to determine whether the charges are justified and, more importantly, whether the facts support the extremity of the criticisms leveled. This we shall attempt to do, followed immediately by a similar evaluation of the views of those who largely rationalize the morality of the status quo.

1. Waste of Talent and Unequal Opportunity

Using the criterion of social efficiency, there is one indictment which the stratification system of the United States cannot escape, namely, the waste of talent due to the inability of the society to find ways to stimulate and/or allow individuals of high intelligence but low parental status to realize their potential for educability,[3] even though part of this failure is admittedly rooted in the low aspirational levels of many. People are not born with low aspirations; they learn them; and they learn them from their experiences and those of their families and peer groups.

Without postulating any utopian society in which everyone's potential is appraised by a psychometrician and his position in society assigned with superhuman wisdom, we find there is still

[3] This point is richly documented in two of the preceding chapters, "Elmtown's Youth" and "Who Shall Be Educated?"

room for improvement in present methods of apprehending, recruiting, and training talent. Our present methods are at best slipshod, and the consequences spell needless inefficiency. On the one hand, we see persons of talent holding inferior positions and, on the other hand, persons of mediocre talent but high aspiration substituting dogged determination for talent, and eventually achieving comparatively high positions of responsibility. Specifically, not a few long-time observers of the American graduate school claim to have observed a slow but clear depreciation of the American Ph.D. degree, offering an explanation closely paralleling what we have just said. They reason that by a gradual substitution of effort for ability and by a rewarding of high effort and mediocre skill, a lower level of over-all creative competency has resulted. Criticisms of this sort are exceedingly difficult to prove, but the hypothesis is at least worthy of consideration. Certainly, we have enough research data to demonstrate that the society is not making the optimal use of talent and that failing to do so lowers its over-all efficiency. America could conceivably go on for a long time this way without courting national disaster, probably because the advantages of technology and abundant natural resources give us a margin of safety so great that we can waste half of our brains and still have enough to "get by." This may not be possible indefinitely, however.

The ethical aspect of the waste of talent warrants consideration. Little elaboration needs to be made, except to point out that if we mean what some of us say, namely, that there is, or ought to be, equality of opportunity in America, then the *fact of unequal opportunity* to develop potential talent is a clear moral breach. Inconsistent practice and preachment, of course, can be resolved in either of two ways. We can improve the practice or we can lower our sights on the preachment. Until we do one or the other, there are likely to be many among us with a disturbed social conscience, particularly when charged with the responsibility of talking equality of opportunity out of one side of the mouth and differential life-chances out of the other.

2. Special-Interest Groups Versus the Public Interest

Certain special-interest groups present a companion problem. Members of pressure groups tend to get rewarded not so much by the intrinsic merits of their real objectives as by their effectiveness in wielding decisive power. Gradually we have come to recognize that in physical matters might does not make right, but in the more genteel piracy of interest-group struggle the old axiom persists largely unchallenged. Politicians, editorial writers, and professors follow a pacifying convention of deference to what is politely called "the public interest," but in the melee of pressure group against pressure group, propaganda against propaganda, distortion against counter-distortion, it becomes exceedingly difficult to find this public interest or general welfare, or even to find very many persons with sufficient objectivity to distinguish between the desire of their own pressure groups and some clearly contrasting public interest. There are, however, exceptions to the above, and in these exceptions lies whatever hope may be realistically entertained that we may sometime get beyond the law of the jungle in the reallocation of power privilege in American society.

3. Unequal Power

This raises even broader questions regarding social power, a concept which social scientists still sense more clearly than they can define. Whatever consensus exists in the definition of "social power" seems to reside in the idea that persons are able to control, completely or relatively, the behavior of others, that is, are able to bend the overt behavior, if not the wills, of others to conform to their own.[4] As we have seen in a preceding chapter, there are numerous ways of analyzing and classifying power relations among people, and each of these has implications for evaluation. We shall, however, limit ourselves, in this evaluation to only one power dimension, namely, non-legitimate power. The crux of the

[4] Earlier treatments of power are to be found on pages 7-10 and 315-325.

issue seems to be this: How can we circumscribe or meliorate the more naked aspects of non-legitimate power so that persons holding positions of control over others can be induced or required to limit the sphere of their power to the defined operations of their roles?

In government we are quite familiar with the concept "usurpation of power." Many of the sharpest issues in American history have centered on the question of whether or not certain acts constituted usurpation. Currently there are important issues in this category, notably, in regard to the appropriate degree to which congressional investigating committees should go in determining (and/or suggesting) questions of guilt or innocence which have traditionally been regarded as the proper province only of courts of law.

The problem of limitations on non-legitimate forms and sources of power, however, is subtle and pervasive. It operates virtually everywhere: management versus labor, middle-class school teachers versus lower-class children, liberal professors versus ethnocentric parents, mass-media owners versus minority-group viewpoints on national issues. The list is endless. Many persons feel that an urgent problem of our time is that of finding ways to define the necessary scope of operation of various functionaries so that they will not have—or take—undue liberty in the control of those less-empowered people in the society. There are in America still too few and too weak curbs on arbitrary power. Accusations of "a one-party press," of "middle-class bias" in the public schools, of "inequality before the law" are not empty slogans. They are richly documented charges that can be objectively brought against the system. The equally objective fact, often brought out in defense of the status quo, namely, that elsewhere in the world conditions are worse, is quite beside the point. The debate does not refer to the rest of the world, which for the most part does not even pretend to function under representative, constitutional, and democratic government. The American problem here, as in other areas, emanates in part at least from the anachronisms brought out so forcefully by Myrdal in *The American Dilemma:* that our malcontents have a strong case because we promise so much ("democracy"—"equal opportunity"—"classless society"—etc.) and offer, *in fact,* unequal life-chances, virtual disfranchisement, and inequality before the law. The consciences of at least some Americans can hardly be wholly clear when they talk limitations on arbitrary power and then refuse to curb non-legitimate power.

4. Are Differential Privileges "Too Great" in America?

Some critics, essentially functionalistic in their orientation, challenge the *magnitude* of our existing differential privileges. They do not deny, as we have said many times, that differences in talent and ambition are very great. These critics, moreover, acknowledge that societal needs probably require differential privileges, such as income and power as recruiting and sustaining rewards. More specifically, for example, it is granted that a corporation president ought to receive a larger salary than a foreman. But should he receive ten or twenty times as much, to take a by no means extreme illustration? His nutritional, medical, housing, and clothing needs are roughly the same. It is not denied that executive talents are scarce and that such talents are worth a great deal to the employing company. But from the more general point of view of fostering co-operative attitudes and relations in the community, would it not be better if the differences were less gross? So runs the criticism.

It is more than normally difficult to sort the wheat from the chaff in this issue. No one knows, for example, how much willingness to defer immediate gratification stems from the belief that the rewards will be extraordinary. We do not even know, with certainty, that deferment is strongly influenced by the magnitude of the reward at all. What is more, some of the greatest inequities are not in matters of income, but rather are interposed by public opinion—for example, the high status accorded to people in the athletic and entertainment fields and the strong accent on lineage in some communities. The issue is complex, but there is no dearth of critics who see it as simple and regard any other view as simply the stupidity of the duped or the chicanery of the exploiter.

FAVORABLE FACTORS

There is much that can be said about the American system of distributing prestige, privilege, and power which is commendatory, if not even laudatory.

1. No Categorical Distinctions

First, with the exception of "persons of color," and diminishing even for them, persons in the United States are almost completely free from *categorical* (caste) disprivileges due to lineage, possessions, or wealth. We are not overlooking the fact that *life-chances* are still and may always be markedly different.[5] But despite the poorer odds for the person of low status to achieve some higher status or privilege or power by his own competitive skill, *the odds are almost never zero*. There is in America today no actual counterpart of the serf or the slave or the commoner or the indentured servant.

2. High Vertical Mobility [6]

There is, moreover, much vertical mobility in contemporary America. The objection might be raised that we do not indicate *how much*. We do not know exactly how much. No one does. But the most casual glance at the occupants of the "reserved seats for parents" at almost any college commencement offers convincing and often poignant evidence of one channel of inter-generation upward social mobility. Not all of the graduates will be

---

[5] See, e.g., Beverly Davis, "Eminence and Level of Social Origin," *American Journal of Sociology*, 59 (July, 1953), pp. 11-19.

[6] A stimulating and original paper bearing on this problem is Gideon Sjoberg, "Are Social Classes in America Becoming More Rigid?" *American Sociological Review*, 16 (December, 1951), pp. 775-783.

wealthy and not all, surely, will be powerful and famous; but many, if not most, will certainly soon stand in very favorable status, income, and power contrast to the positions of their parents. Nor are the colleges and universities the only "rites of passage" to higher position. Other institutions with hierarchical status-systems also show the same processes, although probably less dramatically. "Getting one's wings" or celebrating one's ordination are the counterparts of the college commencement in other institutional settings. Add to these the small businessmen who are no longer really "small," the tenant farmers successfully achieving ownership, and other groups of upwardly mobile persons and the total impact becomes impressive.

It is also well to point out that upward mobility is approximately double what the statistics show. The criterion group most used is men, but these men usually marry and their wives (and children), quite as much as they themselves, share whatever benefits may derive from the improved privileges that accrue to the successful higher-status aspirant.

Instances of those who "do not make the grade" are often cited as if they constitute damaging evidence against the functionality and morality of "the system." Although in some cases this is doubtless a fair interpretation, it seems highly unrealistic to expect that a social system either can or should reward every individual to the full extent of his fantasy aspirations. Rewards to successful competitors unavoidably carry with them the necessity of disappointment and denial to the unsuccessful.

In pointing out that there is appreciable social mobility in the American system, we do not mean to imply that there is necessarily "enough." We do not know how much is enough. And enough for what? Surely it would be impossible for any social system to satisfy all of the insatiable capacities of some people for rewards! The fact that such persons may be articulate, even literary, should not obscure the fact that ambition may extend beyond ability, and aspiration outdistance the capacity of some for deferring their more imperative gratifications.

3. Equalizing Living Levels

We have pointed out several times that there is evidence that, in many respects, the more extreme differentials in some categories of privilege have been and are still being reduced, and that some of the inequities in life-chances are being rectified. The extremes of income in the United States have been reduced during the last thirty years,[7] despite an almost unprecedented prosperity since World War II. What may be more important is that many kinds of material goods, like household appliances, automobiles, and owned homes, are becoming increasingly available almost throughout the status range. While it is true that the wheelbase of the automobile and the size of the TV screen may still vary significantly according to income, there still *is* at least a used automobile and the same telecasts can be seen on the TV with the smaller screen. Also recent innovations in low-down-payment financing of homes has greatly extended the range of Americans who can, *if they wish*, own their own homes. Meanwhile more and more of the total costs of education are being defrayed by public funds. By an elaborate system of scholarships, loans, remissions of fees, and other devices, colleges and universities are becoming something closer to free educational institutions, at least for persons of ability. It is not uncommon, for instance, to find that most of the students enrolled in graduate departments of large universities are in one way or another almost completely subsidized—fellowships, assistantships, "G.I. bill," research assistantships, and other devices—so that the net cost *in money* to their parents or to themselves is negligible. This is a comparatively new development on the present scale.

It is at least an interesting speculation that possibly one of the factors in low aspiration, and an unwillingness to defer gratifica-

[7] See, e.g., Joseph J. Spengler, "Changes in Income Distribution and Social Stratification: A Note," *American Journal of Sociology*, 59 (November, 1953), pp. 247-260. Spengler's handling of this intricate and technical question seems especially lucid. Spengler is an economist. See also Sjoberg, *op. cit.*, relative to this point.

tion in order to achieve higher-status position, is that so many persons can achieve a substantial pattern of privilege without the necessity of advancing higher in the status hierarchy than they already are. Semiskilled workers in factories, with no apprenticeship training whatsoever, frequently receive higher annual incomes than persons in certain professions—after graduation from college. So, they reason, "Why bother?" If, however, individuals also value intangibles like occupational prestige, titles, white collars, and the like, then they may reason that the higher-status position is still "worth the grief."

4. Welfare Government

Finally, there are numerous innovations, in and through government during the last thirty years or so, which have made for rather remarkable shifts in status and power as well as in material position for large groups of American citizens with traditionally low over-all privileges. The gains of organized labor are well known.[8] Several of these "gains" have resulted in increased real wages, and others involve such important principles as tying wage rates to cost of living indices, pensions, vacation benefits, and improved tenure rights. Stated in another way, there now exist curbs on the power of management which did not exist earlier. Moreover, there is currently an elaborate system of social security through which an individual, *even if he is improvident*, is virtually guaranteed at least a minimum income level during his old age. There are also public funds for the support and rehabilitation of crippled people and dependent children. In most large cities the public-welfare agencies are firmly established in the traditions of the community, and virtually everyone supports their programs of service which go largely to the underprivileged. Although we have by no means exhausted this category we have

[8] There is a minority view among social scientists to the contrary. "...Unions appear to have had little influence on the economic position of the organized third of employees through altering the distribution of income." George H. Hildebrand, "American Unionism, Social Stratification, and Power," *American Journal of Sociology*, 58 (January, 1953), pp. 381 ff.

said, we think, enough to indicate that our society has recently become committed both in theory and in fact to the proposition that laissez faire will no longer be allowed to operate as the sole impersonal distributor of privilege.

Americans, particularly those having grown up since the 1930's, tend to take many of these innovations as their inalienable rights. They have not experienced and may only vaguely have heard "how it was in the old time," before veterans had G.I. bills and when the underprivileged had to support their own aged and destitute. It is well to recall that only a minority of the peoples of the world, in North America and Western Europe, operate within a status system with the floors and ceilings on privilege which the United States now has. These remarks are not intended to imply that there still may not be a long way to go before other crudities and inequities in the distribution of privilege are reduced, but rather to place some of the facts of our present system in perspective.

WHAT OF THE FUTURE?

It is a reasonable expectation that a study of this sort should result in some anticipations [9] as to the future of the American status-power-privilege systems. Despite the well-known difficulties which beset social prediction in broad terms, we shall consider at least a principle or two, and venture a few cautious answers to specific questions.

1. Stratification Is Relative to Other Societal Dimensions

A stratification system exists as an integral part of a *total* social system and, therefore, is vitally affected by what takes place in the other interdependent areas. This fact alone greatly complicates our undertaking, if not completely rendering it futile.

[9] For a short, thought-provoking editorial bearing in part upon this problem see Nelson N. Foote, "Destratification and Restratification," *American Journal of Sociology*, 58 (January, 1953), pp. 325 ff.

War or peace? If war, *victory or defeat? Depression or prosperity?* These should be enough to discourage any rash prognostications. Add to these the uncertainty which emanates from the knowledge that in times past *new industries or new forms of exploitation of natural resources* have profoundly affected contemporary stratification.

Then, too, there is the *ideological factor.* Stratification patterns depend on social values, and social values are simply ideas shared by relatively large groups. Ideas have never stood still and there is no reason to think that they will do so now. What is to prevent, for example, the rise and popularization of a strong *equalitarian ethic* in the United States, taking the form of demands, such as the late President Roosevelt's, that a ceiling be placed on incomes at some relatively low figure. Although this would not have much effect upon the size of the incomes of the persons in the lower brackets, the psychological effect of a narrower consumption pattern might have profound consequence upon aspiration levels and upon the entire pattern of recruitment of personnel. Or suppose, on the other hand, that some sort of *neo-fascistic* ideology were to develop and flourish. There would, then, be a new pattern of privilege and disprivilege and a new rationale for explaining and justifying disprivilege. Or, suppose that a great *religious revival with an ascetic emphasis* were to occur. Enough has perhaps been written to indicate that any predictions, or even anticipations, about the systems of stratification are conditioned by what happens in other aspects of the society, and we do not have conclusive indications as to what these innovations might be.

2. Stratification Systems Tend to Persist

In discussing some possibilities above we may have unwittingly given the impression that we expect radical changes in the American stratification system in the near future. Quite the contrary; our judgments tend toward the conclusion that *the present systems of status, power, and privilege will change for the most part slowly and undramatically.* Stratification systems are deeply entrenched both in the habit structures of people and in the codifications of law and government. Change is slow and usually resisted long after the functional requisites for a new order have been demonstrated.

3. Some Specific Queries

Stratification systems, however, do change despite the pressures to perpetuate them. There seem to be a few current trends and/or issues which might be considered as plausible clues to some of the changing dimensions of the emerging pattern.

a. Will there be a continuation and extension of democratic, equalitarian curbs on laissez faire? There seems little indication that many wish to give up such programs as social security, minimum wages, free education, or G.I. bills for veterans. Rather, increasingly Americans seem to want, and get, more of such "socialistic," leveling programs. The issue seems no longer a partisan one, since the present Republican administration seems quite as committed in practice to "health, education and welfare" programs as were their predecessors in office.

b. Will there be a continued, or even extended, abundance of material goods made available to a wider income range? This might be fostered, as it has in the past, not so much by any deep humanitarian desire by those in power to provide an abundant life for everyone, but rather because one of the crucial requirements of large-scale production is a large and continuous outflow of units. Devices to stimulate this may be as radically different from present-day practices as installment buying was from the spending habits of our grandparents. The potentialities appear to be potent, particularly if a "recession" threatens present "full employment" conditions.

c. Are interest-group struggles destined to go on ad infinitum? This balance-of-power procedure has become essentially the "American way." There will apparently continue to be a battle for men's minds and the skill of the propagandist may well become the miracle tool of tomorrow, now that iron lungs and plastic surgery are "old stuff."

d. Have we passed the high tide of the "striver personality?" Marquand's [10] inimitable portrait, so conspicuous in our time, might become, if not a museum piece, at least more of a rarity. It would not be surprising to find a growing percentage of people searching first for the pot of gold in the back yard, rather than pursuing status nostrums in far places. A further leveling of material comforts might go a long way to reduce the pressure on the "eager beaver."

These considerations—we have *not* called them predictions— are to be taken only as hypotheses. We are far less sure about any of them than we are about almost anything else we have said in this book. But they *are* plausible—and with that we rest.

SELECTED READINGS

The following forty-two items constitute a suggested "short" list of readings. They cover a wide scope of subjects but are relevant to the topics treated in these four concluding chapters. Some are recommended primarily because of their readability, others because they are classics. Care has been taken to keep the list modern. *For exhaustive bibliographies the reader is referred to the note on page 42 where three extensive bibliographies are cited.*

BECK, H. P., *Men Who Control Our Universities* (New York, King's Crown Press, 1947).

BIERSTEDT, Robert, "An Analysis of Social Power," *American Sociological Review*, 15 (December, 1950), pp. 730-738.

BRADY, Robert A., *Business as a System of Power* (New York, Columbia University Press, 1943).

CENTERS, Richard, "Children of the New Deal: Social Stratification and Adolescent Attitudes," *International Journal of Opinion and Attitude Research*, 4 (Fall, 1950), pp. 315-335.

---

[10] John P. Marquand, *Point of No Return* (New York, Grossett and Dunlap, 1951).

CENTERS, Richard, "Class Consciousness of the American Woman," *ibid.*, 3 (Fall, 1949), pp. 399-408.

——, "Education and Occupational Mobility," *American Sociological Review*, 14 (February, 1949), pp. 143-144.

——, "Motivational Aspects of Occupational Stratification," *Journal of Social Psychology*, 28 (November, 1948), pp. 187-217.

CLARK, Robert E., "Psychoses, Income and Occupational Prestige," *American Journal of Sociology*, 54 (March, 1949), pp. 433-440.

DAVIS, Kingsley, and MOORE, W. E., "Some Principles of Stratification," *American Sociological Review*, 10 (April, 1945), pp. 242-249.

ELLIS, Evelyn, "Upward Social Mobility Among Unmarried Career Women," *American Sociological Review*, 17 (October, 1952), pp. 558-563.

FOOTE, Nelson, "Destratification and Restratification: An Editorial Foreword," *American Journal of Sociology*, 58 (January, 1953), pp. 325-326.

GOLDSCHMIDT, Walter R., "America's Social Classes: Is Equality a Myth?" *Commentary*, 10 (August, 1950), pp. 175-181.

GORDON, Milton M., "Social Class in American Sociology," *American Journal of Sociology*, 55 (November, 1949), pp. 262-268.

GROSS, Llewellyn, "The Use of Class Concepts in Sociological Research," *American Journal of Sociology*, 54 (March, 1949), pp. 409-421.

HATT, Paul K., "Stratification in the Mass Society," *American Sociological Review*, 15 (April, 1950), pp. 216-222.

——, "Occupation and Social Stratification," *American Journal of Sociology*, 55 (May, 1950), pp. 533-543.

HAVIGHURST, R. J., and RUSSEL, Mary, "Promotion in the Armed Services in Relation to School Attainment and Social Status," *School Review*, 53 (April, 1945), pp. 202-211.

HERTZLER, J. O., "Some Tendencies Toward a Closed Class System in the United States," *Social Forces*, 30 (March, 1952), pp. 313-323.

HETZLER, Stanley, "An Investigation of the Distinctiveness of Social Classes," *American Sociological Review*, 18 (October, 1953), pp. 493-497.

HOULT, Thomas F., "Economic Class Consciousness in American Protestantism," *American Sociological Review*, 15 (February, 1950), pp. 97-100.

HYMAN, Herbert H., "The Relation of the Reference Group to Judgments of Status," in Reinhart Bendix and Seymour Lipset, *Class Status and Power* (Glencoe, Ill., The Free Press, 1953), pp. 263-270.

JOHNSON, E. S., "Social Classes as Fact and Perspective in the Social Sciences," *School Review*, 60 (April, 1952), pp. 203-212.

KEY, V. O., *Politics, Parties and Pressure Groups* (New York, The Thomas Y. Crowell Co., 1942).

KNUPFER, Genevieve, "Portrait of the Underdog," *Public Opinion Quarterly*, 11 (Spring, 1947), pp. 103-114.

LUNDBERG, Ferdinand, *America's Sixty Families* (New York, Vanguard Press, 1937).

LYND, Robert and LYND, Helen, *Middletown in Transition* (New York, Harcourt, Brace and Co., 1937) especially the chapter on "The X Family."

MANNHEIM, Karl, *Freedom, Power and Democratic Planning* (New York, Oxford University Press, 1950), especially pp. 77-107.

MERTON, Robert, "The Role of the Intellectual in Public Bureaucracy," *Social Forces*, 23 (May, 1945), pp. 404-415.

MILLS, C. W., *White Collar* (New York, Oxford University Press, 1951).

———, "The Competitive Personality," *Partisan Review*, 13 (September-October, 1946), pp. 433-441.

———, *The New Men of Power* (New York, Harcourt, Brace and Co., 1948).

MOORE, Barrington, Jr., "The Relation between Social Stratification and Social Control," *Sociometry*, 5 (August, 1942), pp. 230-250.

PAGE, C. H., *Class and American Sociology: From Ward to Ross* (New York, Dial Press, 1940).

PARSONS, Talcott, "A Revised Analytical Approach to The Theory of Social Stratification," in Reinhart Bendix and Seymour Lipset, *Class Status and Power* (Glencoe, Ill., The Free Press, 1953).

Purdue Opinion Panel, "Teen-Age Personality in Our Culture," Report of Poll No. 32, May, 1952, Purdue University, Lafayette, Ind., mimeographed.

REISSMAN, Leonard, "Class, Leisure, and Social Participation," *American Sociological Review*, 19 (February, 1954), pp. 76-85.

RYAN, J. A., *Distributive Justice* (New York, The Macmillan Co., 1942).

SJOBERG, Gideon, "Are American Social Classes Becoming More Rigid?" *American Sociological Review*, 16 (December, 1951), pp. 775-83.

SPENGLER, J. J., "Changes in Income Distribution and Social Stratification: A Note," *American Journal of Sociology*, 59 (November, 1953), pp. 247-260.

SUTHERLAND, Edwin, *White Collar Crime* (New York, Dryden Press, 1949).

TUMIN, Melvin, "Some Principles of Stratification: A Critical Analysis," *American Sociological Review*, 18 (August, 1953), pp. 387-394.

WILLIAMS, Robin, *American Society* (New York, Alfred Knopf, 1951), especially pp. 78-135.

Author Index

349

Subject Index